Berlitz® speaking your language

D1559796

Confident
Russian

Berlitz Publishing
New York London Singapore

Contacting the Editors
Every effort has been made to provide accurate information in this publication, but changes are inevitable. The publisher cannot be responsible for any resulting loss, inconvenience or injury. We would appreciate it if readers would call our attention to any errors or outdated information, please contact us at:
comments@berlitzpublishing.com

All Rights Reserved
© 2014 Berlitz Publishing/APA Publications (UK) Ltd.

Original edition: 2001 by Langenscheidt KG, Berlin and Munich

First printing: 2014

Berlitz Trademark Reg. U.S. Patent Office and other countries. Marca Registrada.
Used under license from Berlitz Investment Corporation

Senior Commissioning Editor: Kate Drynan
Design: Beverley Speight
Picture research: Beverley Speight
Authors: Professor Keith Rawson-Jones; Dr. Alla Leonidovna Nazarenko; Valery Kaminski
Russian Editor: Sophie Cooper
Cover photos: © APA Publications (UK) Ltd. & istockphotos
Interior photos: © All APA Publications (UK) Ltd. except istockphotos on p1,76,103,118,134,149,161,167,178,214,220, 241,252.

Distribution

Worldwide
APA Publications GmbH & Co. Verlag KG
(Singapore branch)
7030 Ang Mo Kio Ave 5
08-65 Northstar @ AMK, Singapore 569880
Email: apasin@signet.com.sg

UK and Ireland
Dorling Kindersley Ltd
(a Penguin Company)
80 Strand, London, WC2R 0RL, UK
Email: sales@uk.dk.com

US
Ingram Publisher Services
One Ingram Blvd,
PO Box 3006
La Vergne, TN 37086-1986
Email: ips@ingramcontent.com

Australia
Woodslane
10 Apollo St
Warriewood, NSW 2102
Email: info@woodslane.com.au

Contents

Introduction

This course is designed for advanced beginner learners or for those who have already had some introduction to Russian. It is divided into sections so that you can easily build up your language skills at your own pace. By the end of the course, you should have a good understanding of the language. You will be able to speak, write and understand basic Russian and you will have the grammar and vocabulary foundations to help you to progress with ease.

How to Use this Book

Listen to the dialogue at the beginning of each lesson. You can follow along with the book which contains the dialogue in Russian, the English translation and, for Lessons 1 to 3, a simplified pronunciation to help you break down the sounds of the words.

You can then move on to the grammar section. Here you will learn how to build sentences and what each component means and how to use it.

Next you will find the vocabulary section. When studying the vocabulary, it is useful to write the words down – this will help you to memorize them faster. Another tip is to try to create sentences that contain the word. This way you will remember the word, what it means, and how to use it. For more on the vocabulary section, see the Online Content section below.

Finally, you will come across the exercises. These are important to complete in order to progress as they allow you the opportunity to put into practice what you have learnt. Do not go on to the next section until you have successfully completed each one. You can refer back to the dialogue and the vocabulary sections to help you. You will be able to check your answers against the Answer Key at the end of the book on page 256.

Online Content

You will notice that each of the vocabulary sections has an audio symbol. You can download the audio version online from our website at **www.berlitzpublishing.com**. Each word is read once in English, and then in the foreign language. This will help you to memorize words and to build your vocabulary more quickly. It will also help you to work on your pronunciation.

Pronunciation

The phonetic transcription in the first half of the course will help you to pronounce Russian correctly. Instead of using complicated phonetic symbols, we've devised recognizable English approximations that, when read aloud, will give you the correct pronunciation of the Russian words. You don't need to memorize the phonetics; just sound the words out and practice their pronunciation until you're comfortable with them.

The phonetic transcription will help you to learn the basic sound of each word; practice full sentences by listening to the audio dialogues and repeating them. This will help you to become accustomed to the flow and speed of the language. You can also use the online vocabulary downloads in the same way, listen to the words and repeat them until the sounds become natural.

1. The Alphabet

In order to learn Russian, it is first important to get to know the Cyrillic alphabet. Some letters represent more than one sound, depending on their position in a word or combination of words. Take the time to familiarize yourself with the pronunciation indicated.

Ру́сский Алфави́т

Note that the letters on the left are capital, while those on the right are lower case.

Letter	Approximate Pronunciation	Symbol
А а	between [a] in car and [u] in cut	ah
Б б	[b] in bed	b
В в	[v] in vodka	v
Г г	[g] in gold	g
Д д	[d] in dot	d

Е е	[ye] in yet	ye, yeh
	[i] in lip (unstressed)	ee
	[e] in get	e, eh
Ё ё	[yo] in yogurt	yo, yoh
Ж ж	[zh] in measure	zh
З з	[s] in please	z
И и	[ee] in street (stressed)	ee
	[i] in sin (unstressed)	ee
Й й	[y] in young	y
К к	[c] in cover	k
Л л	[l] in low	l
М м	[m] in mad	m
Н н	[n] in not	n
О о	[o] in north (stressed)	o, oh
	[a] in attorney (unstressed)	ah
П п	[p] in plot	p
Р р	[r] in grey	r
С с	[s] in salt	s
Т т	[t] in town	t
У у	[oo] in cool	oo

Ф ф	[f] in fee	**f**
Х х	[h] in hurry (see note on next page)	**kh**
Ц ц	[tz] in quartz	**ts**
Ч ч	[ch] in chunk	**ch**
Ш ш	[sh] in shawl	**sh**
Щ щ	[shch] in hush child	**shch**
Ъ ъ	No sound. See note on next page.	
Ы ы	[i] in thing	**ih**
Ь ь	No sound. See note on next page.	
Э э	[e] in every	**e, eh**
Ю ю	[u] in union	**yoo**
Я я	[ya] in Yankee	**yah**

Notes

1. The letter ъ is called the **hard sign**. It is placed between a consonant and either e, ё, ю or я to keep the consonant it follows hard:

подъе́зд	объём	объявле́ние
entrance	volume	announcement
(pahd-<u>yezd</u>)	(ahb-<u>yom</u>)	(ahb-yahv-<u>lyeh</u>-nee-yeh)

2. The letter ь is called the **soft sign**. It has no sound of its own, but it acts to soften the consonant that it follows. Although there is no direct equivalent symbol in English, the English language does differentiate between hard and soft consonants (the **t** in **hat** can be **softer** than the **t** in

top, and the **l** in **liaison** is **softer** than the **l** in **lobster**). Examples of the soft sign in common Russian words:

день	мать	рубль
day	mother	ruble
(dyen')	*(maht')*	*(roobl')*

3. When o is not stressed, it becomes an **ah** sound, like the **a** in **attorney**:

хорошо́	молоко́	Москва́
good	milk	Moscow
(khah-rah-<u>shoh</u>)	*(mah-lah-<u>koh</u>)*	*(mahs-<u>kvah</u>)*

4. The letter x does not have an equivalent sound in English. It is, however, like the Scottish **ch** in **loch** and the German **ch** in **Bach**.

5. At the end of a word, the pronunciation of the following consonants changes:

Letter	Usual	End of a word
Б	[b] as in "bed": Бог God *(bok)*	[p] as in "hip": гроб casket *(grop)*
В	[v] as in "very": вино́ wine *(vee-<u>noh</u>)*	[f] as in "feather": нерв nerve *(nyerf)*
Г	[g] as in "good": год year *(got)*	[k] as in "crook": флаг flag *(flahk)*
Д	[d] as in "dog": дом home/house *(dom)*	[t] as in "cat": сад garden *(saht)*
З	[z] as in "zoo": зуб tooth *(zoop)*	[s] as in "sip": моро́з frost *(mah-<u>ros</u>)*
Ж	[zh] as in "measure": жара́ heat *(zhah-<u>rah</u>)*	[sh] as in "shave": нож knife *(nosh)*

6. The letter г is usually pronounced like the **g** in **good**:

го́род	мно́го	год
city/town	much/many	year
(goh-<u>raht</u>)	*(<u>mnoh</u>-gah)*	*(got)*

In the combination of letters: ero *(yeh-voh)* and oro *(ah-voh)* г is pronounced **v** when the vowel preceding г, either е or о, is not stressed:

Всего хорошего!
All the best!
(fsee-voh khah-roh-sheh-vah)

7. When a letter is not pronounced as you would usually expect, the alternative pronunciation is reflected in the transliteration.

8. Vowel Combinations

Letters	Approximate Pronunciation	Symbol	Example	Pronunciation
Ай	like [y] in "my"	**ie**	май	*mie*
яй	like [y] in "my", preceded by [y] in "yes"	**yie**	негодяй	*nee-gah-dyie*
Ой	like [oy] in "boy"	**oy**	бой	*voy*
Ей	like [ey] in "obey", preceded by [y] in "yes"	**yey**	соловей	*sah-lah-vyey*
Ий	like [ee] in "see", followed by [y] in "yes"	**eey**	ранний	*rahn-neey*
Ый	like [i] in "ill", followed by [y] in "yes"	**iy**	красивый	*krah-see-viy*
Уй	like [oo] in "good", followed by [y] in "yes"	**ooy**	дуй	*dooy*
Юй	like уй above, preceded by [y] in "yes"	**yooy**	плюй	*plyooy*

Transliteration

For the first 10 lessons in this course – apart from review lessons – we give the approximate pronunciation of the complete texts in the Latin alphabet, as well as notes on pronunciation where necessary.

Stress

In Russian words of more than one syllable, only one of the syllables is stressed, and the stress is heavier, more emphatic, than in English. The stress in Russian is only on vowels and is marked in the Russian text with an accent. We advise you to pay particular attention to the stress when you learn a word. Vowels on which the stress falls are pronounced clearly; unstressed vowels are less distinct. The letter Ё / ё is always stressed. During this course, you will encounter some instances where the stress is unexpectedly different. This occurs mainly in set phrases, which you may find useful to memorize.

Grammar

1. NUMBERS 0–10

0
ноль
(nol')

1	2	3	4	5
оди́н	два	три	четы́ре	пять
(ah-_deen_)	(dvah)	(tree)	(chee-_tih_-ryeh)	(pyaht')

6	7	8	9	10
шесть	семь	во́семь	де́вять	де́сять
(shest')	(syem')	(_voh_-seem')	(_dyeh_-vyaht')	(_dyeh_-syaht')

Remember that т is very soft /faint when followed by a soft sign (ь).

Useful Expressions

да (dah)	yes
нет (nyet)	no
хорошо́ (khah-rah-_shoh_)	good (unstressed **o** = **a** in attorney)
спаси́бо (spah-_see_-bah)	thank you (unstressed **o** again)
до свида́ния (dah-svee-_dah_-nee-yah)	goodbye (until we meet again), _pronounced as one word, so the_ **o** _in до is unstressed: ah._
Росси́я (rah-_see_-yah)	Russia (unstressed **o**)
Аме́рика (ah-_myeh_-ree-kah)	America

президе́нт *(pree-zee-<u>dyent</u>)* president (different from English stress)

ко́фе *(<u>koh</u>-fyeh)* coffee

чай *(chie)* tea (Pronounced just like *chai*, but refers to simple black tea.)

Exercises

Exercise A

You may be surprised to find that you already know some Russian words. Here are a few words we think you will recognize. Write down the English equivalents and check them against the Answer Key on page 256.

Example: КО́ЛА = *(koh-lah)* = COLA.

1. ТЕ́ННИС

....

2. ДО́ЛЛАР

....

3. БАСКЕТБО́Л

....

4. ДО́КТОР

....

5. НЬЮ-ЙО́РК

....

6. КАЛИФО́РНИЯ

....

7. БЕЙСБО́Л

....

8. УНИВЕРСИТЕ́Т

....

9. А́ДРЕС

....

10. КО́ЛА

....

11. О́ФИС

....

12. ФУТБО́Л

....

13. ПРЕЗИДЕ́НТ КЛИНТОН О́БАМА

....

14. ПРЕЗИДЕ́НТ БУШ

....

15. ТЕЛЕФО́Н

....

16. БАР

....

17. РЕСТОРА́Н

....

18. ВЛАДИ́МИР ПУ́ТИН

....

19. МА́ФИЯ

....

20. ТАКСИ́

....

A lot of Russian words are similar to English ones. There are more in later lessons.

Exercise B

The following exercise will help you to become familiar with some of the letters of the Russian alphabet. Writing the letters down will help you to remember them. The approximate English equivalent sound is given. Give the Russian letter twice, in both capital and lower case.

For example: [y] in young = Й й

1. [a] in car

....

2. [ya] in yankee

....

3. [e] in every

....

4. [ye] in yet

....

5. [i] in thing

....

6. [ee] in street

....

7. [o] in north

....

8. [yo] in yogurt

....

9. [oo] in cool

....

10. [u] in union

....

Did you notice that these letters are vowels, and that they are in pairs? The first in each pair is hard and the second soft.

Exercise C

Here are some words that you have already seen. Each has a letter missing. Write down the complete word, with the stress mark, and check your answer against the answer key.

1. Пре–идéнт

....

5. – аксú

....

9. ó–ис

....

13. д– сви–áния

....

2. А–éрика

....

6. дóлла–

....

10. дéс–ть

....

14. кó–е

....

3. спа–йбо

....

7. дó–тор

....

11. хо–ошó

....

15. ча–

....

4. четы́–е

....

8. вóсем–

....

12. Рос–úя

....

16. рес–орáн

....

Exercise D

Let's do some simple math in Russian. Write out your answers in full, complete with stress marks.

1. одúн + три = ...

2. пять + пять = ...

3. вóсемь + одúн = ...

4. дéсять – два = ...

5. пять – пять = ...

6. шесть – два = ...

7. дéвять + одúн = ...

8. четы́ре + три = ...

9. дéсять – пять = ...

10. нуль + шесть = ...

2: Hello

Welcome to Russia! Be prepared to immerse yourself in the Russian language, starting with an overview of the basics. Listen to the audio, become accustomed to the rhythm of the language and just start speaking – don't forget to download the audio vocabulary online too!

ЗДРА́ВСТВУЙТЕ* HELLO

*In Здра́вствуйте, the first в is not pronounced.
In this lesson we have two characters. А́нна *(ahn-nah)* = Anna Ива́новна *(ee-vah-nahv-nah)* = daughter of Ivan Смирно́ва *(smeer-noh-vah)*, and Пол *(pol)* = Paul. Paul is an American studying Russian.

А́нна *ahn-nah*	Здра́вствуйте, Пол. Как ва́ши дела́? *(zdrah-stvooy-tyeh pol. kahk vah-shih dee-lah)* Hello, Paul. How are things?)
Пол *pol*	Здра́вствуйте. У меня́ всё хорошо́, спаси́бо. А как ва́ши дела́? *(zdrah-stvooy-tyeh. oo mee-nyah fsyoh khah-rah-shoh spah-see-bah. ah kahk vah-shih dee-lah)* Hello. Everything's fine with me, thank you. And how are things with you?
А́нна	Спаси́бо, хорошо́. Сади́тесь, пожа́луйста. Дава́йте начнём наш уро́к. *(spah-see-bah khah-rah-shoh. sah-dee-tees' pah-zhahl-stah. dah-vie-tyeh nahch-nyom nahsh oo-rok)* Fine, thank you. Sit down, please. Let's begin our lesson.
Пол	С удово́льствием.

(soo-dah-<u>vol</u>'-stvee-yem)
With pleasure.

Áнна   Оди́н вопро́с, Пол.
(ah-<u>deen</u> vah-<u>pros</u> pol)
One question, Paul.

Пол   Да, пожа́луйста.
(dah pah-<u>zhahl</u>-stah)
Yes, please by all means.

Áнна   Вот, посмотри́те. Э́то ру́чка?
(vot pah-smah-<u>tree</u>-tyeh. <u>eh</u>-tah <u>rooch</u>-kah)
Look at this. Is this a pen?

Пол   Да, э́то ру́чка.
(dah <u>eh</u>-tah <u>rooch</u>-kah)
Yes, it's a pen.

Áнна   А э́то? Э́то ру́чка и́ли ключ?
(ah <u>eh</u>-tah. <u>eh</u>-tah <u>rooch</u>-kah <u>ee</u>-lee klyooch)
And this? Is it a pen or a key?

Пол   Э́то ключ.
(<u>eh</u>-tah klyooch)
It's a key.

Áнна   А э́то? Э́то то́же ключ?
(ah <u>eh</u>-tah. <u>eh</u>-tah <u>toh</u>-zheh klyooch)
And this? Is this a key too?

Пол   Нет, э́то не ключ.
(nyet <u>eh</u>-tah nyeh klyooch)
No, it's not a key.

Áнна   Что э́то?
shtoh <u>eh</u>-tah (Usually ч is pronounced "ch"—here it is "sh".)
What is it?

Пол   Э́то кни́га. Э́то кни́га на ру́сском языке́.
(<u>eh</u>-tah <u>knee</u>-gah. <u>eh</u>-tah <u>knee</u>-gah nah <u>roos</u>-kahm yah-zih-<u>kyeh</u>)
It's a book. It's a book in Russian.

Áнна   О́чень хорошо́, Пол. До свида́ния.
(<u>oh</u>-chen' khah-rah-<u>shoh</u> pol. dah-svee-<u>dah</u>-nee-yah)
Very good, Paul. Goodbye.

Пол   До свида́ния, Áнна Ива́новна. До ско́рой встре́чи!
(dah-svee-<u>dah</u>-nee-yah <u>ahn</u>-nah ee-<u>vah</u>-nahv-nah. dah <u>skoh</u>-rie <u>fstryeh</u>-chee)
Goodbye, Anna Ivanovna. See you soon.

Questions and Answers

Вопрос:	Что это?	
vahp-ros	*shtoh eh-tah*	
Question	What is this?	

Ответ:	Это ру́чка.	ру́чка
aht-vyet	*eh-tah rooch-kah*	*rooch-kah*
Answer	It's a pen.	a pen

Вопрос:	Что это?	
	shtoh eh-tah	
	What is this?	

Ответ:	Это кни́га.	кни́га
	eh-tah knee-gah	*knee-gah*
	It's a book.	a book

Вопрос:	Что это?	
	shtoh eh-tah	
	What is this?	

Ответ:	Это стол.	стол
	eh-tah stol	*stol*
	It's a table.	a table

Вопрос:	Что это?	
	shtoh eh-tah	
	What is this?	

Ответ:	Это стул.	стул
	eh-tah stool	*stool*
	It's a chair.	a chair

Yes or No?

Вопрос:	Это кни́га?
vahp-ros	*eh-tah knee-gah*
Question	Is this a book?

Ответ:	Да, это кни́га.
aht-vyet	*dah eh-tah knee-gah*
Answer	Yes, it's a book.

Вопрос:	Это стол?
	eh-tah stol
	Is this a table?

Отве́т:	Нет, э́то не стол. Э́то стул. *nyet eh-tah nyeh stol. eh-tah stool* No, it's not a table. It's a chair.
Вопро́с:	Э́то стол? *eh-tah stol* Is this a table?
Отве́т:	Да, э́то стол. *dah eh-tah stol* Yes, it's a table.
Вопро́с:	Э́то кни́га? *eh-tah knee-gah* Is this a book?
Отве́т:	Нет, э́то не кни́га. Э́то ру́чка. *nyet eh-tah nyeh knee-gah. eh-tah rooch-kah* No, it's not a book. It's a pen.

Grammar

1. THE VERB "TO BE"

Russians rarely use the present tense of the verb **to be** (**am**, **are**, **is**).

Э́то кни́га.	*It is a book* or *This is a book*, depending on the context.
Э́то	*it* or *this*
кни́га	*book*

2. THE DEFINITE AND INDEFINITE ARTICLES: THE AND A

As you have just seen, кни́га = **book**. There are no articles in Russian. So кни́га can mean **a book** or **the book**, depending on the context.

3. QUESTIONS IN RUSSIAN

| Э́то стул. | *It is a chair?* or *This is a chair?*, according to the context. |
| Э́то стул? | *Is it a chair?* or *Is this a chair?* |

We can do the same in English by altering the intonation:

He's at home. (statement)   **He's at home?** (question)

a) Read aloud, in English, **He's at home**. (statement)
 Now, in the same way read Он дóма *(on doh-mah)* = **He (is) at home**.
 The way you read it will have been rather flat, with no ups or downs in your speech.

b) Now read aloud: **He's at home?** (Question.) Your intonation automatically expresses a question.

c) And now, in the same way, read Он дóма? *(on doh-mah)* = **(Is) he at home?**

 Similarly, compare:

Да. *(dah)* = **Yes.**
(statement)

Да? *(dah)* = **Yes?**
(question)

Нет. *(nyet)* = **No.**
(statement)

Нет? *(nyet)* = **No?**
(question)

Just as in English, questions can be asked by using:

How? как? *(kahk)*, **What?** что? *(shtoh)*, **When?** когдá? *(kahg-dah)*, etc.

4. THE NEGATIVE

Это не кнúга.
(eh-tah nyeh knee-gah)

It is not a book/this is not the book.

This is a good example of how to form a negative sentence. In general, just add не to a positive sentence before the main relevant word:

Это хорошó.
(eh-tah khah-rah-shoh).

It's good.

Это не хорошó. It's not good.
(eh-tah nyeh khah-rah-shoh)

5. FORMAL AND INFORMAL YOU

In English there is no distinction between the formal and informal use of you. Russian, like many other languages, still expresses this distinction.

вы *(vih)* = formal you, and ты *(tih)* = informal you ('thou'). Only close friends, members of the same family, and older people talking to younger people use ты *(tih)*.
Other uses are considered rude, as is the inappropriate use of ты *(tih)*.

In the dialogue, Anna Ivanovna and Paul say Здрáвствуйте *(zdrah-stvooy-tyeh)* to each other (the first в is not pronounced).

If Paul had been a child, Anna would have said здрáвствуй *(zdrah-stvooy)* to him, using the informal form of address.

When you are in Russia, you will often hear ты *(tih)*. But you should use the вы *(vih)* form until you know someone well.

6. PATRONYMICS

In Lesson 1 you met a couple of American Presidents. Here is another: Джо́нсон *(dzhon-sahn)* Johnson. This surname originally signified **son of John**. All Russians have a middle name based on their father's first name: son of . . . , daughter of . . . . This middle name is called a **patronymic**.

If the father's first name ends in a **hard consonant**, the ending -ович *(ah-veech)* is added for males, -овна *(ahv-nah)* for females:

Ива́н + ович *ee-vahn*	Ива́нович *ee-vah-nah-veech*	son of Ivan
Ива́н + овна *ee-vahn*	Ива́новна *ee-vah-nahv-nah*	daughter of Ivan
Леони́д + ович *lee-ah-neet*	Леони́дович *lee-ah-nee-dah-veech*	son of Leonid
Леони́д + овна *lee-ah-neet*	Леони́довна *lee-ah-nee-dahv-nah*	daughter of Leonid

If the father's first name ends in -й, or ь, the й or ь is dropped and -евич *(yeh-veech)* is added for males, and -евна *(yev-nah)* for females.

If the father's first name ends in -a or -я, these endings are dropped, and replaced by -ич *(eech)*, and -инична *(ee-neech-nah)* or -ична *(eech-nah)* for females:

Серге́й *syer-gyey*	Серге + евич	Серге́евич *syer-gyeh-yeh-veech*
Серге́й *syer-gyey*	Серге + евна	Серге́евна *syer-gyeh-yev-nah*
И́горь *ee-gahr'*	И́гор + евич	И́горевич *ee-gar-eh-veech*
И́горь *ee-gahr'*	И́гор + евна	И́горевна *ee-gah-rehv-nah*

Илья́	Иль + ич	Ильи́ч
eel'-yah		*eel'-yeech*
Илья́	Иль + инична	Ильи́нична
eel'-yah		*eel'-yee-neech-nah*
Ники́та	Ники́т + ич	Ники́тич
nee-kee-tah		*nee-kee-teech*
Ники́та	Ники́т + ична	Ники́тична
nee-kee-tah		*nee-kee-teech-nah*

Russians usually use the first name and patronymic when addressing anybody who is not a child, close friend or member of the family.

7. NUMBERS 11–20

The numbers **11–19** are formed by putting **1–9** before **-надцать** *(nah-tsaht')*: **на** *(nah)* means **on**, and **дцать** *(tsaht')*, which is a form of **де́сять** *(dyeh-syaht')*, means **ten**. **One on ten**, **two on ten**, etc. Some letters are dropped or changed before **-на**. The **д** in **-дцать** is not pronounced.

The final **-ть** *(-t')* is pronounced very softly, like **t** in **steer** rather than in **top** – only softer, more faintly.

11	12	13	14
оди́ннадцать	двена́дцать	трина́дцать	четы́рнадцать
(ah-dee-nah-tsaht')	*(dvee-nah-tsaht')*	*(tree-nah-tsaht')*	*(cheh-tir-nah-tsaht')*

15	16	17	18
пятна́дцать	шестна́дцать	семна́дцать	восемна́дцать
(pyaht-nah-tsaht')	*(shes-nah-tsaht')*	*(seem-nah-tsaht')*	*(vah-syem-nah-tsaht')*

19	20		
девятна́дцать	два́дцать		
(dee-veet-nah-tsaht')	*(dvah-tsaht')*		

Note that there is no **на** before **20** and that **2**, **два** *(dvah)*, changes to **две** *(dveh)* in **12**.

Useful Expressions

Я говорю́ по-ру́сски.
(yah gah-vah-ryoo pah-roos-kee)

I speak Russian.

Я говорю́ по-англи́йски.
yah gah-vah-ryoo pah-ahn-gleey-skee

I speak English.

Я не говорю́ по-ру́сски.
yah nyeh gah-vah-ryoo pah-roos-kee

I don't speak Russian.

Вы говори́те по-ру́сски?
vih gah-vah-ree-tyeh pah-roos-kee

Do you speak Russian?

Вы говори́те по-англи́йски?
vih gah-vah-ree-tyeh pah-ahn-gleey-skee

Do you speak English?

Vocabulary

Remember that there are no articles in Russian, so уро́к *(oo-rok)* can mean "a lesson" or "the lesson", and so on. Note: Throughout this book, *m.* = masculine, *f.* = feminine, and *n.* = neuter.

уро́к *(oo-rok)* lesson
Здра́вствуйте. *(zdrah-stvooy-teh)* Hello.
как? *(kahk)* how?
дела́ *(dee-lah)* things/affairs/business
Как ва́ши дела́? *(kahk vah-shih dee-lah)* How are things?
у *(oo)* can mean *at, beside, by, near* or *on*, depending on the context. It is used to indicate possession, proximity or a close connection.
у меня́ *(oo mee-nyah)* I have
У меня́ кни́йга. *(oo mee-nyah knee-gah)* I have a book

всё *(fsyoh)* everything
хорошо́ *(khah-rah-shoh)* good, fine
У меня́ всё хорошо́. *(oo mee-nyah fsyoh khah-rah-shoh)* Everything's fine (with me)
спаси́о *(spah-see-bah)* thank you
а *(ah)* but, and
сади́тесь *(sah-dee-tees')* Sit down. (This is the formal or plural form of the "you" imperative.)
дава́йте *(dah-vie-tyeh)* let us, let's
дава́йте начнём *(dah-vie-tyeh nahch-nyom)* Let's begin.
наш *(nahsh)* our
с *(s)* with
удово́льствие *(oo-dah-vol'-stvee-yeh)* pleasure
с удово́льствием *(s oo-dah-vol'-stvee-yem)* with pleasure

оди́н (ah-<u>deen</u>) one

вопро́с (vahp-<u>ros</u>) question

да (dah) yes

пожа́луйста (pah-<u>zhahl</u>-stah) please, by all means

вот (vot) there is/are, here is/are

Посмотри́те! (pah-smah-<u>tree</u>-tyeh) Look! (This is the formal/plural form of the imperative)

э́то (<u>eh</u>-tah) this, that, it; this is, that is, it is

ру́чка (<u>rooch</u>-kah) pen

и́ли (<u>ee</u>-lee) or

ключ (klyooch) key

то́же (<u>toh</u>-zheh) also

что? (shtoh) what?

кни́га (<u>knee</u>-gah) book

на (nah) on (can also mean "in" with certain nouns)

на ру́сском языке́ (nah <u>roos</u>-kahm yah-zih-<u>kyeh</u>) in Russian

до (dah) until, to

до свида́ния (dah svee-<u>dah</u>-nee-yah) goodbye

до ско́рой встре́чи (dah <u>skoh</u>-rie <u>fstryeh</u>-chee) See you soon.

вопро́с (vahp-<u>ros</u>) question

отве́т (aht-<u>vyet</u>) answer

стол (stol) table

стул (stool) chair

нет (nyet) no

не (nyeh) Used to form negative sentences

он (on) he, it m.

она́ (ah-<u>nah</u>) she, it f.

оно́ (ah-<u>noh</u>) it n.

до́ма (<u>doh</u>-mah) at home

вы (vih) you (The polite form with one person, or like "y'all" with multiple people)

ты (tih) you (Can only refer to one person)

я ¨говорю́ (yah gah-vah-<u>ryoo</u>) I speak

вы ¨говори́те (vih gah-vah-<u>ree</u>-tyeh) you speak

по-ру́сски (pah-<u>roos</u>-kee) in Russian

по-англи́йски (pah-ahn-<u>gleey</u>-skee) in English

Exercises

Exercise A

Write down the English equivalents of these words and check your answers against the answer key.

1. во́дка

2. факт

3. план

4. профе́ссор

5. класс

6. Ле́нин

7. Горачёв   10. Большо́й Бале́т   13. бага́ж

....

8. кана́л   11. порт   14. база́р

....

9. студе́нт   12. фильм

....

Exercise B

Name the items listed in English. Give a full sentence, complete with stress marks where appropriate. For example:

book   Что э́то?   You write: Э́то кни́га.

1. pen   Что э́то?   ....

2. suitcase   Что э́то?   ....

3. table   Что э́то?   ....

4. pen   Что э́то?   ....

5. chair   Что э́то?   ....

Exercise C

Give full answers to the following questions that follow. For example, if the English is **a pen** and we ask Э́то ру́чка? (*eh-tah* <u>*rooch*</u>*-kah*) **Is it a pen?**, answer: Да, э́то ру́чка. **Yes, it's a pen.** But if we ask Э́то кни́га? (*eh-tah* <u>*knee*</u>*-gah*) **Is it a book?**, you should reply: Нет, э́то не кни́га. Э́то ру́чка. (*nyet* <u>*eh-tah*</u> *nyeh* <u>*knee*</u>*-gah.* <u>*eh-tah*</u> <u>*rooch*</u>*-kah*) **No, it's not a book. It's a pen.** Remember to put in the stress marks!

1. Paul   Э́то Пол? (*eh-tah pol*) ....

2. table   Э́то кни́га? (*eh-tah* <u>*knee*</u>*-gah*) ....

3. pen   Э́то ру́чка? (*eh-tah* <u>*rooch*</u>*-kah*) ....

4. Paul   Э́то А́нна Ива́новна? (<u>*eh*</u>*-tah* <u>*ahn*</u>*-nah ee-*<u>*vah*</u>*-nahv-nah*) ....

....

5. table   Это стол? (_eh_-tah stol) ....

6. chair   А это стол? (ah _eh_-tah stol) ....

7. Anna   Это Пол? (_eh_-tah pol) ....

Exercise D

Write out the following words in Russian and check them against the answer key. Remember the

stress marks.

1. **America**

   ....

2. **president**

   ....

3. **university**

   ....

4. **cola**

   ....

5. **baseball**

   ....

6. **vodka**

   ....

7. **doctor**

   ....

8. **student**

   ....

9. **California**

   ....

3. Introductions

In this lesson you will continue with basic introductions. You will learn the essential verbs you need to form a solid foundation for speaking Russian and you will increasingly build your knowledge and understanding of grammar and vocabulary.

ЗНАКÓМСТВО INTRODUCTIONS

Пол	Здрáвствуйте. Я – Пол. А вы кто?
	(*zdrah*-*stvooy-tyeh. yah pol. ah vih ktoh*)
	Hello. I'm Paul. And who are you?
Натáлья	А меня́ зову́т Натáлья Петрóвна Иванóва. Я ру́сская. А вы ру́сский?
	(*ah mee-nyah zah-voot nah-tahl'-yah peet-rov-nah ee-vah-noh-vah. yah roos-kah-ya. ah vih roos-keey*)
	And I'm Natalya Petrovna Ivanova. I'm Russian. And are you Russian?
Пол	Я не ру́сский. И не украи́нец, и не белору́с.
	(*yah nyeh roos-keey. ee nyeh oo-krah-ee-neets ee nyeh beh-lah-roos*)
	I'm not Russian. And not a Ukrainian, nor a Belarusian.
Натáлья	Кто вы по национáльности?
	(*ktoh vih pah nah-tsih-ah-nahl'-nahs-tee*)
	What nationality are you?
Пол	Я америкáнец. Я роди́лся в Сан-Франци́ско. А вы отку́да?
	(*yah ah-mee-ree-kah-neets. yah rah-deel-syah v sahn-frahn-tsihs-kah. ah vih aht-koo-dah*)
	I'm American. I was born in San Francisco. And where do you come from?

Наталья	Я из Новосиби́рска. А сейча́с я живу́ здесь, в Москве́. Я рабо́таю в ба́нке. А где вы рабо́таете?
	(yah eez nah-vah-see-<u>beer</u>-skah. ah sey-<u>chahs</u> yah zhih-<u>voo</u> zdyes' v mahs-<u>kvyeh</u>. yah rah-<u>boh</u>-tah-yoo v <u>bahn</u>-kyeh. ah gdyeh vih rah-<u>boh</u>-tah-yeh-tyeh)
	I'm from Novosibirsk. But now I live here, in Moscow. I work in a bank. And where do you work?
Пол	Я? Я не рабо́таю. Я студе́нт. Я учу́ ру́сский язы́к.
	(yah. yah nyeh rah-<u>boh</u>-tah-yoo. yah stoo-<u>dyent</u>. yah oo-<u>choo</u> <u>roos</u>-keey yah-<u>zihk</u>)
	Me? I do not don't work. I'm a student. I'm am studying Russian.
Наталья	Зна́чит, я бухга́лтер, а вы студе́нт … А кто э́та же́нщина?
	(<u>znah</u>-cheet yah boo-<u>gahl</u>-teer ah vih stoo-<u>dyent</u>. ah ktoh <u>eh</u>-tah <u>zhen</u>-shchee-nah)
	So, I'm an accountant and you're a student…And who is this woman?
Пол	Э́то А́нна Ива́новна. Она́ преподава́тель. Она́ белору́ска, из Ми́нска.
	(<u>eh</u>-tah <u>ahn</u>-nah ee-<u>vah</u>-nahv-nah. ah-<u>nah</u> pree-pah-dah-<u>vah</u>-teel'. ah-<u>nah</u> bee-lah-<u>roos</u>-kah eez <u>meen</u>-skah)
	This is Anna Ivanovna. She's a teacher. She's Belarusian, from Minsk.
	А́нна Ива́новна! Иди́те сюда́! … Э́то А́нна Ива́новна. А́нна Ива́новна, э́то Ната́лья Петро́вна. Она́ рабо́тает в ба́нке.
	(<u>ahn</u>-nah ee-<u>vah</u>-nahv-nah. ee-<u>dee</u>-tyeh syoo-<u>dah</u> … <u>eh</u>-tah <u>ahn</u>-nah ee-<u>vah</u>-nahv-nah. <u>ahn</u>-nah ee-<u>vah</u>-nahv-nah <u>eh</u>-tah nah-<u>tal'</u>-yah peet-<u>rov</u>-nah. ah-<u>nah</u> rah-<u>boh</u>-tah-yet v <u>bahn</u>-kyeh)
	Anna Ivanovna! Come here! … This is Anna Ivanovna. Anna Ivanovna, this is Natalya Petrovna. She works in a bank.
Ната́лья	О́чень прия́тно.
	(<u>oh</u>-chen' pree-<u>yaht</u>-nah)
	Nice to meet you.

Grammar

1. NOUNS: MASCULINE, FEMININE AND NEUTER

Russian nouns are masculine, feminine or neuter. You have already come across some masculine and feminine nouns. The gender of nouns is important, and the adjectives that modify them **must agree** with them. With masculine nouns you use the masculine form of the adjectives and with feminine nouns you use the feminine form. For example:

A Russian (male) student = ру́сский студе́нт *(roos-keey stoo-dyent)*

A Russian (female) student = ру́сская студе́нтка *(roos-kah-yah stoo-dyent-kah)*

A new (male) student = но́вый студе́нт *(noh-viy stoo-dyent)*

A new (female) student = но́вая студе́нтка *(noh-vah-yah stoo-dyent-kah)*

A good (male) student = хоро́ший студе́нт *(khah-roh-shiy stoo-dyent)*

A good (female) student = хоро́шая студе́нтка *(khah-roh-shah-yah stoo-dyent-kah)*

MASCULINE NOUNS

All nouns ending in a consonant in the nominative singular case – the form in which they appear in a dictionary – are masculine.

Here are some masculine nouns, some of which you have already seen:

Уро́к *(oo-rok)* lesson	вопро́с *(vahp-ros)* question	отве́т *(aht-vyet)* answer	стол *(stol)* table
бага́ж *(bah-gahzh)* luggage	до́ллар *(doh-lahr)* dollar	това́рищ *(tah-vah-reeshch)* comrade	англича́нин *(ahn-glee-chah-neen)* Englishman
дом *(dom)* house, home	чемода́н *(cheeh-mah-dahn)* suitcase	америка́нец *(ah-mee-ree-kah-neets)* American	

All nouns ending in -й in the nominative singular are masculine:

Чай	бой	геро́й
(chie)	*(boy)*	*(gee-roy)*
tea	battle	hero

Nouns ending in -ь are either masculine or feminine, never neuter. Here are some masculine examples:

слова́рь	день	конь	зверь
(slah-vahr')	*(dyen')*	*(kon')*	*(zvyer')*
dictionary	day	horse	beast

FEMININE NOUNS

Most nouns ending in -a or -я are feminine:

вода́	у́лица	шко́ла	ба́нка
(vah-dah)	*(oo-lee-tsah)*	*(shkoh-lah)*	*(bahn-kah)*
water	street	school	jar/can/tin
война́	газе́та	фа́брика	конфере́нция
(vie-nah)	*(gah-zeh-tah)*	*(fahb-ree-kah)*	*(kahn-fee-ryen-tsih-yah)*
war	newspaper	factory	conference
Земля́	пе́сня	ру́чка	кни́га
(zeem-lyah)	*(pyes-nyah)*	*(rooch-kah)*	*(knee-gah)*
earth/land	song	pen	book

The suffixes -ка and -ница denote the feminine form of some words:

студе́нтка	америка́нка	англича́нка
(stoo-dyent-kah)	*(ah-mee-ree-kahn-kah)*	*(ahn-glee-chahn-kah)*
student (female)	American (female)	Englishwoman
Иностра́нка	украи́нка	учи́тельница
(ee-nah-strahn-kah)	*(oo-krah-een-kah)*	*(oo-chee-tyel'-nee-tsah)*
foreigner (female)	Ukrainian (female)	school teacher (female)

Most nouns ending in -сть are feminine:

гла́сность	национа́льность	сто́имость
(*glahs*-nahst')	(nah-tsih-ah-*nahl'*-nahst')	(*stoh*-ee-mahst')
openness	nationality	cost

An important exception is the masculine noun гость (*gost'*) guest.

Nouns ending in -жь, -чь, -шь, and -щь are feminine:

Рожь	ночь	пу́стошь	вещь
(*rosh*)	(*noch*)	(*poos*-tahsh)	(*vyeshch*)
rye	night	neglected land	thing

NEUTER NOUNS

Nouns ending in -e are neuter:

Упражне́ние	мо́ре	по́ле	со́лнце
(oo-prahzh-*nyeh*-nee-yeh)	(*moh*-ryeh)	(*poh*-lyeh)	(*son*-tseh)
			(л is not pronounced)
exercise	sea	field	sun

Almost all nouns ending in -o are neuter:

село́	письмо́	вино́	яйцо́	сло́во	д'е́ло
(see-*loh*)	(pees'-*moh*)	(vee-*noh*)	(yie-*tsoh*)	(*sloh*-vah)	(*dyeh*-lah)
village	letter	wine	egg	word	affair

A few neuter nouns end in -мя:

вре́мя	и́мя
(*vryeh*-myah)	(*ee*-myah)
time	first name

2. NOUNS: CASES – THE NOMINATIVE

All the nouns given above are in the nominative singular form. In English, nouns have only a singular and plural form:

question	questions
language	languages

In Russian, nouns have several singular and several plural forms. These forms are called **cases**. Here are some examples of the nominative singular and nominative plural:

MASCULINE NOUNS

Nominative Singular	Nominative Plural
унив́ерсит́ет *(oo-nee-veer-see-<u>tyet</u>)* university	унив́ерсит́еты *(oo-nee-veer-see-<u>tyeh</u>-tih)* universities
банк *(bahnk)* bank	б́анки *(<u>bahn</u>-kee)* banks
Язы́к *(yah-<u>zihk</u>)* language	языќи *(yah-zih-<u>kee</u>)* languages
Стол *(stol)* table	стол́ы *(stah-<u>lih</u>)* tables
вопр́ос *(vahp-<u>ros</u>)* question	вопр́осы *(vahp-<u>roh</u>-sih)* questions
отв́ет *(aht-<u>vyet</u>)* answer	отв́еты *(aht-<u>vyeh</u>-tih)* answers

Masculine nouns ending in a consonant add -ы in the plural. If the final consonant is к, г, х, ж, ч, ш, щ, they add -и.

Nominative Singular	Nominative Plural
кни́га *(knee-gah)* book	кни́ги *(knee-gee)* books
студе́нтка *(stoo-dyent-kah)* student	студе́нтки *(stoo-dyent-kee)* students
Америка́нка *(ah-mee-ree-kahn-kah)* American	америка́нки *(ah-mee-ree-kahn-kee)* Americans
газе́та *(gah-zyeh-tah)* newspaper	газе́ты *(gah-zyeh-tih)* newspapers
Шко́ла *(shkoh-lah)* school	шко́лы *(shkoh-lih)* schools
война́ *(vie-nah)* war	во́йны *(voy-nih)* wars

Feminine nouns ending in -а change the last letter to -ы in the plural. If the last consonant is к, г, х, ж, ч, ш, щ, the ending is -и. Nouns ending in -я or -ь change the last letter to -и.

NEUTER NOUNS

Nominative Singular	Nominative Plural
упражне́ние *(oo-prahzh-__nyeh__-nee-yeh)* exercise	упражне́ния *(oo-prahzh-__nye__-nee-yah)* exercises
по́ле *(__poh__-lyeh)* field	поля́ *(pah-__lyah__)* fields
мо́ре *(__moh__-ryeh)* sea	моря́ *(mah-__ryah__)* seas
де́ло *(__dyeh__-lah)* affair, business	дела́ *(dee-__lah__)* affairs, business, things
окно́ *(ahk-__noh__)* window	о́кна *(__ohk__-nah)* windows
сло́во *(__sloh__-vah)* word	слова́ *slah-__vah__* words

In the plural, neuter nouns ending in -e change the last letter to -я, and those ending in -o change it to -a. This is also true in the genitive case. The genitive case in the neuter singular is formed in the same way. Cases will be explained in later lessons.

3. AGREEMENT OF ADJECTIVES AND NOUNS

Russian adjectives have a masculine, a feminine and a neuter form. In Russian, an adjective agrees with the noun it modifies. In the dialogue, Natalya said to Paul "Я ру́сская. А вы ру́сский?"

Ру́сск- *(roosk-)* is the stem of the adjective. -ая *(-ah-yah)* is a feminine ending because Natalya is female. -ий *(eey)* is a masculine ending because Paul is male. There is also a neuter ending for ру́сск: -ое *(-oh-yeh)*.

The adjectives that follow are all in the nominative singular form. Note that there are several different endings. Try to memorize the forms given in the table overleaf.

THE NOMINATIVE SINGULAR OF ADJECTIVES

English	Stem	Masculine	Feminine	Neuter
new	нов- (nov-)	но́вый (<u>noh</u>-viy)	но́вая (<u>noh</u>-vah-yah)	но́вое (<u>noh</u>-vah-yeh)
pleasant	прия́т- (pree-yaht-)	прия́тный (pree-<u>yaht</u>-niy)	прия́тная (pree-<u>yaht</u>-nah-yah)	прия́тное (pree-<u>yaht</u>-nah-yeh)
Russian	ру́сск- (roosk-)	ру́сский (<u>roos</u>-keey)	ру́сская (<u>roos</u>-kah-yah)	ру́сское (<u>roos</u>-kah-yeh)
good	хоро́ш- (khah-rosh-)	хоро́ший (khah-<u>roh</u>-shiy)	хоро́шая (khah-<u>roh</u>-shah-yah)	хоро́шее (khah-<u>roh</u>-sheh-yeh)
young	молод- (mah-lahd-)	молодо́й (mah-lah-<u>doy</u>)	молода́я (mah-lah-<u>dah</u>-yah)	молодо́е (mah-lah-<u>doh</u>-yeh)

Here are some examples of adjectives modifying nouns in the nominative singular:

ADJECTIVE PLUS MASCULINE NOUN

1. Он мой но́вый студе́нт.
   (on moy <u>noh</u>-viy stoo-<u>dyent</u>)

   He is /He's my new student.

2. Пол – о́чень прия́тный америка́нец.
   (pol <u>oh</u>-chen' pree-<u>yaht</u>-niy ah-mee-ree-<u>kah</u>-neets)

   Paul is a very pleasant American.

3. Я преподаю́ ру́сский язы́к.
   (yah pree-pah-dah-<u>yoo</u> <u>roos</u>-keey yah-<u>zihk</u>)

   I teach Russian.

4. Э́то но́вый ру́сский па́спорт?
   (<u>eh</u>-tah <u>noh</u>-viy <u>roos</u>-keey pahs-pahrt)

   Is this a new Russian passport?

5. Ива́н Петро́вич – хоро́ший
   преподава́тель.
   (ee-<u>vahn</u> peet-<u>roh</u>-veech khah-roh-shiy
   pree-pah-dah-<u>vah</u>-tyel')

   Ivan Petrovich is a good teacher.

6. Кто э́тот молодо́й челове́к?
   (ktoh <u>eh</u>-taht mah-lah-<u>doy</u> chee-lah-<u>vyek</u>)

   Who is this young man?

ADJECTIVE PLUS FEMININE NOUN

1. Она́ моя́ но́вая студе́нтка.   She is/She's my new student.
   (ah-<u>nah</u> mah-<u>yah</u> <u>noh</u>-vah-yah stoo-<u>dyent</u>-kah)

2. Она́ о́чень прия́тная америка́нка.   She is/She's a very pleasant American.
   (ah-<u>nah</u> oh-chen' pree-<u>yaht</u>-nah-yah ah-mee-ree-<u>kahn</u>-kah)

3. У меня́ но́вая ру́сская кни́га.   I have a new Russian book.
   (oo mee-<u>nyah</u> <u>noh</u>-vah-yah <u>roos</u>-kah-yah <u>knee</u>-gah)

4. Э́то хоро́шая шко́ла.   It is/It's a good school.
   (<u>eh</u>-tah khah-<u>roh</u>-shah-yah <u>shkoh</u>-lah)

5. Ната́лья Петро́вна не о́чень молода́я.   Natalya Petrovna is not very young.
   (nah-<u>tahl'</u>-yah peet-<u>rov</u>-nah nyeh <u>oh</u>-chen' mah-lah-<u>dah</u>-yah)

6. Молода́я аме́риканка – студе́нтка.   The young (female) American is a student.
   (mah-lah-<u>dah</u>-yah ah-mee-ree-<u>kahn</u>-kah stoo-<u>dyent</u>-kah)

ADJECTIVE PLUS NEUTER NOUN

1. Э́то но́вое упражне́ние.   It is/It's a new exercise.
   (<u>eh</u>-tah <u>noh</u>-vah-yeh oo-prahzh-<u>nyeh</u>-nee-yeh)

2. У меня́ но́вое де́ло.   I have a new business.
   (oo mee-<u>nyah</u> <u>noh</u>-vah-yeh <u>dyeh</u>-lah)

3. Э́то о́чень неприя́тное вре́мя в Москве́.   It is/It's a very unpleasant time in Moscow.
   (<u>eh</u>-tah <u>oh</u>-chen' nyeh-pree-<u>yaht</u>-nah-yeh <u>vryeh</u>-myah v mahs-<u>kvyeh</u>)

4. Э́то о́чень прия́тное ме́сто.   It is it's a very pleasant place.
   (<u>eh</u>-tah <u>oh</u>-chen' pree-<u>yaht</u>-nah-yeh <u>myes</u>-tah)

5. Э́то ру́сское сло́во.   It is/It's a Russian word.
   (<u>eh</u>-tah <u>roos</u>-kah-yeh <u>sloh</u>-vah)

6. Моё и́мя ру́сское.   My first name is Russian.
   (mah-<u>yoh</u> <u>ee</u>-myah <u>roos</u>-kah-yeh)

4. THE POSSESSIVE PRONOUN: MY

The possessive pronoun мой also changes its form to agree with the gender of the noun it modifies.

Masculine: мой: мой оте́ц (moy ah-tyets)   my father
Feminine: моя́: моя́ мать (mah-yah maht')   my mother
Neuter: моё: моё де́ло (mah-yoh dyeh-lah)   my business

5. PERSONAL PRONOUNS

You already know the Russian for **I** – я *(yah)*, **you** (informal), – ты *(tih)*, **he** – он *(on)*, **she** – она́ *(ah-nah)*, and **you** (informal) – вы *(vih)*.

The Russian for **we** is мы *(mih)*, and for **they** is они́ *(ah-nee)*. Here are some short sentences on people's occupations:

Я врач. *(yah vrahch)*	I am/I'm a doctor.
Ты студе́нт. *(tih stoo-dyent)*	You are/You're a student.
Вы пило́т? *(vih pee-lot)*	Are you a pilot?
Он продаве́ц. *(on prah-dah-vyets)*	He is/He's a salesman.
Она́ бухга́лтер. *(ah-nah boo-gahl-teer)*	She's/She is an accountant.
Мы врачи́. *(mih vrah-chee)*	We are doctors.
Вы пило́ты. *(vih pee-loh-tih)*	You are pilots.
Они́ студе́нты. *(ah-nee stoo-dyen-tih)*	They are students. (either all male, or mixed male and female)
Они́ студе́нтки. *(ah-nee stoo-dyent-kee)*	They are students. (all female)

Note that you have learned two words for **doctor**: до́ктор and врач. The word врач is used when talking about medical doctors: **I must see a doctor**. The word до́ктор is used as a form of address, as in: **Doctor, I have a pain in my leg**. It is also used, as in English, to address someone with an advanced degree.

PERSONAL PRONOUNS: NEUTER FORMS ОНО́ *(ah-noh)* IT, ОНИ́ *(ah-nee)* THEY

In English, we usually refer to a place or an object using the neutral word **it**. Russian is more specific: a single masculine object is referred to as он *(on)*, a single feminine object as она́ *(ah-nah)*, and a single neuter object as оно́ *(ah-noh)*. Two or more objects – masculine, feminine, neuter, or a mixture of genders – are referred to as они́ *(ah-nee)*. Here are some questions and answers that illustrate this: где? *(gdyeh)* = **Where?**

1. Где паспорт? Он на столе.
   (gdyeh <u>pahs</u>-pahrt. on nah stah-<u>lyeh</u>)

   Where's is the passport? It's on the table.

2. Где книга? Она на столе.
   (gdyeh <u>knee</u>-gah. ah-<u>nah</u> nah stah-<u>lyeh</u>)

   Where's is the book? It is on the table.

3. Где письмо? Оно на столе.
   (gdyeh pees'-<u>moh</u>. ah-<u>noh</u> nah stah-<u>lyeh</u>)

   Where's is the letter? It's on the table.

4. Где паспорт, книга и письмо?
   Они на столе.
   (gdyeh <u>pahs</u>-pahrt <u>knee</u>-gah ee pees'-<u>moh</u>. ah-<u>nee</u> nah stah-<u>lyeh</u>)

   Where are the passport, the book and the letter?
   They are on the table.

6. NUMBERS 21–30

21	22	23
два́дцать оди́н *(<u>dvah</u>-tsaht' ah-<u>deen</u>)*	два́дцать два *(<u>dvah</u>-tsaht' dvah)*	два́дцать три *(<u>dvah</u>-tsaht' tree)*

24	25	26
два́дцать четы́ре *(<u>dvah</u>-tsaht' chee-tih-ryeh)*	два́дцать пять *(<u>dvah</u>-tsaht' pyaht')*	два́дцать шесть *(<u>dvah</u>-tsaht' shest')*

27	28	29
два́дцать семь *(<u>dvah</u>-tsaht' syem')*	два́дцать во́семь *(<u>dvah</u>-tsaht' <u>voh</u>-seem')*	два́дцать де́вять *(<u>dvah</u>-tsaht' <u>dyeh</u>-vyat')*

30
три́дцать *(<u>treet</u>-tsaht')*

Useful Expressions

Я америка́нец.
(yah ah-mee-ree-<u>kah</u>-neets)

I'm American (male).

Я америка́нка.
(yah ah-mee-ree-<u>kahn</u>-kah)

I'm American (female).

Я живу́ в Вашингто́не.
(yah zhih-voo v vah-shihng-<u>toh</u>-nyeh)

I live in Washington.

Где вы живёте?
(gdyeh vih zhih-<u>vyoh</u>-tyeh)

Where do you live?

Где вы работаете?
(gdyeh vih rah-boh-tah-yeh-tyeh)

Where do you work?

Я работаю в Филаде́льфии.
(yah rah-boh-tah-yoo f fee-lah-del'-fee-ee)

I work in Philadelphia.

Vocabulary

m. = masculine, f. = feminine,
n. = neuter

знако́мство *(znah-kom-stvah)*
introductions
Кто? *(ktoh) Who?*
Меня́ зову́т . . . *(mee-nyah zah-voot . . .) My*
name is . . .
Ру́сский *m.* **ру́сская** *f.* **ру́сское** *n. (roos-keey*
m. roos-kah-yah f. roos-kah-yeh n.) Russian
Украи́нец *m.* **украи́нка** *f. (oo-krah-ee-neets*
m. oo-krah-een-kah f.) a Ukrainian
по *(pah) on, by*
национа́льность *f. (nah-tsih-ah-nahl'-*
nahst') nationality
кто вы по национа́льности? *(ktoh vih*
pahnah-tsih-ah-nahl'-nahs-tee) What is your
nationality?
белору́с *m.* **белору́ска** *f. (bee-lah-roos*
m. bee-lah-roos-kah f.) a Belarusian
Я роди́лся в Ми́нске *(yah rah-deel-syah v*
meen-skyeh) I was born in Minsk.
Отку́да? *(aht-koo-dah) Where are you from?*
из *(eez) from, out of*
сейча́с *(seey-chahs) now*
Я живу́ в . . . *(yah zhih-voo v . . .) I live in . . .*
здесь *(zdyes') here*
банк *(bahnk) bank*

Я рабо́таю в ба́нке. *(yah rah-boh-tah-yoo*
v bahn-kyeh) I work in a bank.
Где? *(gdyeh) Where?*
университе́т *(oo-nee-vyer-see-tyet)*
university
Я преподаю́ *(yah pree-pah-dah-yoo) I teach*
язы́к *(yah-zihk) language, tongue*
зна́чит *(znah-cheet) it means, so*
бухга́лтер *(m. or f.) (boo-gahl-teer)*
accountant
преподава́тель *(pree-pah-dah-vah-tyel')*
teacher
же́нщина *(zhen-shchee-nah) a woman*
мой *m.* **моя́** *f.* **моё** *n. (moy m. mah-yah f.*
mah-yoh n.) my
но́вый *m.* **но́вая** *f.* **но́вое** *n. (noh-viy m.*
noh-vah-yah f. noh-vah-yeh n.) new
он *m.* **она́** *f.* **у́чит . . .** *(on/ah-nah oo-cheet*
. . .) he, she teaches . . .
англи́йский *m.* **англи́йская** *f.* **англи́йское**
n. (ahn-gleey-skeey m. ahn-gleey-skah-yah f.
ahn-gleey-skah-yeh n.) English
францу́зский *m.* **францу́зская** *f.*
францу́зское *n. (frahn-tsoos-keey m.*
frahn-tsoos-kah-yah f. frahn-tsoos-kah-yeh
n.) French
коне́чно *(kah-nyesh-nah) of course*
иди́те сюда́ *(ee-dee-tyeh syoo-dah) come*

here

он *m.* **она** *f.* **работает** *(on m.ah-nah f. rah-boh-tah-yet) he/she works*

очень *(oh-chen') very*

приятно *(pree-yaht-nah) pleasant*

рад *m.* **рада** *f. (raht m. rah-dah f.) pleased*

познакомиться *(pah-znah-koh-mee-tsah) to meet, to get to know someone*

с вами *(s vah-mee) with you*

числа *(chees-lah) numbers*

багаж *(bah-gahsh) baggage*

доллар *(doh-lahr) dollar*

Американец *m.* **американка** *f. (ah-mee-ree-kah-neets m. ah-mee-ree-kahn-kah f.) an American*

англичанин *m.* **англичанка** *f. (ahn-glee-chah-neen m.ahn-glee-chahn-kah f.) Englishman/Englishwoman*

дом *(dom) house*

чемодан *(chee-mah-dahn) suitcase*

товарищ *(m. or f.) (tah-vah-reeshch) comrade*

чай *(chie) tea*

бой *(boy) battle*

герой *(gee-roy) hero*

словарь *(slah-vahr') dictionary*

день *(dyen') day*

гость *(gost') guest*

вода *(vah-dah) water*

улица *(oo-lee-tsah) street*

школа *(shkoh-lah) school*

банка *(bahn-kah) jar, can, tin*

война *(vie-nah) war*

газета *(gah-zyeh-tah) newspaper*

фабрика *(fahb-ree-kah) factory*

песня *(pyes-nyah) song*

студент *m.* **студентка** *f. (stoo-dyent m. stoo-dyent-kah f.) student*

иностранец *m.* **иностранка** *f. (ee-nah-strahn-neets m.ee-nah-strahn-kah f.) foreigner*

земля *(zeem-lyah) earth, land*

конференция *(kahn-fee-ryen-tsih-yah) conference*

гласность *(glahs-nahst') openness*

стоимость *(stoh-ee-mahst') cost, value*

вещь *(vyeshch) thing*

письмо *(pees'-moh) letter*

солнце *(son-tseh) sun*

дело *(dyeh-lah) affair, work, business*

село *(see-loh) village*

вино *(vee-noh) wine*

яйцо *(yie-tsoh) egg*

слово *(sloh-vah) word*

время *(vryeh-myah) time*

упражнение *(oo-prahzh-nyeh-nee-yeh) exercise*

море *(moh-ryeh) sea*

поле *(poh-lyeh) field*

имя *(ee-myah) first name*

мы *(mih) we*

они *(ah-nee) they*

пилот *(pee-lot) pilot*

хороший *m.* **хорошая** *f.* **хорошее** *n. (kha-roh-shiy m. kha-roh-shah-yah f. kha-roh-sheh-yeh n.) good*

молодой *m.* **молодая** *f.* **молодое** *n. (mah-lah-doy m. mah-lah-dah-yah f. mah-lah-doh-yeh n.) young*

Exercises

Exercise A

Write down the English equivalents of these words and check your answers against the answer key.

1. спорт

  ....

2. фильм

  ....

3. такси́

  ....

4. телефо́н

  ....

5. центр

  ....

6. а́втомоби́ль

  ....

7. футбо́л

  ....

8. царь

  ....

9. экску́рсия

  ....

10. теа́тр

  ....

11. а́йсберг

  ....

12. а́втор

  ....

Exercise B

Are you from . . . ? Reply to the following questions in the negative.

For example:

Вы из Новосиби́рска? Are you from Novosibirsk?
(vih eez nah-vah-see-beer-skah)

You reply:

Нет, я не из Новосиби́рска.   No, I'm not from Novosibirsk.
(nyet yah nyeh eez nah-vah-see-beer-skah)

Note how the endings of the words change after из. Минск – из Минска.

1. **Вы из Ло́ндон<u>а</u>?**

   ....

2. **Он из Новосиби́рск<u>а</u>?**

   ....

3. **Она́ из Москвы́?**

   ....

4. **Они́ из Аме́рики?**

   ....

5. **Вы из А́нглии?**

   ....

6. **Он из Берлина?**

   ....

7. **Она́ из Сан-Франциско?** (no change from the nominative).

   ....

8. **Они из Нью-Йо́рка?**

   ....

Exercise C

Are you a . . . ? Give a positive reply to these questions.

For example:

Он врач?   Is he a doctor?
(on vrahch)

You reply:

Да, он врач.   Yes, he's a doctor.
(dah on vrahch)

Note the changes in endings in the plural. **Он врач – они врачи́**.

1. **Вы профе́ссор?**

   ....

2. **Он бухга́лтер?**

   ....

3. Она́ студе́нтка?

....

4. Они́ врачи́?

....

5. Вы преподава́тель?

....

6. Он пило́т?

....

7. Она́ преподава́тель?

....

8. Они́ пило́ты?

....

Exercise D

Agreement of adjectives and nouns. Remember, adjectives take the gender of the noun. Tick А *(ah)*,

Б *(beh)* or В *(veh)* as appropriate.

большо́й big
(bahl'-shoy)

ма́ленький small
(mah-leen'-keey)

1. Пол	А: молодо́й	Б: молода́я	В: молодо́е
2. Ната́лья	А: ру́сский	Б: ру́сская	В: ру́сское
3. кни́га	А: но́вый	Б: но́вая	В: но́вое
4. стол	А: большо́й	Б: больша́я	В: большо́е
5. село́	А: ма́ленький	Б: ма́ленькая	В: ма́ленькое
6. мо́ре	А: большо́й	Б: больша́я	В: большо́е
7. чемода́н	А: но́вый	Б: но́вая	В: но́вое
8. упражне́ние	А: хоро́ший	Б: хоро́шая	В: хоро́шее

Exercise E

Translate the following sentences into English.

1. Я о́чень рад (ра́да) познако́миться с ва́ми.

   ....

2. Ната́лья Ива́новна рабо́тает в банке.

   ....

3. Пол живёт в Москве́, но он роди́лся в Сан-Франци́ско.

   ....

4. А́нна Ива́новна не бухга́лтер. Она́ преподаёт в университе́те.

   ....

5. Он не из Москвы́, но он рабо́тает в Москве́.

   ....

6. Я рабо́таю в Аме́рике.

   ....

7. А́нна не америка́нка и не ру́сская. Она́ белору́ска.

   ....

8. Она́ ру́сская и́ли америка́нка?

   ....

9. Э́та кни́га на ру́сском и́ли на англи́йском языке́?

   ....

Exercise F

True or false? Here are some statements based on the dialogue. Check your answers against the

answer key.

1. **Ната́лья Петро́вна ру́сская.**   **T/F**
   (nah-*tahl'*-yah peet-*rov*-nah *roos*-kah-yah)

2. **А́нна Ива́новна ру́сская.**   **T/F**
   (*ahn*-nah ee-*vah*-nov-nah *roos*-kah-yah)

3. **Пол студе́нт.**   **T/F**
   (pol stoo-*dyent*)

4. **Ната́лья Петро́вна рабо́тает в университе́те.**   **T/F**
   (nah-*tahl'*-yah peet-*rov*-nah rah-*boh*-tah-yet v oo-nee-veer-see-*tyeh*-tyeh)

5. **Пол рабо́тает в ба́нке.**   **T/F**
   (pol rah-*boh*-tah-yet v *bahn*-kyeh)

6. **Ната́лья Петро́вна бухга́лтер.**   **T/F**
   (nah-*tahl'*-yah peet-*rov*-nah boo-*gahl*-teer)

7. **А́нна Ива́новна преподава́тель.**   **T/F**
   (*ahn*-nah ee-*vah*-nov-nah pree-pah-dah-*vah*-tyel')

8. **Она́ преподаёт ру́сский язы́к.**   **T/F**
   (ah-*nah* pree-pah-dah-*yot roos*-keey yah-*zihk*)

9. **Пол у́чит англи́йский язы́к.**   **T/F**
   (pol *oo*-cheet ahn-*gleey*-skeey yah-*zihk*)

10. **Вы у́чите ру́сский язы́к.**   **T/F**
    (vih *oo*-chee-tyeh *roos*-keey yah-*zihk*)

4. Getting Around

Lesson 4 introduces more verbs to aid your conversation skills. The dialogue focuses on travel and the vocabulary you need to talk about it. You will already learn the present tense and lots of prepositions and you will get used to answering questions.

НАТА́ЛЬЯ Е́ДЕТ В КОМАНДИРО́ВКУ NATALYA GOES ON A BUSINESS TRIP

Anna Ivanovna Smirnova tells you a little about herself and Natalya Petrovna, and Natalya has a conversation with Paul:

Áнна   Как вы зна́ете, я белору́ска. Я живу́ и рабо́таю в Москве́. Я о́чень люблю́ Москву́. Но я люблю́ и Минск, где живу́т мой оте́ц и моя́ мать.
(kahk vih <u>znah</u>-yeh-tyeh yah beeh-lah-<u>roos</u>-kah. yah zhih-<u>voo</u> ee rah-<u>boh</u>-tah-yoo v mahs-<u>kvyeh</u>. yah <u>oh</u>-chen' lyoob-<u>lyoo</u> mahs-kvoo. noh yah lyoob-<u>lyoo</u> ee meensk gdyeh zhih-<u>voot</u> moy ah-<u>tyets</u> ee mah-<u>yah</u> maht')
As you know, I'm Belarusian. I live and work in Moscow. I like Moscow very much. But I also like Minsk too, where my father and my mother live.
Вы та́кже зна́ете, что Ната́лья Петро́вна из Новосиби́рска. Но сейча́с она́ живёт в Москве́. У неё своя́ отде́льная кварти́ра. Ей нра́вится жить в Москве́. Она́ рабо́тает в ба́нке. Она́ о́чень лю́бит свою́ рабо́ту.
(vih <u>tahk</u>-zheh <u>znah</u>-yeh-tyeh shtoh nah-<u>tahl'</u>-yah peet-<u>rov</u>-nah eez nah-vah-see-<u>beer</u>-skah. noh sey-<u>chahs</u> ah-<u>nah</u> zhih-<u>vyot</u> v mahs-<u>kvyeh</u>. oo nee-<u>yoh</u> svah-<u>yah</u> aht-<u>dyel'</u>-nah-yah kvahr-<u>tee</u>-rah. yey

nrah-vee-tsah zhiht' v mahs-<u>kvyeh</u>. ah-<u>nah</u> rah-<u>boh</u>-tah-yet v <u>bahn</u>-kyeh. ah-<u>nah</u> <u>oh</u>-chen' <u>lyoo</u>-beet svah-<u>yoo</u> rah-<u>boh</u>-too)

You also know that Natalya Petrovna is from Novosibirsk. But now she lives in Moscow. She has her own separate apartment. She likes living in Moscow. She works in a bank. She likes her work very much.

Сего́дня она́ е́дет в командиро́вку в Санкт-Петербу́рг. Сейча́с она́ говори́т с По́лом …

(see-<u>vod</u>-nyah ah-<u>nah</u> <u>yeh</u>-deet f kah-mahn-dee-<u>rof</u>-koo f sahnkt-pee-teer-<u>boork</u>. sey-<u>chahs</u> ah-<u>nah</u> gah-vah-<u>reet</u> s poh-lahm …)

Today she's going on a business trip to St. Petersburg. Just now she's talking with Paul …

Пол	Как вы е́дете в Санкт-Петербу́рг?
	(kahk vih <u>yeh</u>-dee-tyeh f sahnkt-pee-teer-<u>boork</u>)
	How are you going to St. Petersburg?
Ната́лья	Я лечу́ туда́ на самолёте, а возвраща́юсь на по́езде.
	(yah lee-<u>choo</u> too-<u>dah</u> nah sah-mah-<u>lyoh</u>-tyeh ah vahz-vrah-<u>shchah</u>-yoos' nah <u>poh</u>-eez-dyeh)
	I'm flying there by plane, but I'm returning by train.
Пол	У вас есть биле́т на самолёт?
	(oo vahs yest' bee-<u>lyet</u> nah sah-mah-<u>lyot</u>)
	Do you have a ticket for the plane?
Ната́лья	Да. У меня́ есть биле́т на самолёт и обра́тный биле́т на по́езд.
	(dah. oo mee-<u>nyah</u> yest' bee-<u>lyet</u> nah sah-mah-<u>lyot</u> ee ahb-<u>raht</u>-niy bee-<u>lyet</u> nah <u>poh</u>-eest)
	Yes. I have a plane ticket, and a return ticket on the train.
Пол	Вы до́лго бу́дете в Санкт-Петербу́рге?
	(vih <u>dol</u>-gah <u>boo</u>-dee-tyeh f sahnkt-pee-teer-<u>boor</u>-gyeh)
	Will you be long in St. Petersburg?
Ната́лья	Я бу́ду там три дня. У меня́ там мно́го дел.
	(yah <u>boo</u>-doo tahm tree dnyah. oo mee-<u>nyah</u> tahm <u>mnoh</u>-gah dyel)
	I will be there for three days. I have a lot of things to do there.
Пол	Вы ча́сто туда́ е́здите?
	(vih <u>chahs</u>-tah too-<u>dah</u> <u>yez</u>-dee-tyeh)
	Do you go there often?
Ната́лья	Да, дово́льно ча́сто. Я там быва́ю три-четы́ре дня ка́ждый ме́сяц.
	(dah dah-<u>vol</u>'-nah <u>chahs</u>-tah. yah tahm bih-<u>vah</u>-yoo tree-chee-<u>tih</u>-ryeh dnyah <u>kahzh</u>-diy <u>myeh</u>-syahts.)
	Yes, fairly often. I am there three to four days every month.
Пол	Я о́чень хочу́ побыва́ть в Санкт-Петербу́рге.
	(yah <u>oh</u>-chen' khah-<u>choo</u> pah-bih-<u>vaht</u>'f sahnkt-pee-teer-<u>boor</u>-gyeh)
	I really want to spend some time in St. Petersburg.
	Говоря́т, э́то о́чень интере́сный и краси́вый го́род.
	(gah-vah-<u>ryaht</u> <u>eh</u>-tah <u>oh</u>-chen' een-tee-<u>ryes</u>-niy ee krah-<u>see</u>-viy

goh-raht)
They say that it's a very interesting and beautiful city.

Наталья Да, это правда. Но у меня никогда нет времени там гулять.
(dah eh-tah prahv-dah. noh oo mee-nyah ńee-kahg-dah nyet vryeh-myeh-nee tahm goo-lyaht')
Yes, that's true. But I never have time to wander around there.

Пол А почему? *(ah pah-chee-moo)*
But why?

Наталья Потому что у меня много работы.
(pah-tah-moo shtah oo mee-nyah mnoh-gah rah-boh-tih)
Because I have a lot of work.

Пол Когда улетает ваш самолёт?
(kahg-dah oo-lyeh-tah-yet vahsh sah-mah-lyot)
When does your plane leave?

Наталья Через четыре часа. Из аэропорта Шереметьево-1.
(cheh-ryes chee-tih-ryeh chah-sah. eez ah-eh-rah-por-tah sheh-ree-myet'-yeh-vah ah-deen)
In four hours. From Sheryemyetyevo 1 Airport.

Пол И как вы туда едете?
(ee kahk vih too-dah yeh-dee-tyeh)
And how are you getting there?

Наталья Обычно я иду к автобусной остановке и еду в аэропорт на автобусе. Но сегодня я еду на такси.
(ah-bihch-nah yah ee-doo k ahf-toh-boos-nie ahs-tah-nof-kyeh ee yeh-doo v ah-eh-rah-port nah ahf-toh-boo-syeh. noh see-vod-nyah yah yeh-doo nah tahk-see)
Usually I walk to the bus stop and go to the airport by bus. But today I' am going by taxi.

Пол Я поеду с вами, если хотите. Я хочу помочь вам нести ваши чемоданы.
(yah pah-yeh-doo s vah-mee yes-lee khah-tee-tyeh. yah khah-choo pah-moch vahm nees-tee vah-shih chee-mah-dah-nih)
I'll go with you, if you like. I want to help you carry your suitcases.

Наталья Большое спасибо, но у меня только один чемоданчик, и он не тяжёлый. Он очень лёгкий. Но проводить меня за компанию – пожалуйста.
(bahl'-shoh-yeh spah-see-bah noh oo mee-nyah tol'-kah ah-deen chee-mah-dahn-cheek ee on nyeh tyah-zhoh-liy. on oh-chen' lyokh-keey. noh prah-vah-deet'mee-nyah zah kahm-pah-nee-yoo. pah-zhahl-stah)
Thanks a lot, but I have only one little suitcase, and it's not heavy. It's very light. But please come with me for the company by all means.

Пол Да. С удовольствием. *(dah. s oo-dah-vol'-stvee-yem)*
Yes. With pleasure.

Capital Letters in Russian

As you have seen, the use of capital letters in Russian is not always the same as in English. Compare the Russian and English use of capitals in the two sentences which follow:

А я А́нна Ива́новна Смирно́ва.   And I am Anna Ivanovna Smirnova.

Я белору́ска, но я живу́ в Москве́.   I am a Belarusian, but I live in Moscow.

Although in English **I** is always written as a capital letter, я is only capitalized Я at the beginning of a sentence.

In English, the adjective forms of country names and nouns denoting nationality are capitalized, but not in Russian (Russian language, ру́сский язы́к/Belarusian, белору́ска). Proper nouns, as in English, are capitalized: А́нна, Москва́.

Grammar

1. THE INFINITIVE OF VERBS

The infinitive - the **to ...** form - i.e. **to** work, **to** live, etc.) of most Russian verbs ends in -ть. For example:

рабо́тать *(rah-boh-taht')* to work   жить *(zhiht')* to live

люби́ть *(lyoo-beet')* to love/to like   говори́ть *(gah-vah-reet')* to speak

Note that the **t** in ть is made soft by the soft sign that follows it, and is pronounced similarly to the **t** in **steer**.

Some verbs do not end in -ть, for example, идти́ *(eet-tee)*, **to go** (on foot). This verb will be introduced later in the lesson.

2. THE PRESENT TENSE

Just as different subjects take different verb forms in English (e.g., **I go**, **he goes**), Russian verbs also change forms. Here are the infinitives of the verbs **to work**, **to live**, **to love/like** and **to speak**. Note the different endings.

рабо́тать	Жить	люби́ть	говори́ть
(rah-<u>boh</u>-taht')	(zhiht')	(lyoo-<u>beet</u>')	(gah-vah-<u>reet</u>')
to work	to live	to love/like	to speak

Most Russian verbs end in -ю in the first person singular: я любл<u>ю</u>. Sometimes the ending is -у: я живу́, я иду́, but the first person singular (я …) always ends in -ю after a vowel: я рабо́таю.

я	рабо́та<u>ю</u>	жив<u>у́</u>	любл<u>ю́</u>	говор<u>ю́</u>
(yah)	(rah-<u>boh</u>-tah-yoo)	(zhih-<u>voo</u>)	(lyoob-<u>lyoo</u>)	(gah-vah-<u>ryoo</u>)
I	work	live	love/like	speak

The second person singular endings are -ешь, -ёшь or -ишь:

ты	рабо́та<u>ешь</u>	жив<u>ёшь</u>	лю́б<u>ишь</u>	говор<u>и́шь</u>
(tih)	(rah-<u>boh</u>-tah-yesh)	(zhih-<u>vyosh</u>)	(<u>lyoo</u>-beesh)	(gah-vah-<u>reesh</u>)
you	work	live	love/like	speak

The third person singular ending is -ет, -ёт or -ит:

Он				
(on)				
he				
она́	рабо́та<u>ет</u>	жив<u>ёт</u>	лю́б<u>ит</u>	говор<u>и́т</u>
(ah-<u>nah</u>)	(rah-<u>boh</u>-tah-yet)	(zhih-<u>vyot</u>)	(<u>lyoo</u>-beet)	(gah-vah-<u>reet</u>)
she	works	lives	loves/likes	speaks
Оно́				
(ano)				
it				

The first person plural endings are **-ем**, **-ём** or **-им**:

мы	рабо́таем	живём	лю́бим	говори́м
(mih)	*(rah-boh-tah-yem)*	*(zhih-vyom)*	*(lyoo-beem)*	*(gah-vah-reem)*
we	work	live	love/like	speak

The second person plural endings are **-ете**, **-ёте** or **-ите**:

вы	рабо́таете	живёте	лю́бите	говори́те
(vih)	*(rah-boh-tah-yeh-tyeh)*	*(zhih-vyoh-tyeh)*	*(lyoo-bee-tyeh)*	*(gah-vah-ree-tyeh)*
you	work	live	love/like	speak

The third person plural endings are **-ют**, **-ут** or **-ят**:

они́	рабо́тают	живу́т	лю́бят	говоря́т
(ah-nee)	*(rah-boh-tah-yoot)*	*(zhih-voot)*	*(lyoo-byaht)*	*(gah-vah-ryaht)*
they	work	live	love/like	speak

The present tense in Russian is similar to the same as the English present tense (**I work**) and present continuous (**I am working**). Like English, it can also indicate describe an action in the future:

За́втра я рабо́таю в библиоте́ке.
(zahf-trah yah rah-boh-tah-yoo v bee-blee-ah-tyeh-kyeh)
Tomorrow I am working (will work) in the library.

Here are some examples:

present:
Я рабо́таю в Москве́.
(yah rah-boh-tah-yoo v mahs-kvyeh)
I work in Moscow.

present continuous:
Сейча́с он живёт в Ми́нске.
(sey-chahs on zhih-vyot v meen-skyeh)
He is currently living in Minsk.

future meaning:
За́втра она́ е́дет в Москву́.
(zahf-trah ah-nah yeh-dyet v mahs-kvoo)
Tomorrow she is going to Moscow.

3. VERBS OF MOTION

Russian has two distinct verbs for the English **to go – to go on foot and to go by transport**.

In the dialogue, Paul asks Natalya how she is going to the airport: **И как вы туда́ е́дете?**

She replies that she usually goes on foot (**я иду́**) to the bus stop, but that today she is going (**я е́ду**) by taxi. These are two different verbs. **я иду́** means **I am going on foot**. **я е́ду** means **I am going on some form of transport**.

TO GO ON FOOT

идти *(eet-tee)*	To go on foot:
Я иду́. *(yah ee-doo)*	I'm going.

To go on foot to a specific destination:

Я иду́ домо́й. *(yah ee-doo dah-moy)*	I'm going home.

It can also have a future meaning:

Я иду́ домо́й че́рез час. *(yah ee-doo dah-moy chyeh-rees chahs)*	I am going home in an hour.
ходи́ть *(khah-deet')*	To go on foot frequently or habitually.
Я ча́сто хожу́ в теа́тр. *(yah chahs-tah khah-zhoo f tee-ahtr)*	I often go to the theater.

TO GO BY TRANSPORT

е́хать *(yeh-khat')*	To be going by transport:
Я е́ду. *(yah yeh-doo)*	I'm going. *(not on foot)*

To be going to a specified place:

Я е́ду домо́й. *(yah yeh-doo dah-moy)*	I am going home. *(not on foot)*

It can also have a future meaning:

Я éду домóй чéрез час. (*yah* <u>*yeh*</u>-*doo dah-*<u>*moy*</u> <u>*chyeh*</u>-*rees chahs*)	I'm going home in an hour. (*not* on foot)
éздить (<u>*yez*</u>-*deet'*)	To go frequently or habitually by some means of transport:
Он чáсто éздит в Москвý. (*on* <u>*chahs*</u>-*tah* <u>*yez*</u>-*deet v mahs-*<u>*kvoo*</u>)	He often goes (travels) to Moscow.

TO FLY

летéть (*lee-*<u>*tyet'*</u>)	To be flying, to fly, be flying to a specific destination:
Онá летит в Минск. (*ah-*<u>*nah*</u> *lee-*<u>*teet*</u> *v meensk*)	She is flying to Minsk.

It can also have a future meaning:

Он летит в Москвý чéрез час. (*on lee-*<u>*teet*</u> *v mahs-*<u>*kvoo*</u> <u>*chyeh*</u>-*rees chahs*)	He is flying to Moscow in an hour.
летáть (*lee-*<u>*taht'*</u>)	To fly frequently or habitually:
Онá чáсто летáет в Москвý. (*ah-*<u>*nah*</u> <u>*chahs*</u>-*tah lee-*<u>*tah*</u>-*yet v mahs-*<u>*kvoo*</u>)	She often flies to Moscow.

4. THE PRESENT TENSE OF VERBS OF MOTION

These are frequently used verbs. Try to memorize them.

	ИДТИ́ to go (once) on foot (eet-<u>tee</u>)	Е́ХАТЬ to go (once) (<u>yeh</u>-khat')	ЛЕТЕ́ТЬ to fly (once) (lee-<u>tyet'</u>)
Я	иду́ (ee-<u>doo</u>)	е́ду (<u>yeh</u>-doo)	Лечу́ (lee-<u>choo</u>)
Ты	идёшь (ee-<u>dyosh</u>)	е́дешь (<u>yeh</u>-dyesh)	лети́шь (lee-<u>teesh</u>)
Он/она́/оно́	идёт (ee-<u>dyot</u>)	е́дет (<u>yeh</u>-dyet)	лети́т (lee-<u>teet</u>)
Мы	идём (ee-<u>dyom</u>)	е́дем (<u>yeh</u>-dyem)	Лети́м (lee-<u>teem</u>)
вы	идёте (ee-<u>dyoh</u>-tye)	е́дете (<u>yeh</u>-dee-tyeh)	лети́те (lee-<u>tee</u>-tyeh)
Они́	иду́т (ee-doot)	е́дут (<u>yeh</u>-doot)	Летя́т (lee-tyaht)
	ХОДИ́ТЬ to go (habitually) on foot (khah-deet')	Е́ЗДИТЬ to go (habitually) (yez-deet')	ЛЕТА́ТЬ to fly (habitually) (lee-taht'
Я	Хожу́ (khah-<u>zhoo</u>)	Е́зжу (<u>yezh</u>-zhoo)	Лета́ю (lee-<u>tah</u>-yoo)
Ты	хо́дишь (<u>khoh</u>-deesh)	е́здишь (<u>yez</u>-deesh)	лета́ешь (lee-<u>tah</u>-yesh)
Он/она́/оно́	хо́дит (<u>khoh</u>-deet)	е́здит (<u>yez</u>-deet)	лета́ет (lee-<u>tah</u>-yet)
Мы	хо́дим (<u>khoh</u>-deem)	е́здим (<u>yez</u>-deem)	Лета́ем (lee-<u>tah</u>-yem)
"''вы	хо́дите (<u>khoh</u>-dee-tyeh)	е́здите (<u>yez</u>-dee-tyeh)	лета́ете (lee-<u>tah</u>-yeh-teh)
Они́	хо́дят (<u>khoh</u>-dyat)	е́здят (<u>yez</u>-dyat)	Лета́ют (lee-<u>tah</u>-yoot)

5. PREPOSITIONS

Here are some common Russian prepositions. Each can have several meanings in English, depending on the context in which they are used. Some of the most common meanings are given below, with examples. Note that the form of the noun following a preposition changes from the nominative case – the case in which it is given in a dictionary. These changes are explained in the next section.

ДО   to, up to, as far as, until, before:

До Москвы́ 30 киломе́тров.   It is 30 kilometers to Moscow.
(dah mahs-kvih tree-tsaht' kee-lah-myet-rahf)
До за́втра!   See you tomorrow! ('until tomorrow')
(dah zahf-trah)   (за́втра = tomorrow)
До свида́ния!   Goodbye! ('until the next meeting')
(dah svee-dah-nee-yah)   (свида́ние = meeting)

НА   on, onto, in, to, by, for, during:

на у́лице   on the street, outside (у́лица = street)
(nah oo-lee-tseh)
на по́езде   on the train, by train (по́езд = train)
(nah poh-eez-dyeh)
биле́т на по́езд   a train ticket
(bee-lyet nah poh-eest)
Они́ живу́т на Кавка́зе.   They live in the Caucasus. (Кавка́з = Caucasus)
(ah-nee zhih-voot nah kahf-kah-zyeh)
по́езд на Кавка́з   a train to the Caucasus
(poh-eest nah kahf-kahs)
на неде́лю   for a week (неде́ля = week)
(nah nee-dyeh-lyoo)

У   at, (can indicate possession), by:

у окна́   at/by the window (окно́ = window)
(oo ahk-nah)
Она́ у Ива́на.   She's at Ivan's.
(ah-nah oo ee-vah-nah)
У меня́ биле́т на самолёт.   I have a plane ticket.
(oo mee-nyah bee-lyet nah sah-mah-lyot)

ПО   along, by, on, in, in a language

идти́ по у́лице   to walk along/down the street
(eet-tee pah oo-lee-tsyeh)
по телефо́ну   by phone (телефо́н = telephone)
(pah tee-lee-foh-noo)
кни́га по матема́тике   a math book (a book on math)
(knee-gah pah mah-tee-mah-tee-kyeh) (матема́тика = math)
по-америка́нски   in the American way
(pah ah-mee-ree-kahn-skee)
она́ говори́т по-англи́йски   she speaks English
(ah-nah gah-vah-reet pah ahn-gleey-skee)

В   in, to, at,

в Москве́   in Moscow
(v mahs-kvyeh)

в Москву́   to Moscow
(v mahs-kvoo)

в 2 часа́   at 2 o'clock (час = hour)
(v dvah chah-sah)

С   from, and/with (sometimes **со** before a consonant: **со мной** = with me).

с мо́ря   from the sea (мо́ре = sea)
(s moh-ryah)

с утра́ до но́чи   from morning till night (у́тро = morning)
(s oot-rah dah noh-chee)   (ночь = night)

два с полови́ной   two and a half (полови́на = half)
(dvah s pah-lah-vee-nie)

иди́те со мной   go with me
(ee-dee-tyeh sah mnoy)

ИЗ   from, out of, of

Они́ из Ми́нска.   They are from Minsk.
(ah-nee eez meens-kah)

из уважéния   out of respect (уважéние = respect)
(eez oo-vah-zheh-nee-yah)

букéт из роз   a bouquet of roses (ро́за a rose)
(boo-kyet eez ros)

К   to, towards, by, for,

éхать к бра́ту   to go to one's brother's, to go and to see one's
(yeh-khat' k brah-too)   brother (брат = brother)

к утру́   towards/by morning (у́тро = morning)
(k oot-roo)

к вéчеру   towards/by evening (вéчер = evening)
(k vyeh-chee-roo)

ходи́ть от до́ма к до́му   to go from house to house
(khah-deet'aht doh-mah k doh-moo)

О   about, on,

кни́га о Москвé   a book about Moscow
(knee-gah ah mahs-kvyeh)

О чём вы говори́те?   What are you talking about?
(ah chyom vih gah-vah-ree-tyeh)   (чём = что? = what?)

6. THE SIX CASES OF NOUNS IN THE SINGULAR

When nouns follow prepositions, they change their endings from the nominative form and are **declined** (put into cases). There are six of these cases in both the singular and the plural. In Russian, case endings (the endings tacked onto the noun stem) can have the same function as prepositions serve the same sorts of functions prepositions serve. A good example of this is:

Письмо́ напи́сано преподава́телем.   The letter was written by the teacher.
(pees'-<u>moh</u> nah-<u>pee</u>-sah-noh pree-pah-dah-<u>vah</u>-tee-lyem)

The nominative form of **teacher** is преподава́тель. The -ем ending on преподава́телем expresses the concept of **by**: by the teacher. There are many examples of such constructions in this course where the preposition is expressed via through in the noun ending.

EXAMPLES OF SINGULAR FORMS OF NOUNS IN THE SIX CASES:

NOMINATIVE

masculine	feminine	neuter
стол table *(stol)*	Москва́ Moscow *(mahs-<u>kvah</u>)*	мо́ре sea *(<u>moh</u>-ryeh)*

The nominative is mainly used for the subject of a sentence:

Стол большо́й.
(stol bahl'-<u>shoy</u>)   The table is big.

Москва́ большо́й го́род.
(mahs-<u>kvah</u> bahl'-<u>shoy</u> goh-raht)   Moscow is a big city.

The nominative is used for a predicative noun:

Ната́лья бухга́лтер.
(nah-<u>tahl</u>'-yah boo-<u>gahl</u>-teer)   Natalya is an accountant.

А́нна преподава́тельница.
(<u>ahn</u>-nah pree-pah-dah-<u>vah</u>-teel'-nee-tsa)   Anna is a teacher.

The nominative is also used in forms of address:

Пол! Иди́те сюда́!
(pol. ee-<u>dee</u>-tye syoo-<u>dah</u>)   Paul! Come here!

ACCUSATIVE

masculine	feminine	neuter
стол	Москву́	мо́ре
(stol)	(mahs-_kvoo_)	(_moh_-ryeh)

Without a preposition, the accusative is used for the **direct object** of an action or feeling:

Я не о́чень люблю́ Москву́.
(yah nyeh _oh_-chen' lyoob-_lyoo_ mahs-_kvoo_)

I don't like Moscow very much.

Я о́чень люблю́ Минск.
(yah _oh_-chen' lyoob-_lyoo_ meensk)

I like Minsk a lot.

Where в and на are used to indicate motion, nouns also take the accusative:

Сего́дня она́ е́дет в Москву́.
(see-_vod_-nyah ah-_nah_ yeh-dyet v mahs-_kvoo_)

Today she is going to Moscow.

А́нна е́дет в Минск.
(_ahn_-nah _yeh_-dyet v meensk)

Anna is going to Minsk.

Они́ е́дут на́ мо́ре.
(ah-_nee_ _yeh_-doot nah _moh_-ryeh)

They are going to the sea/coast.

GENITIVE

masculine	feminine	neuter
стола́	Москвы́	мо́ря
(stah-_lah_)	(mahs-_kvih_)	(_moh_-ryah)

The genitive without a preposition indicates **of**:

чемода́н Ива́на
(chee-mah-_dahn_ ee-_vah_-nah)

Ivan's suitcase (nominative Иван)

центр Москвы́
(tsentr mahs-_kvih_)

the center of Moscow

The genitive is used after из, до, у, с:

Я из Новосибирска.
(yah eez nah-vah-see-<u>beer</u>-skah)
I'm from Novosibirsk. (nom. Новосибирск)

до свидания
(dah svee-<u>dah</u>-nee-yah)
goodbye (nom. свидание)

у меня
(oo mee-<u>nyah</u>)
I have (nom. я)

У Ивана есть чемодан.
(oo ee-<u>vah</u>-nah yest' chee-mah-<u>dahn</u>)
Ivan has a suitcase.

у Ивана can also mean **at Ivan's place** - Она у Ивана. **She's at Ivan's.**
(ah-<u>nah</u> oo ee-<u>vah</u>-nah)

Он идёт с работы.
(on ee-<u>dyot</u> s rah-<u>boh</u>-tih)
He is coming from work. (nom. работа)

DATIVE

masculine	feminine	neuter
столу	Москве	морю
(stol-<u>loo</u>)	*(mahs-<u>kvyeh</u>)*	*(<u>moh</u>-ryoo)*

The dative conveys the idea of **to** in the sense of giving, sending or saying something to someone or approaching (going toward) a person or place.

Here are some examples of the dative **without** a preposition:

Я хочу помочь Полу.
(yah khah-<u>choo</u> pah-<u>moch</u> <u>poh</u>-loo)
I want to help Paul.

Помогите Анне, пожалуйста.
(pah-mah-<u>gee</u>-tyeh <u>ahn</u>-nyeh pah-<u>zhahl</u>-stah)
Help Anna, please.

Ивану холодно.
(ee-<u>vah</u>-noo <u>khoh</u>-lahd-nah)
Ivan is cold.

Here are some examples of the dative case **with** the prepositions к and по:

Он говорит по телефону.
(on gah-vah-<u>reet</u> pah tee-lee-<u>foh</u>-noo)
He is talking on the phone.

Она́ идёт по у́лице.		She is walking along the street.
(ah-_nah_ ee-_dyot_ pah _oo_-lee-tseh)		
Я еду к врачу́.		I am going to the doctor.
(yah _yeh_-doo k vrah-_choo_)		

INSTRUMENTAL

masculine	feminine	neuter
столо́м	Москво́й	мо́рем
(stol-_lom_)	(mahs-_kvoy_)	(_moh_-ryem)

Without a preposition, the instrumental is used for the instrument by or with which something is done. In the dialogue, Natalya said:

Я лечу́ туда́ на самолёте …	I am going there by plane …
(yah lee-_choo_ too-_dah_ nah sah-mah-_lyoh_-tyeh …)	
… а возвраща́юсь на по́езде	… but I'm returning by train.
(… ah vahz-vrah-_shchah_-yoos' nah _poh_-eez-dyeh)	

She could have said:

Я лечу́ туда́ самолётом …	I am going there by plane … (nom. самолёт)
(yah lee-_choo_ too-_dah_ sah-mah-_lyoh_-tahm …)	
… а возвраща́юсь по́ездом.	… but I'm returning by train. (nom. по́езд)
(… ah vahz-vrah-_shchah_-yoos' _poh_-eez-dahm.)	

самолётом = by plane
по́ездом = by train

Here are some examples of the instrumental with с:

с удово́льствием	with pleasure (nominative удово́льствие)
(s oo-dah-_vol'_-stvee-yem)	
Пол говори́т с Ната́льей.	Paul is speaking with Natalya.
(pol gah-vah-_reet_ s nah-_tahl'_-yey)	
Я пое́ду с ва́ми.	I will go with you. (nominative вы).
(yah pah-_yeh_-doo s _vah_-mee)	

PREPOSITIONAL

masculine	feminine	neuter
столе́	Москве́	мо́ре
(stol-_lyeh_)	(mahs-_kvyeh_)	(_moh_-ryeh)

This case is always preceded by a preposition. When **в** and **на** are used to indicate being in a place – as opposed to going to a place – they are followed by the prepositional:

Она́ на рабо́те.
(ah-_nah_ nah rah-_boh_-tyeh)

She's at work. (nom. рабо́та)

Он в ба́нке.
(on v _bahn_-kyeh)

He's in the bank. (nom. банк)

Кни́га на столе́.
(_knee_-gah nah stah-_lyeh_)

The book is on the table. (nom. стол)

Профе́ссор в университе́те.
(prah-_fyeh_-sahr v oo-nee-veer-see-_tyeh_-tyeh)

The professor is at the university.
(nom. университе́т)

The preposition **о** means **about**:

Они́ говоря́т о командиро́вке.
(ah-_nee_ gah-vah-_ryaht_ ah kah-mahn-dee-_rof_-kyeh)

They are talking about the business trip.
(nom. командиро́вка)

7. NUMBERS 31–40

31	32	33
три́дцать оди́н	три́дцать два	три́дцать три
(_tree_-tsaht' ah-_deen_)	(_tree_-tsaht' dvah)	(_tree_-tsaht' tree)

34	35	36
три́дцать четы́ре	три́дцать пять	три́дцать шесть
(_tree_-tsaht' chee-_tih_-ryeh)	(_tree_-tsaht' pyat')	(_tree_-tsaht' shest')

37	38	39
три́дцать семь	три́дцать во́семь	три́дцать де́вять
(_tree_-tsaht' syem)	(_tree_-tsaht' _voh_-syem')	(_tree_-tsaht' _dyeh_-vyat')

40
со́рок
(_soh_-rahk)

Useful Expressions

Как вы поживаете? *(kahk vih pah-zhih-<u>vah</u>-yeh-tyeh)*	How are you? How are you getting on?
Нормально. *(nahr-<u>mahl'</u>-nah)*	Alright/Okay.
Всё в порядке. *(fsyoh f pah-<u>ryaht</u>-kyeh)*	Everything's in order/fine.
Как ваша жена? *(kahk <u>vah</u>-shah zheh-<u>nah</u>)*	How is your wife?
Как ваш муж? *(kahk vahsh moosh)*	How is your husband?

Vocabulary

The infinitive of verbs and the nominative singular of nouns, pronouns and adjectives are given in parentheses where necessary.

ехать *(<u>yeh</u>-khat')* to go, be going

в командировку *(командировка) (f. kah-mahn-dee-<u>rof</u>-koo)* on a business trip

как *(kahk)* as, how, like, how is/are

вы знаете *(знать) (vih <u>znah</u>-yeh-tyeh)* you know

любить *(lyoo-<u>beet'</u>)* to love/like

жить *(zhiht')* to live

отец *(ah-<u>tyets</u>)* father

мать *(maht')* mother

также *(<u>tahg</u>-zheh)* also

что *(shtoh)* that, what

но *(noh)* but

у неё *(oo nee-<u>yoh</u>)* she has/at her place

свой *m.*/своя *f.*/своё *n.* *(svoy m./svah-<u>yah</u> f./svah-<u>yoh</u> n.)* reflexive pronoun meaning "one's own".

отдельный *m.*/отдельная *f.*/отдельное *n.* *(aht-<u>dyel'</u>-niy m./aht-<u>dyel'</u>-nah-yah f./aht-<u>dyel'</u>-nah-yeh n.)* separate, individual

квартира *(kvahr-<u>tee</u>-rah)* apartment

ей *(она) (yey)* to her

ей нравится *(нравиться) (yey <u>nrah</u>-vee-tsah)* she likes

работа *(rah-<u>boh</u>-tah)* work

сегодня *(see-<u>vod</u>-nyah)* today

говорить *(gah-vah-<u>reet'</u>)* to speak, be speaking

лететь *(lee-<u>tyet'</u>)* to fly, be flying (now/to a specific place)

туда *(too-<u>dah</u>)* there

самолётом *(самолёт) (sah-mah-<u>lyoh</u>-tahm)* by plane

я возвраща́юсь (возвраща́ться) *(yah vahz-vrah-shchah-yoos') I am returning*

по́ездом *(по́езд) (poh-eez-dahm) by train*

у меня́ есть *(oo mee-nyah yest') I have*

биле́т *(bee-lyet) ticket*

биле́т на самолёт *(bee-lyet nah sah-mah-lyoht) a plane ticket*

обра́тный *m.*/**обра́тная** *f.*/**обра́тное** *n. (ahb-raht-niy m./ahb-raht-nah-yah f./ahb-raht-nah-yeh n.) back, return*

до́лго *(dol-gah) long (time)*

вы бу́дете (быть) *(vih boo-dee-tyeh) you will be*

бу́ду (быть) *(boo-doo) I will be (note that in Russian я is often omitted)*

там *(tahm) there*

три дня *(день) (tree dnyah) three days*

мно́го *(mnoh-gah) a lot, many*

мно́го дел *(де́ло) (mnoh-gah dyel) a lot of things/affairs/work*

ча́сто *(chahs-tah) often*

е́здить *(yez-deet') to go (frequently/ habitually by transport)*

дово́льно *(dah-vol'-nah) enough, sufficiently, rather*

я быва́ю *(yah bih-vah-yoo) I am (somewhere), I spend some time in …*

быва́ть *(bih-vaht') to be in./to visit/to go*

побыва́ть *(pah-bih-vaht') to be in, to spend some time in, to visit*

ка́ждый *m.*/**ка́ждая** *f.*/**ка́ждое** *n. (kahzh-diy m./kahzh-dah-yah f./kahzh-dah-yeh n.) every, each*

ме́сяц *(myeh-syats) month*

мне хо́чется *(mnyeh khoh-chee-tsah) I want*

интере́сный *m.*/**интере́сная** *f.*/

интере́сное *n. (een-tee-ryes-niy m./een-tee-ryes-nah-yah f./een-tee-ryes-nah-yeh n.) interesting*

краси́вый *m.*/**краси́вая** *f.*/**краси́вое** *n. (krah-see-viy m./krah-see-vah-yah f./krah-see-vah-yeh n.) beautiful*

го́род *(goh-raht) town, city*

пра́вда *(prahv-dah) truth, it is true*

никогда́ *(nee-kahg-dah) never*

нет вре́мени (вре́мя) *(nyet vryeh-mee-nee) there is no time*

гуля́ть *(goo-lyat') This is a versatile verb with a lot of idiomatic meanings, such as: **to walk, to enjoy oneself, to go out, to fool around, to do nothing, to be unfaithful to one's husband or wife** …*

Почему́? *(pah-chee-moo) Why?*

потому́ что … *(pah-tah-moo-shtah …) because …*

Когда́? *(kahg-dah) When?*

он улета́ет (улета́ть) *(on oo-lee-tah-yet) he flies away/is flying away*

че́рез *(cheh-rees) in, after, through*

че́рез четы́ре часа́ *(час) (cheh-rees chee-tih-ryeh chah-sah) in four hours*

из аэропо́рта *(аэропо́рт) (eez ah-eh-rah-por-tah) from/out of the airport*

обы́чно *(ah-bihch-nah) usually*

идти́ *(eet-tee) to go, be going*

к *(k) to, towards, up to*

авто́бусная остано́вка *(ahf-toh-boos-nah-yah ahs-tah-nof-kah) bus stop*

на авто́бусе *(авто́бус) (nah ahf-toh-boo-syeh) by bus, on a bus*

я пое́ду (пое́хать) *(yah pah-yeh-doo) I will go*

я хочу́ (хоте́ть) *(yah khah-choo) I want*

помо́чь *(pah-moch)* to help
нести́ *(nees-tee)* to carry
чемода́нчик *(chee-mah-dahn-cheek)* little suitcase *(a diminutive form of* **чемода́н***)*
то́лько *(tol'-kah)* only
тяжёлый *m./*тяжёлая *f./*тяжёлое *n. (tyah-zhoh-liy m./tyah-zhoh-lah-yah f./tyah-zhoh-lah-yeh n.)* heavy, difficult
лёгкий *m./*лёгкая *f./*лёгкое *n. (lyokh-keey m./lyokh-kah-yah f./lyokh-kah-yeh n.)* light, not heavy

проводи́ть *(prah-vah-deet')* to accompany/see off
за компа́нию *(*компа́ния*)* *(zah kahm-pah-nee-yoo)* for the company
с удово́льствием *(*удово́льствие*)* *(s oo-dah-vol'-stvee-yem)* with pleasure
профе́ссор *(m. and f.)* *(prah-fyeh-sahr)* a professor
жена́ *(zheh-nah)* wife
муж *(moosh)* husband

Exercises

Exercise A

In the following sentences, the words given in parentheses are in the nominative. Put them into the correct case, where necessary, and write out the full sentence, complete with stress marks.

For example:

Пол е́дет в (Аме́рика). Пол е́дет в Аме́рику.

1. Ива́н е́дет в (командиро́вка).

   ....

2. А́нна живёт в (Москва́).

   ....

3. Ната́лья рабо́тает в (банк).

   ....

4. У неё есть биле́т на (самолёт).

   ....

5. У (Ива́н) есть чемода́н.

....

6. Ната́лья лю́бит (своя́ рабо́та).

....

7. Сейча́с он на (рабо́та) в (университе́т).

....

8. Они́ е́дут от (Москва́) до (Минск).

....

9. Пол идёт по (у́лица).

....

10. У (я) биле́т на (по́езд).

....

11. Они́ лета́ют на (Кавка́з) (самолёт).

....

12. А́нна говори́т с (Ива́н) по (телефо́н).

....

13. Мы из (Минск), а живём в (Москва́).

....

14. Э́то хоро́шая кни́га по (матема́тика).

....

15. Пол о́чень лю́бит (Москва́), а я о́чень люблю́ (Нью-Йо́рк).

....

Exercice B

Agreement of subject and verb. Put the infinitive of the verb into its in the correct form, and write out the completed sentence.

1. Я (идти́) домо́й.

    ....

2. Ната́лья (е́хать) в Москву́ по́ездом.

    ....

3. Мы (лете́ть) в Вашингто́н че́рез час.

    ....

4. Вы ча́сто (лета́ть) в Ми́нск?

    ....

5. А́нна – профе́ссор. Она́ (рабо́тать) в университе́те.

    ....

6. Я не (люби́ть) Москву́.

    ....

7. Ната́лья (люби́ть) говори́ть с Ива́ном.

    ....

8. Пол (идти́) домо́й.

    ....

9. Мы ча́сто (ходи́ть) в теа́тр.

    ....

10. Оте́ц и мать Ива́на (жить) в Новосиби́рске.

    ....

Exercise C

Translate the following sentences into English.

1. **Я америка́нка.**

   ....

2. **Я живу́ в кварти́ре в Нью-Йо́рке.**

   ....

3. **Мой оте́ц и моя́ мать не живу́т в Нью-Йо́рке.**

   ....

4. **Они́ живу́т и рабо́тают в Калифо́рнии.**

   ....

5. **Мой оте́ц – бухга́лтер, а мать – врач.**

   ....

6. **Я рабо́таю в о́фисе.**

   ....

7. **Я о́чень люблю́ свою́ рабо́ту.**

   ....

8. **Обы́чно я е́ду в аэропо́рт на авто́бусе, но сего́дня я е́ду туда́ на такси́.**

   ....

9. **Моя́ рабо́та тяжёлая, но о́чень интере́сная.**

   ....

10. **Сейча́с я е́ду домо́й с рабо́ты.**

    ....

Exercise D

Translate the following sentences into Russian with stress marks.

1. **My mother and my father live in Moscow.**

   ....

2. **How is your mother?**

   ....

3. **I don'tdo not like St. Petersburg.**

   ....

4. **The big suitcase is heavy.**

   ....

5. **The little suitcase is light.**

   ....

6. **I am in Moscow three to four days a month.**

   ....

7. **Natalya is at Ivan's.**

   ....

8. **We are flying to Moscow in three hours.**

   ....

Exercise E

True or false?

1. Áнна Ивáновна Смирнóва живёт и рабóтает в Минске.   T/F

2. Отéц и мать Анны Ивáновны живýт в Белорýссии.   T/F

3. Натáлья Петрóвна из Новосибирска.   T/F

4. Сегóдня Пол éдет в командирóвку в Санкт-Петербýрг.   T/F

5. Натáлья не лю́бит свою́ рабóту в бáнке.   T/F

6. Натáлья летит в Санкт-Петербýрг на самолёте.   T/F

7. У неё тяжёлый чемодáн.   T/F

8. Онá улетáет из аэропóрта Шеремéтьево-2.   T/F

9. Онá éдет в аэропóрт на автóбусе.   T/F

10. Онá éдет в аэропóрт с Полом.   T/F

5. Conversations

This lesson focuses on conversation skills and phone calls in particular. It's often harder to converse by phone than to speak to someone face-to-face as you cannot use gestures to help yourself be understood. Take the time to listen to the audio and practice repeating it out loud.

ВСТРЕЧА A MEETING

NOTE ON TRANSLITERATION

From this lesson on, you will notice a slight change in the transliteration: we are now indicating where words run together naturally in spoken Russian. Most notably, prepositions often blend with the nouns that follow them, for example: в Санкт-Петербурге = *fsahnkt-pee-teer-boor-gyeh*; в конце концов = *fkahn-tseh kahn-tsof*.

"**Natasha**" and "**Volodya**" are diminutives of "**Natalya**" and "**Vladimir**".

Сегодня Наташа в Санкт-Петербурге. Сейчас она в гостинице. Она пытается позвонить своему коллеге Володе. Но это не легко. Это просто трудно. Иногда номер занят, а иногда никто не отвечает. Это очень досадно! Но в конце концов ей удаётся дозвониться и поговорить с ним ...

(*see-vod-nyah nah-tah-shah fsahnkt-pee-teer-boor-gyeh. sey-chahs ah-nah vgahs-tee-nee-tseh. ah-nah pih-tah-yet-tsah pah-zvah-neet' svah-yeh-moo kah-lyeh-gyeh vah-loh-dyeh. noh eh-tah nyeh lyekh-koh. eh-tah pros-tah trood-nah. ee-nahg-dah noh-meer zah-nyaht ah ee-nahg-dah nee-ktoh nyeh aht-vyeh-chah-yet. eh-tah oh-chen' dah-sahd-nah. noh fkahn-tseh kahn-tsof yey oo-dah-yot-tsah dah-zvah-nee-tsah ee pah-gah-vah-reet' sneem ...*)

Today Natasha is in St. Petersburg. Right now she's in the hotel. She's trying to phone her colleague, Volodya. But it's not easy. It's very difficult. Sometimes the number is busy, and sometimes nobody answers. It's very frustrating! But finally, she manages to get through and speak with him . . .

Воло́дя	Слу́шаю вас.
	(*sloo-shah-yoo vahs*)
	Hello. (Lit. "I'm listening to you".)
Ната́ша	Воло́дя? Здра́вствуйте. Э́то Ната́ша.
	(*vah-loh-dyah. zdrah-stvooy-tyeh. eh-tah nah-tah-shah*)
	Volodya? Hello. This is Natasha.
Воло́дя	До́брый день, Ната́ша. Вы отку́да?
	(*dob-riy dyen' nah-tah-shah. vih aht-koo-dah*)
	Good afternoon, Natasha. Where are you calling from?
Ната́ша	Я здесь, в гости́нице "Нева́". Я уже́ це́лый час звоню́ вам.
	(*yah zdyes' vgahs-tee-nee-tseh nyeh-vah. yah oo-zheh tseh-liy chahs zvah-nyoo vahm*)
	I'm here, in the Hotel Neva. I've been calling you for a whole hour already.
Воло́дя	Я был о́чень за́нят. Майк звони́л мне из Аме́рики. Мы говори́ли о́чень до́лго.
	(*yah bihl oh-chen' zah-nyat. miek zvah-neel mnyeh eez ah-myeh-ree-kee. mih gah-vah-ree-lee oh-chen' dol-gah*)
	I was very busy. Mike called me from America. We talked for a very long time.
Ната́ша	Когда́ мы мо́жем встре́титься? У меня́ к вам мно́го вопро́сов.
	(*kahg-dah mih moh-zhem fstryeh-tee-tsah. oo mee-nyah kvahm mnoh-gah vah-proh-sahf*)
	When can we meet? I have a lot of questions for you.
Воло́дя	Кото́рый час сейча́с?
	(*kah-toh-riy chahs sey-chahs*)
	What time is it now?
Ната́ша	Сейча́с де́сять часо́в.
	(*sey-chahs dyeh-syat' chah-sof*)
	It's ten o'clock.
Воло́дя	Вы мо́жете прие́хать сейча́с?
	(*vih moh-zheh-tyeh pree-yeh-khaht' sey-chas*)
	Can you come now?
Ната́ша	К сожале́нию, сейча́с не могу́. У меня́ ещё одна́ встре́ча сего́дня, в оди́ннадцать часо́в.
	(*k sah-zhah-lyeh-nee-yoo sey-chahs nyeh mah-goo. oo mee-nyah yeh-shchoh ahd-nah f stryeh-chah see-vod-nyah vah-dee-nah-tsat' chah-sof*)
	Unfortunately, I can't right now. I have another meeting today at eleven.
Воло́дя	Мо́жет быть, пообе́даем вме́сте в час дня?
	(*moh-zhet biht' pah-ah-byeh-dah-yem vmyes-tyeh fchas dnyah*)
	Perhaps, we could have lunch together at one?

Ната́ша	Извини́те, но я уже́ договори́лась пообе́дать с колле́гами, с кото́рыми я встреча́юсь в оди́ннадцать. Мо́жет быть, встре́тимся в три?
	(eez-vee-nee-tyeh noh yah oo-zheh dah-gah-vah-ree-lahs' pah-ah-byeh-daht' skah-lyeh-gah-mee skah-toh-rih-mee yah fstryeh-chah-yoos' vah-dee-nah-tsahts. moh-zhet biht' fstryeh-tee-msyah ftree)
	I'm sorry, but I've already agreed to have lunch with the colleagues that I am meeting at eleven. Perhaps we could meet at three?
Воло́дя	В три не могу́. А е́сли в полпя́того? Вам удо́бно?
	(ftree nyeh mah-goo. ah yes-lee fpol-pyah-tah-vah. vahm oo-dob-nah)
	I can't at three. What about half past four? Would that suit?
Ната́ша	Замеча́тельно!
	(zah-mee-chah-teel'-nah)
	Great!
Воло́дя	Договори́лись! Я бу́ду ждать вас в четы́ре три́дцать у себя́ в кабине́те.
	(dah-gah-vah-ree-lees'. yah boo-doo zhdaht' vahs fchee-tih-ryeh tree-tsaht' oo see-byah fkah-bee-nyeh-tyeh)
	Agreed! I will wait for you at four-thirty in my office.
Ната́ша	Воло́дя, я хочу́ спроси́ть, есть ли у вас кака́я-нибу́дь информа́ция о фи́рме, где рабо́тает Майк? Мы хоте́ли бы созда́ть совме́стное предприя́тие с америка́нской фи́рмой.
	(vah-loh-dyah yah khah-choo sprah-seet' yest' lee oo vahs kah-kah-yah-nee-boot' een-fahr-mah-tsih-yah ah feer-myeh gdyeh rah-boh-tah-yet miek. mih khah-tyeh-lee bih sahz-daht'sahv-myes-nah-yeh preet-pree-yah-tee-yeh sah-mee-ree-kahn-skoy feer-mie)
	Volodya, I want to ask if you have any information about the firm where Mike works? We would like to set up a joint venture with an American firm.
Воло́дя	Да, они́ присла́ли нам свой рекла́мные проспе́кты.
	(dah ah-nee pree-slah-lee nahm svah-yee reek-lahm-nih-yeh prahs-pyek-tih)
	Yes, they sent us their promotional brochures.
Ната́ша	Чуде́сно! Тогда́ до встре́чи!
	(choo-dyes-nah. tahg-dah dah-fstryeh-chee)
	Marvelous! So, see you later!
Воло́дя	До встре́чи, Ната́ша! Всего́ до́брого.
	(dah-fstryeh-chee nah-tah-shah. fsyeh-voh dob-rah-vah)
	See you later, Natasha! All the best.
Ната́ша	До свида́ния, Воло́дя!
	(dah-svee-dah-nee-yah vah-loh-dyah)
	Goodbye, Volodya.

Grammar

Note: You will find abbreviations for case names throughout the book.
Nom. = nominative, acc. = accusative, gen. = genitive, dat. = dative, instr. = instrumental, and prep. = prepositional.

1. THE DECLENSION OF PERSONAL PRONOUNS

Lesson 4 looked at the declension of nouns in the singular. Pronouns also have several forms in both the singular and the plural. You will see that we have put н in parentheses before его, ему, им, её, ей, их, им and ими. This is because sometimes in Russian, an "n" sound is inserted to make it easier to pronounce a combination of letters: for example, у его *(oo yeh-voh)* has two vowel sounds together and is more difficult to pronounce than у него *(oo nyeh-voh)*, which slides more easily off the tongue.

Remember that, whereas in English there is only one genderless form of the pronoun **it**, in Russian **it** must agree in gender with the object it represents: книга is feminine and referred to as она, and стол is masculine and referred to as он. Море, on the other hand, is neuter and is referred to as оно.

PERSONAL PRONOUNS

Singular:	I	you	he/it	she/it
Nom.	я (yah)	ты (tih)	он/оно (on/ah-_noh_)	она (ah-_nah_)
acc.	меня (mee-_nyah_)	тебя (tee-_byah_)	(н)его ((n)yeh-_voh_)	(н)её ((n)yeh-_yoh_)
Gen.	меня (mee-nyah)	тебя (tee-byah)	(н)его ((n)yeh-voh)	(н)её ((n)yeh-yoh)
Dat.	мне (mnyeh)	тебе (tee-_byeh_)	(н)ему ((n)yeh-_moo_)	(н)ей ((n)yey)
Instr.	мной * (mnoy)	тобой * (tah-_boy_)	(н)им ((n)eem)	(н)ей * ((n)yey)
Prep.	мне (mnyeh)	тебе (tee-_byeh_)	нём (nyom)	ней (nyey)

* The instrumental forms мною, тобою, ею, нею also exist, but are less common.

Plural:	we	you	they
Nom.	мы	вы	они́
	(mih)	(vih)	(ah-<u>nee</u>)
ăcc.	нас	вас	(н)их
	(nahs)	(vahs)	((n)eekh)
Gen.	нас	вас	(н)их
	(nahs)	(vahs)	((n)eekh)
Dat.	нам	вам	(н)им
	(nahm)	(vahm)	((n)eem)
Instr.	на́ми	ва́ми	(н)и́ми
	(<u>nah</u>-mee)	(<u>vah</u>-mee)	(<u>(n)eeh</u>-mee)
Prep.	нас	вас	них
	(nahs)	(vahs)	(neekh)

Here are some examples of how personal pronouns change depending on the case.

Nominative:

Я иду́ домо́й.
(yah ee-<u>doo</u> dah-<u>moy</u>)

I am going home.

Ты идёшь домо́й.
(tih ee-<u>dyosh</u> dah-<u>moy</u>)

You are going home.

Он *m.*/она́ *f.* идёт домо́й.
(on *m.*/ah-<u>nah</u> *f.* ee-<u>dyot</u> dah-<u>moy</u>)

He/she is going home.

Мы идём домо́й.
(mih ee-<u>dyom</u> dah-<u>moy</u>)

We are going home.

Вы идёте домо́й.
(vih ee-<u>dyoh</u>-tyeh dah-<u>moy</u>)

You are going home.

Они́ иду́т домо́й.
(ah-<u>nee</u> ee-<u>doot</u> dah-<u>moy</u>)

They are going home.

Accusative:

Воло́дя о́чень лю́бит её
(vah-loh-dyah oh-chen' lyoo-beet yeh-yoh)

Volodya likes her a lot.

Ната́ша о́чень лю́бит его́.
(nah-tah-shah oh-chen' lyoo-beet yeh-voh)

Natasha likes him very much.

Я люблю́ тебя́.
(yah lyoob-lyoo tee-byah)

I love you. (Here you **must** use the ты form!)

Пол проводи́л нас в аэропо́рт.
(pol prah-vah-deel nahs vah-eh-rah-port)

Paul accompanied us to the airport.

Genitive:

У меня́ есть па́спорт.
(oo mee-nyah yest' pahs-pahrt)

I have a passport.

У тебя́ есть па́спорт?
(oo tee-byah yest' pahs-pahrt)

Do you have a passport?

У него́ есть биле́т на самолёт.
(oo nyeh-voh yest' bee-lyet nah sah-mah-lyot)

He has a plane ticket.

У неё есть большо́й чемода́н.
(oo nyeh-yoh yest' bahl'-shoy chee-mah-dahn)

She has a big suitcase.

У нас есть хоро́шая кварти́ра.
(oo nahs yest' khah-roh-shah-yah kvahr-tee-rah)

We have a good apartment.

У вас есть биле́ты в теа́тр?
(oo vahs yest' bee-lye-tih fteh-yahtr)

Do you have tickets for the theater?

У них есть но́вая маши́на.
(oo neekh yest' noh-vah-yah mah-shih-nah)

They have a new car.

Note the expressions:

Его́ нет в Москве́.
(yeh-voh nyet vmahs-kvyeh)

He's not in Moscow.

Её нет до́ма.
(yeh-yoh nyet doh-mah)

She's not at home.

Их нет в о́фисе.
(eekh nyet voh-fee-syeh)

They're not in the office.

Dative:

Мне нра́вится жить в Москве́.
(mnyeh nrah-vee-tsah zhiht' vmahs-kvyeh)

I like living in Moscow.

Ему́ нра́вится рабо́тать в университе́те.
(yeh-moo nrah-vee-tsah rah-boh-taht' voo-nee-veer-see-tyeh-tyeh)

He likes to work in the university.

Они́ присла́ли нам свой проспе́кты.
(ah-nee pree-slah-lee nahm svah-ee prahs-pyek-tih)

They sent us their brochures.

Мы присла́ли им биле́ты на самолёт.
(mih pree-slah-lee eem bee-lyeh-tih nah sah-mah-lyot)

We sent them (some) plane tickets.

Я хочу́ помо́чь вам.
(yah khah-choo pah-moch vahm)

I want to help you.

Instrumental:

Я пое́ду с ва́ми.
(yah pah-yeh-doo svah-mee)

I'll go with you.

Она́ говори́ла с ни́ми.
(ah-nah gah-vah-ree-lah snee-mee)

She was talking with them.

Иди́те с не́й.
(ee-dee-tyeh snyey)

Go with her.

Ната́ша идёт со мно́й в теа́тр.
(nah-tah-shah ee-dyot sah-mnoy fteh-y ahtr)

Natasha is going with me to the theater.

Prepositional:

Пол и Ната́ша говоря́т о них.
(pol ee nah-tah-shah gah-vah-ryaht ah neekh)

Paul and Natasha are talking about them.

Не говори́те обо мне́!
(nyeh gah-vah-ree-tyeh ah-bah-mnyeh)

Don't speak about me!

информа́ция о не́й
(een-fahr-mah-tsih-yah ah-nyey)

information about her

2. THE DECLENSION OF NOUNS

As you know, Russian nouns have three genders: masculine, feminine and neuter. We will now look at examples of all three in some detail. Do not try to memorize them. You will have lots of practical examples in the dialogues that follow. Use this section for reference, as necessary, as you work through the course.

MASCULINE NOUNS

All nouns that end with **-й** or with a consonant in the nominative are masculine: **сарáй** *(sah-rie)* shed, **герóй** *(gee-roy)* hero, **крáй** *(krie)* edge/border, **дом** *(dom)* house/home, **автóбус** *(ahf-toh-boos)* bus, **пóезд** *(poh-yeest)* train.

Some nouns ending in **-ь** are masculine, such as **преподавáтель** *(pree-pah-dah-vah-tyel')* teacher, **день** *(dyen')* day, **словáрь** *(slah-vahr')* dictionary, **рубль** *(roobl')* ruble.

A few nouns ending in **-а** or **-я** are masculine, such as **мужчи́на** *(moosh-chee-nah)* man, **дя́дя** *(dyah-dyah)* uncle. Although they are masculine, they are declined like feminine nouns. Here are some examples:

Singular:	table	border	day	uncle
Nom.	стол (stol)	крáй (krie)	день (dyen')	дя́дя (dyah-dyah)
Ăcc.	стол (stol)	крáй (krie)	день (dyen')	дя́дю (dyah-dyah)
Gen.	столá (stah-lah)	крáя (krah-yah)	дня (dnyah)	дя́ди (dyah-dee)
Dat.	столý (stah-loo)	крáю (krah-yoo)	дню (dnyoo)	дя́де (dyah-dyeh)
Instr.	столóм (stah-lom)	крáем (krah-yem)	днём (dnyom)	дя́дей (dyah-dyey)
Prep.	столé (stah-lyeh)	крáе (krah-yeh)	дне (dnyeh)	дя́де (dyah-dyeh)

Plural:	tables	borders	days	uncles
Nom.	столы́ (stoh-_lih_)	края́ (krah-_yah_)	дни (dnee)	дя́ди (_dyah_-dee)
Åcc.	столы́ (stoh-_lih_)	края́ (krah-_yah_)	дни (dnee)	дя́дей (_dyah_-dee)
Gen.	столо́в (stoh-_lof_)	краёв (krah-_yof_)	дне́й (dnyey)	дя́дей (_dyah_-dyey)
Dat.	стола́м (stah-_lahm_)	края́м (krah-_yahm_)	дням (dnyahm)	дя́дям (_dyah_-dyahm)
Instr.	стола́ми (stah-_lah_-mee)	края́ми (krah-_yah_-mee)	дня́ми (_dnyah_-mee)	дя́дями (_dyah_-dyah-mee)
Prep.	стола́х (stah-_lahkh_)	края́х (krah-_yakh_)	днях (dnyakh)	дя́дях (_dyah_-dyahkh)

FEMININE NOUNS

All nouns ending in -ия are feminine: исто́рия (ees-_toh_-ree-yah) history, фами́лия (fah-_mee_-lee-yah) surname, Росси́я (rahs-_see_-yah) Russia, А́нглия (_ahng_-lee-yah) England.

All nouns ending in -сть are feminine. The only common exception is гость (gost'), guest, which is masculine, whether the guest is male or female. They include гла́сность (_glahs_-nahst') openness, кре́пость (_kryeh_-pahst') castle, скро́мность (_skrom_-nahst') modesty, уста́лость (oo-_stah_-lahst') tiredness.

Almost all nouns ending in -а or -я are feminine: кни́га (_knee_-gah) book, доро́га (dah-_roh_-gah) road, земля́ (zeem-_lyah_) land, семья́ (seem'-_yah_) family, ку́хня (_kookh_-nyah) kitchen.

The tables opposite show some examples of the declension of feminine nouns.

Singular:	history	castle	road	land
Nom.	ист´øрия (ees-*toh*-ree-yah)	крéпость (*kryeh*-pahst′)	дорóга (dah-*roh*-gah)	земля́ (zeem-lyah)
ăcc.	истóрию (ees-*toh*-ree-yoo)	крéпость (*kryeh*-pahst′)	дорóгу (dah-*roh*-goo)	зéмлю (*zyem*-lyoo)
Gen.	истóрии (ees-*toh*-ree-ee)	крéпости (*kryeh*-pahs-tee)	дорóги (dah-*roh*-gee)	земли́ (zeem-*lee*)
Dat.	истóрии (ees-*toh*-ree-ee)	крéпости (*kryeh*-pahs-tee)	дорóге (dah-*roh*-gyeh)	землé (zeem-*lyeh*)
Instr.	истóрией (ees-*toh*-ree-yey)	крéпостью (*kryeh*-pahs-tyoo)	дорóгой (dah-*roh*-gie)	землёй (zeem-*lyoy*)
Prep.	истóрии (ees-*toh*-ree-ee)	крéпости (*kryeh*-pahs-tee)	дорóге (dah-*roh*-gyeh)	землé (zeem-*lyeh*)

Plural:	histories	castles	roads	lands
Nom.	истóрии (ees-*toh*-ree-ee)	крéпости (*kryeh*-pahs-tee)	дорóги (dah-*roh*-gee)	зéмли (*zyem*-lee)
ăcc.	истóрии (ees-*toh*-ree-ee)	крéпости (*kryeh*-pahs-tee)	дорóги (dah-*roh*-gee)	зéмли (*zyem*-lee)
Gen.	истóрий (ees-*toh*-reey)	крéпостей (*kryeh*-pahs-tyey)	дорóг (dah-*rog*)	земéль (zee-*myel*′)
Dat.	истóриям (ees-*toh*-ree-yahm)	крéпостям (*kryeh*-pahs-tyahm)	дорóгам (dah-*roh*-gahm)	зéмлям (*zyem*-lyahm)
Instr.	истóриями (ees-*toh*-ree-yah-mee)	крéпостями (*kryeh*-pahs-tyah-mee)	дорóгами (dah-*roh*-gah-mee)	зéмлями (*zyem*-lyah-mee)
Prep.	истóриях (ees-*toh*-ree-yahkh)	крéпостях (*kryeh*-pahs-tyahkh	дорóгах (dah-*roh*-gahkh)	зéмлях (*zyem*-lyahkh)

NEUTER NOUNS

Neuter nouns have no **shared endings** with masculine and feminine nouns. They all end in one of the following:

-о : село *(see-loh)* village, вино́ *(vee-noh)* wine, де́ло *(dyeh-lah)* affair/business

-е : со́лнце *(son-tseh)* sun, мо́ре *(moh-ryeh)* sea, по́ле *(poh-lyeh)* field

-ие : зда́ние *(zdah-nee-yeh)* building, собра́ние *(sah-brah-nee-yeh)* meeting

-ье : ожере́лье *(ah-zheh-ryel'-yeh)* necklace

-ьё : враньё *(vrahn'-yoh)* a lie, мытьё *(miht'-yoh)* (the process of) washing

-мя: вре́мя *(vryeh-myah)* time, и́мя *(ee-myah)* first name

Here are some examples of the declension of neuter nouns:

Singular:	affair	field	first name
Nom.	де́ло *(dyeh-lah)*	по́ле *(poh-lyeh)*	и́мя *(ee-myah)*
ăcc.	де́ло *(dyeh-lah)*	по́ле *(poh-lyeh)*	и́мя *(ee-myah)*
Gen.	де́ла *(dyeh-lah)*	по́ля *(poh-lyah)*	и́мени *(ee-mee-nee)*
Dat.	де́лу *(dyeh-loo)*	по́лю *(poh-lyoo)*	и́мени *(ee-mee-nee)*
Instr.	де́лом *(dyeh-lahm)*	по́лем *(poh-lyem)*	и́менем *(ee-mee-nyem)*
Prep.	де́ле *(dyeh-lyeh)*	по́ле *(poh-lyeh)*	и́мени *(ee-mee-nee)*

Plural:	affairs	fields	first names
Nom.	дела́ (dee-<u>lah</u>)	поля́ (pah-<u>lyah</u>)	имена́ (ee-mee-<u>nah</u>)
ăcc.	дела́ (dee-<u>lah</u>)	поля́ (pah-<u>lyah</u>)	имена́ (ee-mee-<u>nah</u>)
Gen.	дел (dyel)	поле́й (pah-<u>lyey</u>)	имён (ee-<u>myon</u>)
Dat.	дела́м (dee-<u>lahm</u>)	поля́м (pah-<u>lyahm</u>)	имена́м (ee-mee-<u>nahm</u>)
Instr.	дела́ми (dee-<u>lah</u>-mee)	поля́ми (pah-<u>lyah</u>-mee)	имена́ми (ee-mee-<u>nah</u>-mee)
Prep.	дела́х (dee-<u>lahkh</u>)	поля́х (pah-<u>lyahkh</u>)	имена́х (ee-mee-<u>nahkh</u>)

3. THE FUTURE TENSE OF THE VERB "TO BE"

In Lesson 4, Paul asked Natasha: **Вы до́лго бу́дете в Санкт-Петербу́рге? Will you be in St. Petersburg for long?** She replied: **Я бу́ду там три дня I'll be there for 3 days.**

In Lesson 5, Volodya says: **Я бу́ду ждать вас,** I'll wait for you. (Here **вас** is the genitive form of **вы**.)

The future tense of **быть to be** is not complicated:

Singular	Plural
я бу́ду (yah <u>boo</u>-doo) I will be	мы бу́дем (mih <u>boo</u>-dyem) we will be
ты бу́дешь (tih <u>boo</u>-dyesh) you (informal) will be	вы бу́дете (vih <u>boo</u>-dee-tyeh) you will be
он/она́/оно́ бу́дет (on/ah-<u>nah</u>/ah-<u>noh</u> <u>boo</u>-dyet) he, she, it will be	они́ бу́дут (ah-<u>nee</u> <u>boo</u>-doot) they will be

A compound future tense can be formed using the future of **быть** + the infinitive of another verb as in **Я бу́ду ждать вас, I'll wait for you**.

Here are some more examples of the future tense of **быть**:

Где вы бу́дете за́втра ве́чером?
(gdyeh vih <u>boo</u>-dee-tyeh <u>zahf</u>-trah <u>vyeh</u>-chee-rahm)
Where will you be tomorrow evening?

Я бу́ду до́ма.
(yah <u>boo</u>-doo <u>doh</u>-mah)
I'll be at home.

Мы бу́дем жить в Москве́.
(mih <u>boo</u>-dyem zhiht' v mahs-<u>kvyeh</u>)
We will live in Moscow./We are going to live in Moscow.

Они́ бу́дут рабо́тать в Санкт-Петербу́рге.
(ah-<u>nee boo</u>-doot rah-<u>boh</u>-taht' fsahnkt-pee-teer-<u>boor</u>-gyeh)
They will work in St. Petersburg./They are going to work in St. Petersburg.

You are already familiar with **у меня́ есть**. There is also a future form:

У меня́ бу́дет своя́ отде́льная кварти́ра.
(oo mee-<u>nyah boo</u>-dyet svah-<u>yah</u> aht-<u>dyel</u>'-nah-yah kvahr-<u>tee</u>-rah)
I will have my own separate apartment.

За́втра у них бу́дут биле́ты.
(<u>zahft</u>-rah oo neekh <u>boo</u>-doot bee-<u>lyeh</u>-tih)
Tomorrow they will have tickets.

4. THE PAST TENSE OF VERBS

The past tense of Russian verbs is less complicated than the present tense. For most verbs, it is formed by removing the **-ть** from the infinitive and adding:
-л (masculine singular)
-ла (feminine singular)
-ло (neuter singular)
-ли for all genders of all plural forms.

Opposite, you will see some examples of conugations for commonly used verbs.

Plural:	to work	to live	to love/like	to speak
	работать (rah-<u>boh</u>-taht')	жи́ть (zhiht')	люби́ть (lyoo-<u>beet</u>')	говори́ть (gah-vah-<u>reet</u>')
я *m.*	рабо́тал (rah-<u>boh</u>-tahl)	жил (zhihl)	люби́л (lyoo-<u>beel</u>)	говори́л (gah-vah-<u>reel</u>)
я *f.*	рабо́тала (rah-<u>boh</u>-tah-lah)	жила́ (zhih-<u>lah</u>)	люби́ла (lyoo-<u>bee</u>-lah)	говори́ла (gah-vah-<u>reeh</u>-lah)
ты *m.*	рабо́тал (rah-<u>boh</u>-tahl)	жил (zhihl)	люби́л (lyoo-<u>beel</u>)	говори́л (gah-vah-<u>reel</u>)
ты *f.*	рабо́тала (rah-boh-tah-lah)	жила́ (zhih-<u>lah</u>)	люби́ла (lyoo-<u>bee</u>-lah)	говори́ла (gah-vah-<u>reeh</u>-lah)
Он	рабо́тал (rah-<u>boh</u>-tahl)	жил (zhihl)	люби́л (lyoo-<u>beel</u>)	говори́л (gah-vah-<u>reel</u>)
она	рабо́тала (rah-<u>boh</u>-tah-lah)	жила́ (zhih-<u>lah</u>)	люби́ла (lyoo-<u>bee</u>-lah)	говори́ла (gah-vah-<u>reeh</u>-lah)
Оно	рабо́тало (rah-<u>boh</u>-tah-lah)	жи́ло (<u>zhih</u>-lah)	люби́ло (lyoo-<u>bee</u>-lah)	говори́ло (gah-vah-<u>reeh</u>-lah)
Мы вы Они	рабо́тали (rah-<u>boh</u>-tah-lee)	жи́ли (<u>zhih</u>-lee)	люби́ли (lyoo-<u>bee</u>-lee)	говори́ли (gah-vah-<u>ree</u>-lee)

Examples:

Вчера́ мы рабо́тали в Ми́нске.
(fchee-<u>rah</u> mih rah-<u>boh</u>-tah-lee <u>fmeens</u>-kyeh)

Yesterday we worked in Minsk.

В про́шлом году́ я жил в Москве́.
(f <u>prosh</u>-lahm gah-<u>doo</u> yah zhihl fmas-<u>kvye</u>)

Last year I lived in Moscow.

Я о́чень люби́л его́.
(yah <u>oh</u>-chen' lyoo-<u>beel</u> yeh-<u>voh</u>)

I liked him very much.

Ива́н говори́л с Ма́йком.
(ee-<u>vahn</u> gah-vah-<u>reel</u> smie-kahm)

Ivan was talking with Mike.

5. NUMBERS 40–100

40	50	55
со́рок (*soh*-rahk)	пятьдеся́т (pyah-dee-*syaht*)	пятьдеся́т пять (pyah-dee-*syaht* pyaht')

60	63	70
шестьдеся́т (shez-dee-*syaht*)	шестьдеся́т три (shez-dee-*syaht* tree)	се́мьдесят (*syem*-dee-syaht)

73	80	82
се́мьдесят три (*syem*-dee-syaht tree)	во́семьдесят (*voh*-seem-dee-syaht)	во́семьдесят два (*voh*-seem-dee-syaht dvah)

90	91	100
девяно́сто (dee-vyah-*nos*-tah)	девяно́сто оди́н (dee-vyah-*nos*-tah ah-*deen*)	сто (stoh)

Useful Expressions

Кото́рый час?　　　　　　　　　　What time is it?
(kah-*toh*-riy chahs)

В кото́ром часу́ улета́ет самолёт?　　What time does the plane leave?
(fkah-*toh*-rahm chah-*soo* oo-lee-*tah*-yet sah-mah-*lyot*)

В кото́ром часу́ прилета́ет самолёт?　What time does the plane arrive?
(fkah-*toh*-rahm chah-*soo* pree-lee-*tah*-yet sah-mah-*lyot*)

Я вас не понима́ю.　　　　　　　　I don't understand you.
(yah vahs nyeh pah-nee-*mah*-yoo)

Говори́те ме́дленно, пожа́луйста.　　Speak slowly, please.
(gah-vah-*ree*-tyeh *myed*-leen-nah pah-*zhahl*-stah)

Vocabulary

For the rest of the course, verbs will be given in the infinitive and nouns in the nominative singular. The form of the word in the dialogue will also be given if necessary. The gender of the noun will only be given in cases where this is not clear from the form.

договори́ться (*dah-gah-vah-ree-tsah*) to agree (about)

гости́ница (*gahs-tee-nee-tsah*) hotel

пыта́ться (*pih-tah-tsah*) to try

позвони́ть (*pah-zvah-neet'*) to phone (used only in the past or future tenses)

звони́ть (*zvah-neet'*) to phone, to be phoning

дозвони́ться (*dah-zvah-nee-tsah*) to let the phone ring until it is answered, to get through to someone

колле́га (*kah-lyeh-gah*) a colleague

легко́ (*lekh-koh*) easy

про́сто (*pros-tah*) simply

тру́дно (*trood-nah*) difficult

иногда́ (*ee-nahg-dah*) sometimes

но́мер (*noh-meer*) number, hotel room

за́нят (*zah-nyaht*) busy, engaged

никто́ (*nee-ktoh*) nobody

отвеча́ть (*aht-veh-chat'*) to answer, to reply

доса́дно (*dah-sahd-nah*) frustrating

коне́ц (*kah-nyets*) end

в конце́ концо́в (*f kahn-tseh kahn-tsof*) in the end

ей удаётся (*yey oo-dah-yot-tsah*) she succeeds

поговори́ть (*pah-gah-vah-reet'*) to speak,

to have a talk

слу́шать (*sloo-shaht'*) to listen

до́брый *m.*/**до́брая** *f.*/**до́брое** *n.* (*dob-riy m./dob-rah-yah f./dob-rah-yeh n.*) good, kind

Отку́да? (*aht-koo-dah*) Where from?

здесь (*zdyes'*) here

уже́ (*oo-zheh*) already

це́лый *m.*/**це́лая** *f.*/**це́лое** *n.* (*tseh-liy m./tseh-lah-yah f./tseh-lah-yeh n.*) whole

час (*chahs*) hour

до́лго (*dol-gah*) a long time

мочь (*moch*) to be able to

я могу́ (*yah mah-goo*) I can

мы мо́жем (*mih moh-zhem*) we can

вы мо́жете (*vih moh-zheh-tyeh*) you can

мо́жет быть (*moh-zhet biht'*) perhaps, maybe

встре́титься (*fstreh-tee-tsah*) to meet

кото́рый *m.*/**кото́рая** *f.*/**кото́рое** *n.* (*kah-toh-riy m./kah-toh-rah-yah f./ kah-toh-rah-yeh n.*) which

прие́хать (*pree-yeh-khaht'*) to come

сожале́ние (*sah-zhah-lyeh-nee-yeh*) pity, regret

к сожале́нию (*k sah-zhah-lyeh-nee-yoo*) unfortunately, regrettably

пообе́дать (*pah-ah-byeh-daht'*) to have lunch/(dinner)

вме́сте (*vmyes-tyeh*) together

извини́ть (*eez-vee-neet'*) to forgive, to excuse

встреча́ться (*fstryeh-chaht-tsah*) to meet (one another)

удо́бно (*oo-dob-nah*) suitable, convenient

Замеча́тельно! (*zah-mee-chah-teel'-nah*)

Great!, Wonderful!

ждать *(zhdaht') to wait*

кабинéт *(kah-bee-nyet) office*

у себя в кабинéте *(oo see-byah f kah-bee-nyeh-tyeh) in my office*

хотéть *(khah-tyet') to want*

я хочý *(yah khah-choo) I want*

Мы хотéли бы … *(mih khah-tyeh-lee bih …) We would like …*

спросúть *(sprah-seet') to ask*

какóй *m./***какáя** *f./***какóе** *n. (kah-koy m./ kah-kah-yah f./kah-koh-yeh n.) what sort of, what a, which*

какóй-нибýдь *(kah-koy nee-boot') some, any*

информáция *(een-fahr-mah-tsih-yah) information*

фúрма *(feer-mah) firm, company*

создáть *(sahz-daht') to found, to set up*

совмéстный *m./***совмéстная** *f./***совмéстное** *n. (sahv-myes-niy m./ sahv-myes-nah-yah f./sahv-myes-nah-yeh n.) joint*

предприятие *(preet-pree-yah-tee-yeh) enterprise*

прислáть *(pree-slaht') to send*

реклáмный *m./***реклáмная** *f./***реклáмное** *n. (reek-lahm-niy m./reek-lahm-nah-yah f./reek-lahm-nah-yeh n.) advertising, promotional*

проспéкт *(prahs-pyekt) brochure*

чудéсно *(choo-dyes-nah) wonderful, marvelous*

тогдá *(tahg-dah) then*

всегó дóброго *(fsee-voh dob-rah-vah) all the best*

сарáй *(sah-rie) shed*

герóй *(gee-roy) hero*

крáй *(krie) border, edge, territory*

день *m. (dyen') day*

дядя *m. (dyah-dyah) uncle*

истóрия *(ees-toh-ree-yah) history*

фамúлия *(fah-mee-lee-yah) surname*

скрóмность *(skrom-nahst') modesty*

земля *(zeem-lyah) land*

семья *(seem'-yah) family*

кýхня *(kookh-nyah) kitchen*

винó *(vee-noh) wine*

здáние *(zdah-nee-yeh) building*

собрáние *(sahb-rah-nee-yeh) meeting*

ожерéлье *(ah-zheh-ryel'-yeh) necklace*

úмя *n. (ee-myah) first name*

улетáть *(oo-lee-taht') to fly out*

прилетáть *(pree-lee-taht') to fly in*

понимáть *(pah-nee-maht') to understand*

мéдленно *(myed-leen-nah) slowly*

зáвтра *(zahf-trah) tomorrow*

вчерá *(fchyeh-rah) yesterday*

вéчер *(vyeh-cher) evening*

вéчером *(vyeh-chee-rahm) in the evening*

Exercises

Exercise A

Translate the following sentences into Russian.

1. **Mike lives and works in New York.**

   ....

2. **Natasha works in a bank in Moscow.**

   ....

3. **Her father and her mother live in Minsk.**

   ....

4. **I have my own separate apartment.**

   ....

5. **Right now, Natasha is in a hotel.**

   ....

6. **It is difficult for her to call her colleague, Volodya.**

   ....

7. **Volodya and Mike were very busy.**

   ....

8. **When can we meet?** ....

Exercise B

Put the word in parentheses into the appropriate case.

1. **Я иду́ (дом).** ....

2. **Ната́ша в (кабине́т) Воло́ди.** ....

3. **Воло́дя не рабо́тает. Он (дом).** ....

4. Кни́га на (стол). ....

5. (Я) не нра́вится жить в (Москва́). ....

6. Ива́н о́чень лю́бит (она́). ....

7. У (я) есть па́спорт. ....

8. У (мы) больша́я кварти́ра. ....

9. (Он) нет в (Москва́). ....

Exercise C

Give the appropriate form of the verb, so that subject and verb agree.

1. За́втра я (быть) рабо́тать до́ма. ....

2. Вчера́ они́ (рабо́тать) в ба́нке. ....

3. Сейча́с Ната́ша (говори́ть) с Ива́ном. ....

4. Где они́ (быть) вчера́ ве́чером? ....

5. Сего́дня я (идти́) в теа́тр. ....

6. Воло́дя ча́сто (е́здить) в Москву́. ....

7. Сейча́с Пол (жить) в Москве́. ....

8. За́втра у меня́ (быть) биле́т на самолёт. ....

9. Вчера́ Воло́дя (быть) о́чень за́нят. ....

10. Вчера́ Ма́йк (звони́ть) мне из Аме́рики. ....

Exercise D

Translate the following sentences into English.

1. Мне не нра́вится рабо́тать в Москве́.

    ....

2. Сейча́с во́семь часо́в. ....

3. Вам удо́бно встре́титься в три часа́?

....

4. Они́ бу́дут ждать нас в пять три́дцать в ба́нке.

....

5. Ма́йк присла́л нам мно́го вина́.

....

6. Мой оте́ц о́чень лю́бит свою́ рабо́ту.

....

7. У меня́ есть четы́ре биле́та в теа́тр.

....

8. Где Андре́й? Его́ нет до́ма. ....

9. Воло́дя пое́дет с ва́ми, е́сли хоти́те.

....

Exercise E

True or false?

1. Сего́дня Ната́ша не в Москве́.	T/F
2. Ната́ше о́чень тру́дно позвони́ть своему́ колле́ге Воло́де.	T/F
3. Ма́йк звони́л Ната́ше из Аме́рики.	T/F
4. Ната́ше не удаётся поговори́ть с Воло́дей.	T/F
5. У Ната́ши к Воло́де мно́го вопро́сов.	T/F
6. Сего́дня у Ната́ши ещё одна́ встре́ча.	T/F
7. Ната́ша договори́лась пообе́дать с Воло́дей.	T/F
8. Воло́дя бу́дет ждать Ната́шу в 4.30.	T/F

6. Review: Lessons 1–5

This review section is a revision of what you have learnt so far. Take the time to listen to the audio dialogues again and see how much you can understand without turning back to the English versions in the previous chapters! Don't forget to do the short exercise section too!

DIALOGUE 2: ЗДРА́ВСТВУЙТЕ

А́нна	Здра́вствуйте, Пол. Как ва́ши дела́?
Пол	Здра́вствуйте. У меня́ всё хорошо́, спаси́бо. А как ва́ши дела́?
А́нна	Спаси́бо, хорошо́. Сади́тесь, пожа́луйста. Дава́йте начнём наш уро́к.
Пол	С удово́льствием.
А́нна	Оди́н вопро́с, Пол.
Пол	Да, пожа́луйста.
А́нна	Вот, посмотри́те. Э́то ру́чка?
Пол	Да, э́то ру́чка.
А́нна	А э́то? Э́то ру́чка и́ли ключ?
Пол	Э́то ключ.
А́нна	А э́то? Э́то то́же ключ?
Пол	Нет, э́то не ключ.
А́нна	Что э́то?
Пол	Э́то кни́га. Э́то кни́га на ру́сском языке́.
А́нна	О́чень хорошо́, Пол. До свида́ния.
Пол	До свида́ния, А́нна Ива́новна. До ско́рой встре́чи!

DIALOGUE 3: ЗНАКÓМСТВО

Пол	Здрáвствуйте. Я – Пол. А вы кто?
Натáлья	А меня́ зову́т Натáлья Петрóвна Ивáнова. Я ру́сская. А вы ру́сский?
Пол	Я не ру́сский. И не украи́нец, и не белору́с.
Натáлья	Кто вы по национáльности?
Пол	Я америкáнец. Я роди́лся в Сан-Франци́ско. А вы откýда?
Натáлья	Я из Новосиби́рска. А сейчáс я живý здесь, в Москвé. Я рабóтаю в бáнке. А где вы рабóтаете?
Пол	Я? Я не рабóтаю. Я студéнт. Я учý ру́сский язы́к.
Натáлья	Знáчит, я бухгáлтер, а вы студéнт ... А кто эта жéнщина?
Пол	Это Áнна Ивáновна. Она преподавáтель. Она белору́ска, из Ми́нска. Áнна Ивáновна! Иди́те сюдá! ... Это Áнна Ивáновна. Áнна Ивáновна, это Натáлья Петрóвна. Онá рабóтает в бáнке.
Натáлья	Óчень прия́тно.

DIALOGUE 4: НАТÁЛЬЯ ПЕТРÓ ВНА ÉДЕТ В КОМАНДИРÓВКУ

Áнна	Как вы знáете, я белору́ска. Я живý и рабóтаю в Москвé. Я óчень люблю́ Москвý. Но я люблю́ и Минск, где живýт мой отéц и моя́ мать. Вы тáкже знáете, что Натáлья Петрóвна из Новосиби́рска. Но сейчáс онá живёт в Москвé. У неё своя́ отдéльная кварти́ра. Ей нрáвится жить в Москвé. Онá рабóтает в бáнке. Онá óчень лю́бит свою́ рабóту.
	Сегóдня онá éдет в командирóвку в Санкт-Петербýрг. Сейчáс онá говори́т с Пóлом ...
Пол	Как вы éдете в Санкт-Петербýрг?
Натáлья	Я лечý тудá на самолёте, а возвращáюсь на пóезде.
Пол	У вас есть билéт на самолёт?
Натáлья	Да. У меня́ есть билéт на самолёт и обрáтный билéт на пóезд.
Пол	Вы дóлго бýдете в Санкт-Петербýрге?
Натáлья	Я бýду там три дня. У меня́ там мнóго дел.
Пол	Вы чáсто тудá éздите?
Натáлья	Да, довóльно чáсто. Я там бывáю три-четы́ре дня кáждый мéсяц.
Пол	Я óчень хочý побывáть в Санкт-Петербýрге.
	Говоря́т, это óчень интерéсный и краси́вый гóрод.
Натáлья	Да, это прáвда. Но у меня́ никогдá нет врéмени там гуля́ть.
Пол	А почемý?

Ната́лья	Потому́ что у меня́ мно́го рабо́ты.
Пол	Когда́ улета́ет ваш самолёт?
Ната́лья	Че́рез четы́ре часа́. Из аэропо́рта Шереме́тьево-1.
Пол	И как вы туда́ е́дете?
Ната́лья	Обы́чно я иду́ к авто́бусной остано́вке и е́ду в аэропо́рт на авто́бусе. Но сего́дня я е́ду на такси́.
Пол	Я пое́ду с ва́ми, е́сли хоти́те. Я хочу́ помо́чь вам нести́ ва́ши чемода́ны.
Ната́лья	Большо́е спаси́бо, но у меня́ то́лько оди́н чемода́нчик, и он не тяжёлый. Он о́чень лёгкий. Но проводи́ть меня́ за компа́нию – пожа́луйста.
Пол	Да. С удово́льствием.

DIALOGUE 5: ВСТРЕ́ЧА

Сего́дня Ната́ша в Санкт-Петербу́ рге. Сейча́с она́ в гости́ нице. Она́ пыта́ется позвони́ ть своему́ колле́ге Воло́де. Но э́ то не легко́. Э́ то про́сто тру́ дно. Иногда́ но́мер за́нят, а иногда́ никто́ не отвеча́ет. Э́ то о́чень доса́дно! Но в конце́ концо́в ей удаётся дозвони́ ться и поговори́ ть с ним …

Воло́дя	Слу́шаю вас.
Ната́ша	Воло́дя? Здра́вствуйте! Э́то Ната́ша.
Воло́дя	До́брый день, Ната́ша. Вы отку́да?
Ната́ша	Я здесь, в гости́нице "Нева́". Я уже́ це́лый час звоню́ вам.
Воло́дя	Я был о́чень за́нят. Майк звони́л мне из Аме́рики. Мы говори́ли о́чень до́лго.
Ната́ша	Когда́ мы мо́жем встре́титься? У меня́ к вам мно́го вопро́сов.
Воло́дя	Кото́рый час сейча́с?
Ната́ша	Сейча́с де́сять часо́в.
Воло́дя	Вы мо́жете прие́хать сейча́с?
Ната́ша	К сожале́нию, сейча́с не могу́. У меня́ ещё одна́ встре́ча сего́дня, в оди́ннадцать часо́в.
Воло́дя	Мо́жет быть, пообе́даем вме́сте в час дня?
Ната́ша	Извини́те, но я уже́ договори́лась пообе́дать с колле́гами, с кото́рыми я встреча́юсь в оди́ннадцать. Мо́жет быть, встре́тимся в три?
Воло́дя	В три не могу́. А е́сли в полпя́того? Вам удо́бно?
Ната́ша	Замеча́тельно!
Воло́дя	Договори́лись! Я бу́ду ждать вас в четы́ре три́дцать у себя́ в кабине́те.
Ната́ша	Воло́дя, я хочу́ спроси́ть, есть ли у вас кака́я-нибу́дь

	информа́ция о фи́рме, где рабо́тает Майк? Мы хоте́ли бы созда́ть совме́стное предприя́тие с америка́нской фи́рмой.
Воло́дя	Да, они́ присла́ли нам свои́ рекла́мные проспе́кты.
Ната́ша	Чуде́сно! Тогда́ до встре́чи!
Воло́дя	До встре́чи, Ната́ша! Всего́ до́брого.
Ната́ша	До свида́ния, Воло́дя!

Exercises

Exercise A

Here are some English words that are the same – or almost the same – as their Russian counterparts.

Translate them into Russian and check your answers against the key.

1. **America** ....

2. **New York** ....

3. **the president** ....

4. **an office** ....

5. **(a male) student** ....

6. **(a female) student** ....

7. vodka ....

8. a pilot ....

9. students (male, or male and female) ....

10. airport ....

Exercise B

Read these Russian numbers aloud and then write them down (1, 5, etc).

А. во́семь ....
Б. три ....
В. семь ....
Г. четы́ре ....
Д. два ....
Е. оди́н ....
Ё. пять ....
Ж. шесть ....
З. де́вять ....
И. де́сять ....
Й. два́дцать два ....

К. три́дцать шесть ....
Л. со́рок ....
М. пятьдеся́т пять ....
Н. шестьдеся́т де́вять .....
О. се́мьдесят ....
П. сто ....
Р. девяно́сто четы́ре ....
С. во́семьдесят ....
Т. се́мьдесят три ....
У. четы́рнадцать ....
Ф. двена́дцать ....

Х. пятна́дцать ....
Ц. со́рок четы́ре ....
Ч. се́мьдесят оди́н ....
Ш. восемна́дцать ....
Щ. шестьдеся́т во́семь .....
Ь. три́дцать семь ....
Ы. со́рок два ....
Ъ. оди́ннадцать ....
Э. во́семьдесят три ....
Ю. девятна́дцать ....
Я. два́дцать де́вять ....

Exercise C

Put the nouns and pronouns given in parentheses into the appropriate case where necessary.

1. Ива́н и Ната́ша е́дут в (Москва́) .... в (командиро́вка)

    ....

2. Сейча́с Воло́дя и Ната́ша на (рабо́та) .... в (банк) .... в

    (Минск) ....

3. Ива́н не лю́бит (своя́ рабо́та) .... в (университе́т)

....

4. Ната́ша говори́т с (Майк) ....

5. Э́то чемода́н (Ива́н) ....

6. А́нна Ива́новна Смирно́ва живёт в (кварти́ра) .... в

(центр) .... (Москва́) ....

7. Ната́ша из (Новосиби́рск) ....

8. Сейча́с А́нна Ива́новна идёт (дом) .... с (рабо́та) ....

9. Я хочу́ помо́чь (вы) ....

11. Сейча́с Ната́ша у (Ива́н) ....

12. Да, с (удово́льствие) ....

13. Мы пое́дем с (вы) ....

14. Пол и Ната́ша говори́ли о (командиро́вка) .... (Ната́ша)

....

15. В (коне́ц) .... (коне́ц) ....

Exercise D

Agreement of subject and verb: put the verb into the correct form.

1. Сейча́с Пол о́чень (люби́ть) Москву́, и я то́же (люби́ть) .... Москву́.

2. Сейча́с мой оте́ц (жить) .... в Ми́нске, а я (жить)

.... в Ло́ндоне.

3. Вчера́ мы (рабо́тать) .... в Ми́нске, а сего́дня мы (рабо́тать)

.... в Москве́.

4. Вчера́ мы (быть) .... в Аме́рике, где сейча́с (рабо́тать)

.... Майк и Ива́н.

5. Вчера́ Майк (звони́ть) .... Воло́де из Аме́рики, но Воло́ди не (быть)

    .... до́ма.

6. Где вы (быть) .... за́втра ве́чером, и где вы (быть)

    .... вчера́ ве́чером?

7. За́втра ве́чером я (быть) .... до́ма, а вчера́ ве́чером я (быть)

    .... у Ива́на.

8. Мы (быть) .... ждать вас за́втра ве́чером в шесть у нас до́ма.

7. Official Business

Lesson 7 is all about evolving your command of the Russian language, both written and spoken. You will delve deeper into the use of verbs, and learn how to use and form the perfective and imperfective.

НА РАБО́ТЕ AT THE OFFICE

Воло́дя рабо́тает недалеко́ от гости́ницы "Нева́". Ната́ша идёт к нему́ на рабо́ту пешко́м. По пути́ она́ покупа́ет газе́ту. Она́ прихо́дит то́чно в полпя́того . . .
(vah-loh-dyah rah-boh-tah-yet nyeh-dah-lee-koh aht-gahs-tee-nee-tsih nyeh-vah. nah-tah-shah ee-dyot knyeh-moo nah-rah-boh-too peesh-kom. pah-poo-tee ah-nah pah-koo-pah-yet gah-zyeh-too. ah-nah pree-khoh-deet toch-nah fpol-pyah-tah-vah . . .)
Volodya works not far from the Hotel Neva. Natasha goes to his workplace on foot. On the way she buys a newspaper. She arrives at exactly four-thirty . . .

Воло́дя	Здра́вствуйте, Ната́ша!
	(zdrah-stvooy-tyeh nah-tah-shah)
	Hello, Natasha.
Ната́ша	Здра́вствуйте, Воло́дя! Как дела́?
	(zdrah-stvooy-tyeh vah-loh-dyah. kahk dyeh-lah)
	Hello, Volodya. How are things?
Воло́дя	Норма́льно. А что но́вого у вас?
	(nahr-mahl'-nah. ah shtoh noh-vah-vah oo vahs)
	Okay. And what's new with you?

Ната́ша	У меня́ всё по-ста́рому. Как всегда́ мно́го рабо́ты. (oo-mee-<u>nyah</u> fsyoh pah-<u>stah</u>-rah-moo. kahk fseeg-<u>dah</u> <u>mnoh</u>-gah rah-<u>boh</u>-tih) The same old. As always, a lot of work.
Воло́дя	Хоти́те ча́ю? Йли ко́фе? (khah-<u>tee</u>-tyeh <u>chah</u>-yoo. ee-lee <u>koh</u>-fyeh) Would you like some tea? Or coffee?
Ната́ша	Нет, спаси́бо. Я о́чень мно́го пила́ ко́фе сего́дня. (nyet spah-<u>see</u>-bah. yah <u>oh</u>-chen' <u>mnoh</u>-gah pee-<u>lah</u> <u>koh</u>-fyeh see-<u>vod</u>-nyah) No, thank you. I've drank a lot of coffee today.
	Мо́жно минера́льную во́ду? (<u>mozh</u>-nah mee-nee-<u>rahl</u>'-noo-yoo <u>voh</u>-doo) Can I have some mineral water?
Воло́дя	Коне́чно! Вот минера́льная во́да, а вот ко́пии рекла́мных проспе́ктов из Аме́рики. (kah-<u>nyesh</u>-nah. vot mee-nee-<u>rahl</u>'-nah-yah vah-<u>dah</u> ah vot <u>koh</u>-pee-ee reek-<u>lahm</u>-nihkh prahs-<u>pyek</u>-tahf eez-ah-<u>myeh</u>-ree-kee) Of course! Here's is some mineral water, and here are copies of the promotional brochures from America.
Ната́ша	Спаси́бо. Хмм … интере́сно. Я ду́маю, э́то как раз то, что нам ну́жно … Здесь жа́рко. Мо́жно откры́ть окно́? (spah-<u>see</u>-bah. khmm … een-tee-<u>ryes</u>-nah. yah <u>doo</u>-mah-yoo <u>eh</u>-tah kahk rahs toh shtoh nahm <u>noozh</u>-nah … zdyes' <u>zhahr</u>-kah. <u>mozh</u>-nah aht-<u>kriht</u>'ahk-<u>noh</u>) Thanks. Hmm … interesting. I think this it is just what we need … It's hot here. Can we open the window?
Воло́дя	Коне́чно. Я откро́ю. (kah-<u>nyesh</u>-nah. yah aht-<u>kroh</u>-yoo) Of course. I'll open it.
Ната́ша	Когда́ вы смо́жете прие́хать к нам в Москву́? Мы с ва́ми должны́ обсуди́ть вопро́с о совме́стном предприя́тии с мои́м но́вым нача́льником, Ники́той Серге́евичем Кали́ниным. (kahg-<u>dah</u> vih <u>smoh</u>-zheh-tyeh pree-<u>yeh</u>-khaht' knahm vmahs-<u>kvoo</u>. mih <u>svah</u>-mee dahlzh-<u>nih</u> ahp-soo-<u>deet</u>'vahp-<u>ros</u> ah-sahv-<u>myes</u>-nahm preed-pree-<u>yah</u>-tee-ee smah-<u>eem</u> <u>noh</u>-vihm nah-<u>chahl</u>'-nee-kahm nee-<u>kee</u>-tie seer-<u>gyeh</u>-yeh-vee-chem kah-<u>lee</u>-nee-nihm) When will you be able to come and see to us in Moscow? You and I have to discuss the question of the joint venture with my new boss, Nikita Sergeyevich Kalinin.
Воло́дя	Како́е сего́дня число́? Два́дцать пе́рвое? (kah-<u>koh</u>-yeh see-<u>vod</u>-nyah chees-<u>loh</u> <u>dvah</u>-tsaht' <u>pyer</u>-vah-yeh) What's the date today? The twenty-first?
Ната́ша	Два́дцать пе́рвое ноября́, вто́рник.

(*dvah-tsaht' pyer-vah-yeh nah-yahb-ryah ftor-neek*)
The twenty-first of November, Tuesday.

Волóдя — Я смогу́ прие́хать к вам че́рез неде́лю. Ска́жем, в сре́ду, два́дцать девя́того.
(*yah smah-goo pree-yeh-khaht' kvahm cheh-ryes nee-dyeh-lyoo. skah-zhem fsryeh-doo dvah-tsaht' dee-vyah-tah-vah*)
I'll be able to come (to you) in a week's time. Let's say on Wednesday, the twenty-ninth.

Ната́ша — Отли́чно! Я зна́ю, что Ники́та Серге́евич бу́дет свобо́ден в сре́ду.
(*aht-leech-nah. yah znah-yoo shtoh nee-keet-ah seer-gyeh-yeh-veech boo-deet svah-boh-deen fsryeh-doo.*)
Great! I know that Nikita Sergeyevich will be free on Wednesday.

Grammar

1. ASPECTS OF THE VERB: IMPERFECTIVE & PERFECTIVE

Most Russian verbs have two aspects: the **imperfective** aspect and the **perfective** aspect. It's is important to learn these together in in their corresponding pairs.

Broadly speaking, the imperfective indicates that an action is not completed or **imperfect**, while the perfective indicates that an action is completed or **perfect**.

The Russian language therefore has two verbs for every action: for example the verb де́лать (*dyeh-laht'*) is imperfective and means **to do** in the sense of **to be doing**, and the verb сде́лать (*zdyeh-laht'*) is perfective and means **to do completely or once only**.

Compare the following examples: if someone asks poses the question, что де́лать? (*shtoh dyeh-laht'*) **What to do?/What should we (I) be doing?**, the answer will be in the imperfective aspect:

чита́ть кни́гу (*chee-taht' knee-goo*)   to read a book, to be reading a book

писа́ть письмо́ (*pee-saht' pees'-moh*)   to write a letter, to be writing a letter

| пить ко́фе (peet' koh-fyeh) | to drink coffee, to be drinking coffee |

In contrast, the question **что сде́лать?** (shtoh zdyeh-laht') implies completion of the action, and the answer will be in the perfective aspect:

прочита́ть кни́гу (prah-chee-taht' knee-goo)	to read a book, to have read a book, to read a book from the beginning to the end
написа́ть письмо́ (nah-pee-saht' pees'-moh)	to write a letter, to have written a letter, to completely write a letter
вы́пить ко́фе (vih-peet' koh-fyeh)	to drink coffee, to have drunk coffee, to drink a cup of coffee to the last drop

Most perfective verbs are formed by adding a prefix to the corresponding imperfective verb. Common prefixes of perfective verbs are **вы-** (vih-), **за-** (zah-), **по-** (pah-), **про-** (prah-), **при-** (pree-), **с-** (s-) and **со-** (sah-). However, sometimes the suffix changes:

дава́ть (dah-vaht') (impf)	to give, to be giving
дать (daht') (perf)	to give, to have given
начина́ть (nah-chee-naht') (impf)	to begin, to be beginning
нача́ть (nah-chaht') (perf)	to begin, to have begun
сообща́ть (sah-ahp-shchaht') (impf)	to inform, to be informing; to communicate, to be communicating
сообщи́ть (sah-ahp-shcheet') (perf)	to inform, to have informed; to communicate, to have communicated

Sometimes the **stem** itself changes:

встреча́ть (fstree-chat') (impf)	to meet, to be meeting
встре́тить (fstryeh-teet') (perf)	to meet, to have met
крича́ть (kree-chaht') (impf)	to shout, to be shouting
кри́кнуть (kreek-noot') (perf)	to shout, to have shouted

Usually, the imperfective and perfective verbs are similar to one another, and it is easy to learn them in pairs. However, this is not always the case. You are already familiar with the imperfective verb **говори́ть** (gah-vah-reet') **to talk, to be talking**. The perfective is **поговори́ть** (pah-gah-vah-reet') **to talk, to have talked**. But when **говори́ть** means **to say, to be saying** or **to tell, to be telling**, it is paired with the perfective verb **сказа́ть** (skah-zaht') **to say, to have said; to tell, to have told**.

Here are some examples:

Ната́ша говори́ла с Ива́ном. *(nah-tah-shah gah-vah-ree-lah s ee-vah-nahm)*
Natasha talked/was talking to Ivan.

Ната́ша поговори́ла с Ива́ном. *(nah-tah-shah pah-gah-vah-ree-lah s ee-vah-nahm)*
Natasha talked/has talked to Ivan.

Ната́ша говори́ла Ива́ну, что … *(nah-tah-shah gah-vah-ree-lah ee-vah-noo shtoh …)*
Natasha was saying to/telling Ivan that …

Ната́ша сказа́ла Ива́ну, что … *(nah-tah-shah skah-zah-lah ee-vah-noo shtoh …)*
Natasha said to/told Ivan that …

USAGE OF IMPERFECTIVE VERBS:

1. To express unfinished or continuous action:

Ива́н пи́шет кни́гу. *(ee-vahn pee-shet knee-goo)*
Ivan is writing a book.

Ива́н писа́л кни́гу. *(ee-vahn pee-sahl knee-goo)*
Ivan was writing a book.

Ива́н бу́дет писа́ть кни́гу. *(ee-vahn boo-deet pee-saht' knee-goo)*
Ivan will be writing a book.

2. To express habitual or repetitive action:

Она́ пьёт ко́фе по утра́м.
(ah-nah pyot koh-fyeh pah-oot-rahm)
She drinks coffee in the morning.

Он е́здит в Санкт-Петербу́рг ка́ждый ме́сяц.
(on yez-deet fsahnkt-pee-teer-boork kahzh-diy myeh-syahts)
He travels to St. Petersburg every month.

Ра́ньше она́ пила́ ко́фе по утра́м, а тепе́рь она́ пьёт чай.
(rahn'-sheh ah-nah pee-lah koh-fyeh pah-oot-rahm ah tee-pyer' ah-nah pyot chie)
Before, she used to drink coffee in the morning, but now she drinks tea.

В про́шлом году́ он е́здил в Минск ка́ждый ме́сяц.
(fprosh-lahm gah-doo on yez-deel vmeensk kahzh-diy myeh-syahts)
Last year he traveled to Minsk every month.

Вско́ре он бу́дет е́здить в Минск ка́ждую неде́лю.
(fskoh-ryeh on boo-deet yez-deet' vmeensk kahzh-doo-yoo nee-dyeh-lyoo)
Soon he will travel to Minsk every week.

THE USE OF PERFECTIVE VERBS:

1. To express the completion of an action:

Ивáн написáл кнѝгу. *(ee-vahn nah-pee-sahl knee-goo)*
Ivan wrote/has written a book.

2. To express the definite completion of an action in the future:

Скóро Ивáн напѝшет кнѝгу. *(skoh-rah ee-vahn nah-pee-shet knee-goo)*
Soon Ivan will write a book.

3. To express instantaneous actions:

Пол открѝл дверь. *(pol aht-krihl dvyer')*
Paul opened the door.

Натáша вскрѝкнула. *(nah-tah-shah fskreek-noo-lah)*
Natasha screamed.

TENSES OF IMPERFECTIVE AND PERFECTIVE VERBS:

Imperfective verbs have past, present and future tenses. Perfective verbs have past and future tenses, but no present tense, since they describe only completed actions. An action taking place in the present is, by definition, incomplete and therefore imperfect.

The future tense of an imperfective verb is formed with бýду *(boo-doo)*, бýдешь *(boo-dyesh)*, бýдет *(boo-deet)*, бýдем *(boo-deem)*, бýдете *(boo-dee-tye)*, бýдут *(boo-doot)* plus the infinitive of the imperfective verb:

Мы бýдем ждать вас здесь. *(mih boo-deem zhdaht' vahs zdyes')*
We are going to wait/will be waiting for you here.

The future tense of a perfective verb is similar in conjugation to the present tense of imperfective verbs.

Let's have a look at the verbs писáть *(pee-saht')* – **to write, to be writing** (imperfective) – and написáть *(nah-pee-saht')* – **to write, to have written** (perfective).

ПИСА́ТЬ (imperfective)	НАПИСА́ТЬ (perfective)
Present tense	
я пишу́ (yah pee-<u>shoo</u>)	THE
ты пи́шешь (tih <u>pee</u>-shesh)	PERFECTIVE
он/она́ пи́шет (on/ah-<u>nah</u> <u>pee</u>-shet)	HAS
мы пи́шем (mih <u>pee</u>-shem)	NO
вы пи́шете (vih <u>pee</u>-sheh-tyeh)	PRESENT
они пи́шут (ah-<u>nee</u> <u>pee</u>-shoot)	TENSE

ПИСА́ТЬ (imperfective)	НАПИСА́ТЬ (perfective)
Future tense	
я бу́ду писа́ть (yah <u>boo</u>-doo pee-saht')	я напишу́ (yah nah-pee-<u>shoo</u>)
ты бу́дешь писа́ть (tih <u>boo</u>-deesh pee-<u>saht'</u>)	ты напи́шешь (tih nah-<u>pee</u>-shesh)
он/она́ бу́дет писа́ть (on/ah-<u>nah</u> <u>boo</u>-deet pee-<u>saht'</u>)	он/она́ напи́шет (on/ah-<u>nah</u> nah-<u>pee</u>-shet)
мы бу́дем писа́ть (mih <u>boo</u>-deem pee-<u>saht'</u>)	мы напи́шем (mih nah-<u>pee</u>-shem)
вы бу́дете писа́ть (vih <u>boo</u>-dee-tyeh pee-<u>saht'</u>)	вы напи́шете (vih nah-<u>pee</u>-sheh-tyeh
они бу́дут писа́ть (ah-<u>nee</u> <u>boo</u>-doot pee-<u>saht'</u>)	они напи́шут (ah-<u>nee</u> nah-<u>pee</u>-shoot)

ПИСА́ТЬ (imperfective)	НАПИСА́ТЬ (perfective)

Past tense

я писа́л
(yah pee-_sahl_)

ты писа́л
(tih pee-_sahl_)

он писа́л
(on pee-_sahl_)

она́ писа́ла
(ah-_nah_ pee-_sah_-lah)

мы писа́ли
(mih pee-_sah_-lee)

вы писа́ли
(vih pee-_sah_-lee)

они́ писа́ли
(ah-_nee_ pee-_sah_-lee)

я написа́л
(yah nah-pee-_sahl_)

ты написа́л
(tih nah-pee-_sahl_)

он написа́л
(on nah-pee-_sahl_)

она́ написа́ла
(ah-_nah_ nah-pee-_sah_-lah)

мы написа́ли
(mih nah-pee-_sah_-lee)

вы написа́ли
(vih nah-pee-_sah_-lee)

они́ написа́ли
(ah-_nee_ nah-pee-_sah_-lee)

NOTE ON THE USE OF ПО-

Sometimes the prefix по- conveys the idea of spending a little time doing something. For example: погуля́ть pah-goo-_lyaht'_ (perfective):

Они́ погуля́ли в па́рке. (ah-_nee_ pah-goo-_lyah_-lee _fpahr_-kyeh)
They strolled in the park for a while.

посиде́ть (pah-see-_dyet'_) (perfective):

Воло́дя посиде́л с Ната́шей. (vah-_loh_-dyah pah-see-_dyel_ snah-_tah_-shey)
Volodya sat a while with Natasha.

There is, however, one commonly used verb that is an exception and should be memorized:

покупа́ть (pah-koo-_paht'_) **to buy, to be buying**: imperfective despite the prefix по-

купи́ть (koo-_peet'_) (perfective) **to buy, to have bought/to complete the action of buying**

2. THE OMISSION OF VOWELS IN MASCULINE NOUNS

Some masculine nouns with the letters o, ё, and e in the last syllable in the nominative case drop these letters when they are declined. In Lesson 5 we saw this happen to конéц *(kah-nyets)* (end):

в концé концóв *(fkahn-tseh kahn-tsof)*
Eventually, in the end

Similarly:

отéц *(ah-tyets)*
father

с отцóм *(saht-tsom)*
with father

продавéц *(prah-dah-vyets)*
salesperson

продавцá *(prah-dahf-tsah)*
of the salesperson

ýгол *(oo-gahl)*
corner

в углý *(voog-loo)*
in the corner

3. NUMBERS 100–1,000

100	101	102
сто	сто одúн	сто дéва
(stoh)	*(stoh ah-deen)*	*(stoh dvah)*
105	110	150
сто пять	сто дéсять	сто пятьдесят
(stoh pyaht')	*(stoh dyeh-syaht')*	*(stoh pyaht'-dyeh-syaht)*
200	299	
дéвéсти	дéвéсти дééвянóсто дééвять	
(dvyes-tee)	*(dvyes-tee dee-vyah-nos-tah dyeh-vyaht')*	
300	340	430
трúста	трúста сóрок	четыреста трúдцать
(tree-stah)	*(tree-stah soh-rahk)*	*(chee-tih-rees-tah tree-tsaht')*
500	555	600
пятьсóт	пятьсóт пятьдесят пять	шестьсóт
(pyaht'-sot)	*(pyaht'-sot pyaht'-dee-syaht pyaht')*	*(shes-sot)*
622	700	800
шестьсóт дéвáдцать дéва	семьсóт	éвосемьсóт
(shes-sot dvah-tsat' dvah)	*(seem-sot)*	*(vah-seem-sot)*

900	999
деевятьсот	деевятьсот деевяносто деевять
(dee-vyaht-sot)	*(dee-vyaht-sot dee-vyah-nos-tah dyeh-vyaht')*

1,000
одна тысяча
(ahd-nah tih-syah-chah)

Useful Expressions

Я вас не понимаю.
(yah vahs nyeh pah-nee-mah-yoo) — I don't understand you.

Повторите, пожалуйста.
(pahf-tah-ree-tyeh pah-zhahl-stah) — Repeat, please.

Где здесь туалет?
(gdyeh zdyes' too-ah-lyet) — Where is the restroom (here)?

Когда мы встретимся?
(kahg-dah mih fstryeh-teem-syah) — When shall will we meet?

Когда я смогу приехать к вам?
(kahg-dah yah smah-goo pree-yeh-khaht' kvahm) — When can I come to (visit) you?

Days

Note that these are not capitalized in Russian except at the beginning of a sentence.

понедельник	*(pah-nee-dyel'-neek)*	Monday
вторник	*(ftor-neek)*	Tuesday
среда	*(sree-dah)*	Wednesday
четверг	*(chet-vyerk)*	Thursday
Пятница	*(pyaht-nee-tsah)*	Friday
суббота	*(soo-boh-tah)*	Saturday
воскресенье	*(vahs-kree-syen'-yeh)*	Sunday

Vocabulary

на рабо́те *(nah rah-boh-tyeh) at work, at the office*

рабо́тать *(impf) (rah-boh-taht') to work*

далеко́ *(dah-lee-koh) far, a long way, far away*

недалеко́ *(nee-dah-lee-koh) not far*

от *(aht) from*

идти́ пешко́м *(eet-tee peesh-kom) to go on foot, to walk*

путь *(poot') way, path, route*

по пути́ *(pah poo-tee) on the way*

покупа́ть *(impf) (pah-koo-paht') to buy*

газе́та *(gah-zyeh-tah) newspaper*

приходи́ть *(perf) (pree-khah-deet') to arrive, to come*

то́чно *(toch-nah) exactly*

полпя́того *(pol-pyah-tah-vah) half past four*

норма́льно *(nahr-mahl'-nah) okay, normal*

Что но́вого у вас? *(shtoh noh-vah-vah oo vahs) What's new (with you)?*

ста́рый *m.*/**ста́рая** *f.*/**ста́рое** *n. (stah-riy m.*/*stah-rah-yah f.*/*stah-rah-yeh n.) old*

по-ста́рому *(pah-stah-rah-moo) as before, as usual*

всегда́ *(fseeg-dah) always*

как всегда́ *(kahk fseeg-dah) as always, as usual*

хоте́ть *(impf) (khah-tyet') to want*

пить *(impf) (peet') to drink*

минера́льный *m.*/**минера́льная** *f.*/**минера́льное** *n. (mee-nee-rahl'-niy m.*/ *mee-nee-rahl'-nah-yah f.*/*mee-nee-rahl'-nah-yeh n.) mineral*

вода́ *(vah-dah) water*

коне́чно *(kah-nyesh-nah) of course*

ко́пия *(koh-pee-yah) copy, duplicate*

проспе́кт *(prahs-pyekt) brochure, prospectus*

интере́сный *m.*/**интере́сная** *f.*/ **интере́сное** *n. (een-tee-ryes-niy m.*/*een-tee-ryes-nah-yah f.*/*een-tee-ryes-nah-yeh n.) interesting*

интере́сно *(een-tee-ryes-nah) it is interesting*

ду́мать *(impf) (doo-maht') to think*

как раз то, что … *(kahk rahs toh, shtoh …) just what …*

здесь *(zdyes') here*

Мо́жно? *(mozh-nah) Is it possible?, May I …?*

открыва́ть *(impf) (aht-krih-vaht') to open*

откры́ть *(perf) (aht-kriht') to open*

окно́ *(ahk-noh) window*

мочь *(impf) (moch) to be able to*

смочь *(perf) (smoch) to be able to*

смо́жете *(smoh-zhih-tyeh) you will be able to*

е́хать *(impf) (yeh-khaht') to go (by transport), to drive*

прие́хать *(perf) (pree-yeh-khaht') to come (by transport)*

я/он до́лжен *m. (yah/on dol-zhen) I/he must*

я/она́ должна́ *f. (yah/ah-nah dahlzh-nah) I/she must*

мы/вы/они́ должны́ *(mih/vih/ah-nee dahlzh-nih) we/you/they must*

обсуди́ть *(perf) (ahp-soo-deet') to discuss*

вме́сте *(vmyes-tyeh) together*

нача́льник (nah-_chahl'_-neek) chief, boss
число́ (chees-_loh_) number, date
че́рез (_cheh_-rees) through, in (of time)
неде́ля (nee-_dyeh_-lyah) week
че́рез неде́лю (_cheh_-rees nee-_dyeh_-lyoo)
in a week
сказа́ть (perf) (_skah_-zaht') to say
ска́жем (_skah_-zhem) let's say, we'll say
отли́чно (aht-_leech_-nah) it's excellent, great
знать (impf) (znaht') to know

свобо́дный m./**свобо́дная** f./**свобо́дное**
n. (svah-_bod_-niy m./svah-_bod_-nah-yah f./
svah-_bod_-nah-yeh n.) free
я/он свобо́ден m. (yah/on svah-_boh_-dyen)
I am/he is free
я/она́ свобо́дна f. (yah/ah-_nah_ svah-_bod_-
nah) I am/she is free
мы/вы/они́ свобо́дны (mih/vih/ah-_nee_
svah-_bod_-nih) we/you/they are free

Exercises

Exercise A

Perfective or imperfective? Write **impf.** or **perf.**

1. **Вчера́ Воло́дя <u>чита́л</u> кни́гу.**   ....

2. **Сего́дня у́тром Ната́ша <u>прочита́ла</u> но́вую кни́гу.**   ....

3. **Что <u>де́лать</u>?**   ....

4. **Что <u>сде́лать</u>?**   ....

5. **Мы <u>дава́ли</u> ему́ кни́ги ка́ждый ме́сяц.**   ....

6. **Они́ <u>да́ли</u> ей кни́гу вчера́.**   ....

7. **Ната́ша и Воло́дя <u>рабо́тают</u> в ба́нке.**   ....

8. **Ка́ждый день она́ <u>покупа́ет</u> минера́льную во́ду.**   ....

9. **Вчера́ Ната́ша <u>купи́ла</u> англи́йскую газе́ту.**   ....

10. **Когда́ Майк <u>смо́жет</u> прие́хать к нам в Москву́?**   ....

Exercise B

Numbers. Write out the following numbers in Russian and check your answers against the key.

А 5 .... Л 65 ....

Б 10 .... М 70 ....

В 15 .... Н 75 ....

Г 20 .... О 80 ....

Д 25 .... П 85 ....

Е 30 .... Р 90 ....

Ё 35 .... С 95 ....

Ж 40 .... Т 100 ....

З 45 .... У 101 ....

И 50 .... Ф 111 ....

Й 55 .... Х 200 ....

К 60 .... Ц 222 ....

Exercise C

Translate the following sentences into English.

1. **Хотúте чáю, кóфе, минерáльную вóду или вóдку?**

    ....

2. **Какóе сегóдня числó?**

    ....

3. **Сегóдня двáдцать девя́тое апрéля.**

    ....

4. **Извинúте, пожáлуйста. Здесь есть туалéт?**

    ....

5. Когда́ вы бу́дете свобо́дны?

....

6. Мы бу́дем свобо́дны во вто́рник, в шесть часо́в ве́чера.

....

7. По пути́ к Воло́де Ната́ша купи́ла газе́ту.

....

8. Воло́дя дал Ната́ше ко́пии америка́нских рекла́мных проспе́ктов.

....

9. Ра́ньше я пил ча́й по утра́м, а тепе́рь я пью минера́льную во́ду.

....

10. Воло́дя дал Ната́ше проспе́кты, и она́ поду́мала, что они́ как раз то, что ей

    ну́жно.

....

Exercise D

Translate the following sentences into Russian.

1. Yesterday I was talking with Mike in the office.

....

2. Natasha walks to the bank every day.

....

3. I used to drink tea in the morning, but now I drink coffee.

....

4. The pen and the key are on the table.

....

5. Last year we traveled to New York every week.

....

6. I opened the door.

....

7. We have talked with Mike.

....

8. Soon I will travel to Moscow every month.

....

Exercise E

True or false?

1. Воло́дя рабо́тает о́чень далеко́ от гости́ницы "Нева́".　　T/F

2. Ната́ша е́дет к Воло́де на авто́бусе.　　T/F

3. По пути́ она́ покупа́ет газе́ту.　　T/F

4. Она́ не прихо́дит к Воло́де то́чнов полпя́того.　　T/F

5. У Ната́ши немно́го рабо́ты.　　T/F

6. Сего́дня Ната́ша не пила́ ко́фе.　　T/F

7. У Воло́ди нет минера́льнойводы́.　　T/F

8. У Воло́ди есть ко́пии рекла́мных проспе́ктов из Аме́рики.　　T/F

9. Сего́дня два́дцать пя́тое ноября́.　　T/F

8. Shopping

Lesson 8 talks about shopping. You will further look at the future tense and learn how to use the continuous past. By now, you should be able to easily follow the flow of the audio and have a firm grasp of the grammar and a comprehensive vocabulary.

НАТА́ША ДЕ́ЛАЕТ ПОКУ́ПКИ NATASHA GOES SHOPPING

Как мы уже́ зна́ем, у Ната́ши мно́го рабо́ты. Коне́чно, в Москве́ она́ покупа́ет проду́кты в магази́нах. Но у неё почти́ нет вре́мени ходи́ть по магази́нам, что́бы купи́ть оде́жду, о́бувь и други́е ве́щи.

(kahk mih oo-zheh znah-yem oo-nah-tah-shih mnoh-gah rah-boh-tih. kah-nyesh-nah vmahs-k vyeh ah-nah pah-koo-pah-yet prah-dook-tih vmah-gah-zee-nahkh. noh oo nee-yoh pach-tee nyet vryeh-mee-nee khah-deet' pah mah-gah-zee-nahm shtoh-bih koo-peet' ah-dyezh-doo oh-boof' ee droo-gee-yeh vyeh-shchee)

As we already know, Natasha has a lot of work. Of course, in Moscow she buys groceries in stores. But she has almost no time to go shopping to buy clothes, footwear and other things.

Сего́дня она́ всё ещё в Санкт-Петербу́рге. У неё есть немно́го свобо́дного вре́мени. Поэ́тому она́ реши́ла пойти́ по магази́нам и купи́ть себе́ тёплую ша́пку, перча́тки и сапоги́. У нас в Росси́и хо́лодно зимо́й! Ну́жно име́ть тёплые ве́щи, что́бы не замёрзнуть.

(see-vod-nyah ah-nah fsyoh yeh-shchoh fsahnkt-pee-teer-boor-gyeh. oo-nee-yoh yest' neem-noh-gah svah-bod-nah-vah vryeh-mee-nee. pah-eh-tah-moo ah-nah ree-shih-lah pie-tee pah-mah-gah-zee-nahm ee koo-peet' see-byeh tyop-loo-yoo shahp-koo peer-chaht-kee ee sah-pah-gee. oo nahs vrah-see-ee khoh-lahd-nah zee-moy. noozh-nah ee-myet' tyop-lih-yeh vyeh-shchee shtoh-bih nyeh zah-myorz-noot')

Today she is still in St. Petersburg. She has a bit of little free time. She has therefore decided to go shopping and to buy herself a warm hat, gloves and boots. It's cold in the winter here in Russia! You need warm things, in order not to freeze.

Сейча́с Ната́ша в магази́не "Гости́ный Двор". Она́ говори́т с продавцо́м . . .
(seey-chahs nah-tah-shah vmah-gah-zee-nyeh gahs-tee-niy dvor. ah-nah gah-vah-reet sprah-dahf-tsom . . .)
Now Natasha is in the "Gostiniy Dvor" store. She is talking with a salesperson . . .

Ната́ша	Пожа́луйста, покажи́те мне э́ти сапоги́.
	(pah-zhahl-stah pah-kah-zhih-tyeh mnyeh eh-tee sah-pah-gee)
	Show me those boots, please.
Продаве́ц	Каки́е?
	(kah-kee-yeh)
	Which ones?
Ната́ша	Вот те чёрные, в углу́.
	(vot tyeh chor-nih-yeh voog-loo)
	Those black ones, in the corner.
Продаве́ц	Вот э́ти?
	(vot eh-tee)
	These?
Ната́ша	Да, спаси́бо. Ско́лько они́ сто́ят?
	(dah spah-see-bah. skol'-kah ah-nee stoh-yaht)
	Yes, thank you. How much are they?
Продаве́ц	Во́семь ты́сяч.
	(voh-syem' tih-syach)
	Eight thousand (rubles).
Ната́ша	Ой, до́рого! У вас есть подеше́вле?
	(oy doh-rah-gah. oo-vahs yest' pah-dee-shev-lyeh)
	Oh, that's expensive! Do you have anything cheaper?
Продаве́ц	Да. Вот э́ти сто́ят четы́ре ты́сячи.
	(dah. vot eh-tee stoh-yaht chee-tih-ree tih-syah-chee)
	Yes. These cost four thousand.
Ната́ша	Хорошо́. А мо́жно посмотре́ть э́ти перча́тки?
	(khah-rah-shoh. ah mozh-nah pah-smah-tryet' eh-tee peer-chaht-kee)
	Good. And can I have a look at those gloves?
Продаве́ц	Чёрные?
	(chor-nih-yee)
	The black ones?
Ната́ша	Нет, кра́сные, пожа́луйста.
	(nyet krahs-nih-yeh pah-zhahl-stah)
	No, the red ones, please.
Продаве́ц	Пожа́луйста.
	(pah-zhahl-stah)
	Here you are.

Ната́ша	Спаси́бо. Ду́маю, э́ти мне подойду́т. И ещё покажи́те мне, пожа́луйста, ша́пку.
	(spah-<u>see</u>-bah. <u>doo</u>-mah-yoo eh-tee mnyeh pah-die-<u>doot</u>. ee yeh-<u>shchoh</u> pah-kah-<u>zhih</u>-tyeh mnyeh pah-<u>zhahl</u>-stah shah-pkoo)
	Thank you. I think these will suit me. Please also show me a hat.
Продаве́ц	Мехову́ю и́ли шерстяну́ю?
	(mee-khah-<u>voo</u>-yoo ee-lee sher-styah-<u>noo</u>-yoo)
	A fur or woolen one?
Ната́ша	Кра́сную шерстяну́ю. Ско́лько она́ сто́ит?
	(<u>krahs</u>-noo-yoo sher-styah-<u>noo</u>-yoo. <u>skol</u>'-kah ah-<u>nah</u> <u>stoh</u>-eet)
	The red woolen one. How much does it cost?
Продаве́ц	Две ты́сячи.
	(dvyeh <u>tih</u>-syah-chee)
	Two thousand.
Ната́ша	Я возьму́ её, хоть и до́рого. Она́ така́я краси́вая и тёплая! И, коне́чно, сапоги́ и перча́тки. Посчита́йте, пожа́луйста, всё вме́сте.
	(yah vahz'-<u>moo</u> yeh-<u>yoh</u> khot' ee <u>doh</u>-rah-gah. ah-<u>nah</u> tah-<u>kah</u>-yah krah-<u>see</u>-vah-yah ee <u>tyop</u>-lah-yah. ee kah-<u>nyesh</u>-nah sah-pah-<u>gee</u> ee peer-<u>chaht</u>-kee. pah-shchee-<u>tie</u>-tyeh pah-<u>zhahl</u>-stah fsyoh <u>vmyes</u>-tyeh)
	I'll take it, even though it's expensive. It's so beautiful and warm! And of course the boots and the gloves. Please add up everything together.
Продаве́ц	Ша́пка – две ты́сячи, перча́тки – одна́ ты́сяча и четы́ре ты́сячи за сапоги́. Всего́ семь ты́сяч.
	(<u>shahp</u>-kah dveh <u>tih</u>-syah-chee peer-<u>chaht</u>-kee ahd-<u>nah</u> <u>tih</u>-syah-chah ee chee-<u>tih</u>-ryet <u>tih</u>-syah-chee zah sah-pah-<u>gee</u>. fsee-<u>voh</u> syem' <u>tih</u>-syahch)
	The hat, two thousand, the gloves, one thousand and four thousand for the boots. In all, seven thousand.
Ната́ша	Плати́ть вам?
	(plah-<u>teet</u>' vahm)
	Should I pay you?
Продаве́ц	Нет, в ка́ссу.
	(nyet <u>fkah</u>-soo)
	No, (pay) at the cash register/till.
Ната́ша	А где ка́сса?
	(ah gdyeh <u>kah</u>-sah)
	And where is the cash register/till?
Продаве́ц	Вон там, нале́во.
	(von tahm nah-<u>lyeh</u>-vah)
	Over there, on the left.
Ната́ша	Спаси́бо.
	(spah-<u>see</u>-bah)
	Thank you.

Grammar

1. THE TWO CONJUGATIONS OF RUSSIAN VERBS

Most Russian verbs belong to one of two groups: 1st conjugation or 2nd conjugation, depending on their endings.

1ST CONJUGATION VERBS, PRESENT TENSE

The present tense endings for 1st conjugation verbs are:

-у (-oo)/-ю (-yoo), -ешь (-yesh)/-ёшь (yosh), -ет (-yet)/-ёт (-yot), -ем (-yem), -ете (yeh-tyeh)/ -ёте (<u>yoh</u>-tyeh), -ут (oot)/-ют (yoot).

For example: писáть (pee-<u>saht'</u>) **to write, to be writing** and читáть (chee-<u>taht'</u>) **to read, to be reading**:

	Писáть (pee-<u>saht'</u>)	читáть (chee-<u>taht'</u>)
я (yah)	Пишý (pee-<u>shoo</u>)	читáю (chee-<u>tah</u>-yoo)
ты (tih)	Пи́шешь (<u>pee</u>-shesh)	читáешь (chee-<u>tah</u>-yesh)
он/онá/онó (on/ah-<u>nah</u>/ah-<u>noh</u>)	Пи́шет (<u>pee</u>-shet)	читáет (chee-<u>tah</u>-yet)
мы (mih)	Пи́шем (<u>pee</u>-shem)	читáем (chee-<u>tah</u>-yem)
вы (vih)	Пи́шете (<u>pee</u>-sheh-tyeh)	читáете (chee-<u>tah</u>-yeh-tyeh)
они́ (ah-<u>nee</u>)	Пи́шут (<u>pee</u>-shoot)	читáют (chee-<u>tah</u>-yoot)

Here are a couple of similar 1st conjugation verbs that are often confused by people learning Russian: петь (pyet') **to sing, to be singing** and пить (peet') **to drink, to be drinking**:

	Петь (pyet′)	пить (peet′)
я (yah)	Пою (pah-_yoo_)	пью (pyoo)
ты (tih)	Поёшь (pah-_yosh_)	пьёшь (pyosh)
он/она́/оно́ (on/ah-_nah_/ah-_noh_)	Поёт (pah-_yot_)	пьёт (pyot)
мы (mih)	Поём (pah-_yom_)	пьём (pyom)
вы (vih)	Поёте (pah-_yoh_-tyeh)	пьёте (_pyoh_-tyeh)
они́ (ah-_nee_)	Пою́т (pah-_yoot_)	пьют (pyoot)

Remember that the Russian present tense corresponds to both the English present continuous and the present simple. **Я рабо́таю** (yah rah-_boh_-tah-yoo) can be translated as **I am working** or as **I work**, depending on the context.

Remember also that only imperfective verbs can have a present tense. If an action is taking place now, it cannot have been completed or perfected!

2ND CONJUGATION VERBS, PRESENT TENSE

The present tense endings for 2nd conjugation verbs are:

-ю (-yoo)/**-у** (-oo), **-ишь** (-eesh), **-ит** (-eet), **-им** (-eem), **-ите** (-ee-tyeh), **-ат** (aht)/**-ят** (yaht).

Three frequently used 2nd conjugation verbs are:

ходи́ть (khah-_deet′_) **to go, to be going (on foot)**

говори́ть (gah-vah-_reet′_) **to talk/say, to be talking/saying**

крича́ть (kree-_chaht′_) **to shout, to be shouting**

These are conjugated as follows:

	ходи́ть (khah-deet')	говори́ть (gah-vah-reet')	крича́ть (kree-chaht')
я (yah)	хожу́ (khah-zhoo)	говорю́ (gah-vah-ryoo)	кричу́ (kree-choo)
ты (tih)	хо́дишь (khoh-deesh)	говори́шь (gah-vah-reesh)	кричи́шь (kree-cheesh)
он/она́/оно́ (on/ah-nah/ah-noh)	хо́дит (khoh-deet)	говори́т (gah-vah-reet)	кричи́т (kree-cheet)
мы (mih)	хо́дим (khoh-deem)	говори́м (gah-vah-reem)	кричи́м (kree-cheem)
вы (vih)	хо́дите (khoh-dee-tyeh)	говори́те (gah-vah-ree-tyeh)	кричи́те (kree-chee-tyeh)
они́ (ah-nee)	хо́дят (khoh-dyaht)	говоря́т (gah-vah-ryaht)	крича́т (kree-chaht)

Note that **д** changes to **ж** in the first person singular of **ходи́ть**. This occurs in several 2nd conjugation verbs ending in -**дить** (-deet'), -**деть** (dyet'), such as:

води́ть (vah-deet')	"to lead", "to be leading" (e.g., a child by the hand)
води́ть маши́ну (vah-deet' mah-shih-noo)	"to drive/be driving a car"
я вожу́ маши́ну (yah vah-zhoo mah-shih-noo)	I am driving a car.
сиде́ть (see-dyet')	"to sit", "to be sitting"; "to stay", "to be staying"
я сижу́ до́ма (yah see-zhoo doh-mah)	"I am sitting/staying at home"
ви́деть (vee-deet')	"to see", "to be seeing"
я ви́жу его́ ка́ждый день (yah vee-zhoo yeh-voh kahzh-diy dyen')	I see him every day.

Note also that the ending of the first person singular after -**ж**, -**ш**, -**ч**, -**щ** is always -**у**:

я вяжу́ (yah vyah-zhoo) I am knitting (вяза́ть), я служу́ (yah sloo-zhoo) I am serving (in the army, etc.) (служи́ть) я ношу́ *(yah nah-<u>shoo</u>)* I am wearing/carrying (носи́ть), я прошу́ *(yah prah-<u>shoo</u>)* I am asking (проси́ть)

я молчу́ *(yah mahl-<u>choo</u>)* I am remaining silent (молча́ть), я учу́ *(yah oo-<u>choo</u>)* I am learning/ teaching (учи́ть)

я чи́щу *(yah <u>chee</u>-shchoo)* I am cleaning (чи́стить)

Otherwise it is usually -ю but sometimes -у:

я рабо́таю, гуля́ю, лета́ю, покупа́ю *(yah rah-<u>boh</u>-tah-yoo, goo-<u>lyah</u>-yoo, <u>lee</u>-tah-yoo, pah-koo-<u>pah</u>-yoo)*

я веду́ *(yah vee-<u>doo</u>)* I am leading (вести), я несу́ *(yah nee-<u>soo</u>)* I am carrying (нести́), я кладу́ *(yah klah-<u>doo</u>)* I am putting (класть)

2. THE FUTURE TENSE

1. Imperfective verbs use the future of **быть** *(biht')* **to be** with the infinitive to form the future tense. You saw an example in Lesson 5, when Volodya said to Natasha **Я бу́ду ждать вас …** *(yah <u>boo</u>-doo zhdaht' vahs)* **I will wait for you**.

2. As mentioned above, perfective verbs do not have a present tense. They conjugate the same way imperfective verbs do, but this conjugation forms the future tense rather than the present.

3. REFLEXIVE AND RECIPROCAL VERBS

Broadly speaking, a reflexive verb refers back to its subject. The best way to translate reflexive verbs is with the pronoun **oneself**. The infinitive of these verbs ends in **–ться** *(-tsah)*:

умыва́ться *(oo-mih-<u>vah</u>-tsah)*	to wash/wash oneself, to get washed, to wash up
я умыва́юсь *(yah oo-mih-<u>vah</u>-yoos')*	I wash/am washing myself, I am getting washed/washing up
ты умыва́ешся *(tih oo-mih-<u>vah</u>-yesh-syah)*	you wash/are washing yourself, you are getting washed/ washing up
он *m.*/она́ *f.* умыва́ется up *(on m./ah-<u>nah</u> f. oo-mih-<u>vah</u>-yeh-tsah)*	he/she washes/is washing himself/herself, getting washed/washing
мы умыва́емся *(mih oo-mih-vah-yem-syah)*	we wash/are washing ourselves, getting washed/washing up
они́ умыва́ются *(ah-nee oo-<u>mih</u>-vah-yoo-tsah)*	They wash/are washing themselves, getting washed/washing up

A **reciprocal** verb has two or more agents and conveys the idea of the English phrase **one another**. You saw a reciprocal verb in Lesson 3, when Natasha said **I'm very happy to meet you**. In Russian, because the action of meeting or being introduced has been completed, the meaning is **I'm very happy to have met you**:

Я о́чень рад *m.*/ра́да *f.* познако́миться с ва́ми.
(yah <u>oh</u>-chen' raht m./<u>rah</u>-dah f. pah-znah-<u>koh</u>-mee-tsah <u>svah</u>-mee)

познако́миться *(pah-znah-<u>koh</u>-mee-tsah)* **to have met**, **to have been introduced (to one another)** is the perfective form of the imperfective verb знако́миться *(znah-<u>koh</u>-mee-tsah)*.

Reflexive and reciprocal verbs are formed by adding -ся *(-syah)* or -сь *(-s')* to the non-reflexive or non-reciprocal form, for example: умыва́ть *(oo-mih-<u>vaht'</u>)* – умыва́ться *(oo-mih-<u>vah</u>-tsah)*, знако́мить *(znah-<u>koh</u>-meet')* – знако́миться *(znah-<u>koh</u>-mee-tsah)*. After a consonant, ь- or й-, -ся *(-syah)* is added; -сь *(-s')* is added after a vowel. Please note that combinations -тся and -ться are pronounced *-tsah*. Here are two examples, this time without transliteration:

Reflexive		Reciprocal	
одева́ться	to dress oneself	знако́миться	to get to know someone
я одева́юсь		я знако́млюсь	
ты одева́ешься		ты знако́мишься	
он, она́ одева́ется		он, она́ знако́мится	
мы одева́емся		мы знако́мимся	
вы одева́етесь		вы знако́митесь	
они одева́ются		они знако́мятся	

Not all verbs ending in -сь *(-s')* or -ся *(-syah)* are reflexive or reciprocal. For example:

находи́ть *(nah-khah-<u>deet'</u>)*	to find
находи́ться *(nah-khah-<u>dee</u>-tsah)*	to be, to be situated, (to be found)
смея́ться *(smeeh-<u>yah</u>-tsah)*	to laugh

4. СЕБЯ / ONESELF

In the dialogue at the beginning of this lesson, Natasha went shopping:

... купи́ть себе́ тёплую ша́пку ...
(... koo-<u>peet'</u> see-<u>byeh</u> <u>tyop</u>-loo-yoo <u>shahp</u>-koo ...)
... to buy herself a warm hat ...

Себе́ *(see-<u>byeh</u>)* in this phrase is the dative form of the word себя́ *(see-<u>byah</u>)*. себя́, the dictionary form, is the accusative. There is no nominative form of себя́. себя́ can mean myself, yourself, himself, herself, ourselves, yourselves and themselves (you can figure out which one by looking at the subject of the sentence). Note that there is no separate plural form, even though it can have a plural meaning.

Here is its declension, alongside that of я.

Nom.	я (yah)	—
Acc.	меня (mee-nyah)	себя (see-byah)
Gen.	меня (mee-nyah)	себя (see-byah)
Dat.	мне (mnyeh)	себе (see-byeh)
Instr.	мной (mnoy)	собой* (sah-boy)
Prep.	мне (mnyeh)	себе (see-byeh)

* Sometimes мною (mnoh-yoo), собою (sah-boh-yoo)

Here are some examples of the usage of себя:

Я буду ждать вас у себя в кабинете.
(yah boo-doo zhdaht' vahs oo see-byah fkah-bee-nyeh-tyeh)
I will wait for you in my office.

Вчера я купил себе новую шапку.
(fchyeh-rah yah koo-peel see-byeh noh-voo-yoo shahp-koo)
Yesterday I bought myself a new hat.

Он увидел себя в зеркале.
(on oo-vee-dyel see-byah vzyer-kah-lyeh)
He saw himself in the mirror.

Я возьму эту книгу с собой.
(yah vahz'-moo eh-too knee-goo ssah-boy)
I'll take this book with me.

Она всегда говорит о себе.
(ah-nah fseeg-dah gah-vah-reet ah see-byeh)
She always talks about herself.

5. ORDINAL NUMBERS 1ST–10TH

1st первый m./первая f./первое n. (pyer-viy m./pyer-vah-yah f./pyer-vah-yeh n.)

2nd второй m./вторая f./второе n. (ftah-roy m./ftah-rah-yah f./ftah-roh-yeh n.)

3rd третий m./третья f./третье n. (tryeh-teey m./tryeh-tyah f./tryeh-tyeh n.)

4th четвёртый *m.*/четвёртая *f.*/четвёртое *n.* (*chet-<u>vyor</u>-tiy m./chet-<u>vyor</u>-tah-yah f./chet-<u>vyor</u>-tah-yeh n.*)

5th пя́тый *m.*/пя́тая *f.*/пя́тое *n.* (*<u>pyah</u>-tiy m./<u>pyah</u>-tah-yah f./<u>pyah</u>-tah-yeh n.*)

6th шесто́й *m.*/шеста́я *f.*/шесто́е *n.* (*shes-<u>toy</u> m./shes-<u>tah</u>-yah f./shes-<u>toh</u>-yeh n.*)

7th седьмо́й *m.*/седьма́я *f.*/седьмо́е *n.* (*seed'-<u>moy</u> m./seed'-<u>mah</u>-yah f./seed'-<u>moh</u>-yeh n.*)

8th восьмо́й *m.*/восьма́я *f.*/восьмо́е *n.* (*vahs'-<u>moy</u> m./vahs'-<u>mah</u>-yah f./vahs'-<u>moh</u>-yeh n.*)

9th девя́тый *m.*/девя́тая *f.*/девя́тое *n.* (*dee-<u>vyah</u>-tiy m./dee-<u>vyah</u>-tah-yah f./dee-<u>vyah</u>-tah-yeh n.*)

10th деся́тый *m.*/деся́тая *f.*/деся́тое *n.* (*dee-<u>syah</u>-tiy m./dee-<u>syah</u>-tah-yah f./dee-<u>syah</u>-tah-yeh n.*)

In Russian, ordinal numbers decline like adjectives.

6. THE DECLENSION OF ORDINAL NUMBERS

	masculine the first house	feminine the second street	neuter the third window
Nom.	пе́рвый дом (*<u>pyer</u>-viy dom*)	втора́я у́лица (*ftah-<u>rah</u>-yah <u>oo</u>-lee-tsah*)	тре́тье окно́ (*<u>tryet'</u>-yeh ahk-<u>noh</u>*)
Acc.	пе́рвый дом (*<u>pyer</u>-viy dom*)	втору́ю у́лицу (*ftah-<u>roo</u>-yoo <u>oo</u>-lee-tsoo*)	тре́тье окно́ (*<u>tryet'</u>-yeh ahk-<u>noh</u>*)
Gen.	пе́рвого до́ма (*<u>pyer</u>-vah-vah <u>doh</u>-mah*)	второ́й у́лицы (*ftah-<u>roy</u> <u>oo</u>-lee-tsih*)	тре́тьего окна́ (*<u>tryet'</u>-yeh-vah ahk-<u>nah</u>*)
Dat.	пе́рвому до́му (*<u>pyer</u>-vah-moo <u>doh</u>-moo*)	второ́й у́лице (*ftah-<u>roy</u> <u>oo</u>-lee-tseh*)	тре́тьему окну́ (*<u>tryet'</u>-yeh-moo ahk-<u>noo</u>*)
Instr.	пе́рвым до́мом (*<u>pyer</u>-vihm <u>doh</u>-mahm*)	второ́й у́лицей (*ftah-<u>roy</u> <u>oo</u>-lee-tsey*)	тре́тьим окно́м (*<u>tryet'</u>-yeem ahk-<u>nom</u>*)
Prep.	пе́рвом до́ме (*<u>pyer</u>-vahm <u>doh</u>-myeh*)	второ́й у́лице (*ftah-<u>roy</u> <u>oo</u>-lee-tseh*)	тре́тьем окне́ (*<u>tryet'</u>-yem ahk-<u>nyeh</u>*)

поку́пка *(pah-<u>koop</u>-kah) a purchase*

де́лать поку́пки *(<u>dyeh</u>-laht' pah-<u>koop</u>-kee) to go shopping*

магази́н *(mah-gah-<u>zeen</u>) shop, store*

проду́кт *(prah-<u>dookt</u>) product, grocery item*

за проду́ктами *(zah prah-<u>dook</u>-tah-mee) for food, groceries*

оде́жда *(ah-<u>dyezh</u>-dah) clothing*

о́бувь *(<u>oh</u>-boof') footwear*

друго́й *m.*/друга́я *f.*/друго́е *n. (droo-<u>goy</u> m./droo-<u>gah</u>-yah f./droo-<u>goh</u>-yeh n.) other*

вещь *(vyeshch) thing*

реши́ть *(perf) (ree-<u>siht</u>') to decide*

пойти́ *(perf) (pie-<u>tee</u>) to go*

пойти́ по магази́нам *(pie-<u>tee</u> pah mah-gah-<u>zee</u>-nahm) to go from store to store*

себя́ *(see-<u>byah</u>) oneself*

мехово́й *m.*/мехова́я *f.*/мехово́е *n. (meeh-khah-<u>voy</u> m./meeh-khah-<u>vah</u>-yah f./meeh-khah-<u>voh</u>-yeh n.) fur, of fur*

шерстяно́й *m.*/шерстяна́я *f.*/шерстяно́е *n. (sher-styah-<u>noy</u> m./sher-styah-<u>nah</u>-yah f./sher-styah-<u>noh</u>-yeh n.) woolen*

ша́пка *(<u>shahp</u>-kah) hat*

перча́тка *(peer-<u>chaht</u>-kah) glove*

продаве́ц *(prah-dah-<u>vyets</u>) salesperson/ shop assistant*

сапо́г *(sah-<u>pog</u>) boot*

хо́лодно *(<u>khoh</u>-lahd-nah) it is cold*

зима́ *(zee-<u>mah</u>) winter*

зимо́й *(zee-<u>moy</u>) in winter*

ну́жно *(<u>noozh</u>-nah) it is necessary*

име́ть *(impf) (ee-<u>myet</u>') to have, to own*

тёплый *m.*/тёплая *f.*/тёплое *n. (<u>tyop</u>-liy m./<u>tyop</u>-lah-yah f./<u>tyop</u>-lah-yeh n.) warm*

замёрзнуть *(perf) (zah-<u>myorz</u>-noot') to freeze, to be very cold*

показа́ть *(perf) (pah-kah-<u>zaht</u>') to show*

кото́рый *m.*/кото́рая *f.*/кото́рое *n. (kah-<u>toh</u>-riy m./kah-<u>toh</u>-rah-yah f./kah-<u>toh</u>-rah-yeh n.) which*

чёрный *m.*/чёрная *f.*/чёрное *n. (<u>chor</u>-niy m./<u>chor</u>-nah-yah f./<u>chor</u>-nah-yeh n.) black*

у́гол *(<u>oo</u>-gahl) corner*

в углу́ *(v oog-<u>loo</u>) in the corner*

Ско́лько? *(<u>skol</u>'-kah) How much?, How many?*

сто́ить *(impf) (<u>stoh</u>-eet') to cost, to be worth*

дорого́й *m.*/дорога́я *f.*/дорого́е *n. (dah-rah-<u>goy</u> m./dah-rah-<u>gah</u>-yah f./dah-rah-<u>goh</u>-yeh n.) expensive*

до́рого *(<u>doh</u>-rah-gah) it's expensive*

дешёвый *m.*/дешёвая *f.*/дешёвое *n. (dee-shoh-viy m./dee-shoh-vah-yah f./dee-shoh-vah-yeh n.) cheap*

деше́вле *(dee-<u>shev</u>-lyeh) cheaper*

подеше́вле *(pah-dee-<u>shev</u>-lyeh) a bit cheaper*

посмотре́ть *(perf) (pah-smah-<u>tryet</u>') to have a look at*

кра́сный *m.*/кра́сная *f.*/кра́сное *n. (<u>krahs</u>-niy m./<u>krahs</u>-nah-yah f./<u>krahs</u>-nah-yeh n.) red*

ду́мать *(impf) (<u>doo</u>-maht') to think*

подходи́ть *(impf) (paht-khah-<u>deet</u>') to suit, to match, to approach*

подойти́ *(perf) (pah-die-<u>tee</u>) to suit, to match, to approach*

ещё *(yeh-<u>shchoh</u>) also, again*

взять *(perf) (vzyaht') to take*

брать (impf) (braht') to take
возьму́ (vahz'-moo) I'll take
хоть (khot') even though
тако́й m./**така́я** f./**тако́е** n. (tah-koy m./ tah-kah-yah f./tah-koh-yeh n.) such, so
коне́чно (kah-nyesh-nah) of course
счита́ть (impf) (shchee-taht') to calculate, to add up
посчита́ть (perf) (pah-schee-taht') to calculate, to add up
всё (fsyoh) all
вме́сте (vmyes-tyeh) together
всего́ (fsee-voh) in all, of all
плати́ть (impf) (plah-teet') to pay
ка́сса (kah-sah) cash register/till
нале́во (nah-lyeh-vah) to the left
петь (impf) (pyet') to sing
пить (impf) (peet') to drink
крича́ть (impf) (kree-chaht') to shout
умыва́ться (impf) (oo-mih-vah-tsah) to wash oneself

одева́ться (impf) (ah-dee-vah-tsah) to dress oneself
знако́мить (impf) (znah-koh-meet') to introduce
знако́миться (impf) (znah-koh-mee-tsah) to meet, to be introduced, to become acquainted
познако́мить (perf) (pah-znah-koh-meet') to introduce
познако́миться (perf) (pah-znah-koh-mee-tsah) to meet, to be introduced
находи́ть (impf) (nah-khah-deet') to find
находи́ться (impf) (nah-khah-dee-tsah) to be, to be situated
смея́ться (impf) (smee-yah-tsah) to laugh
ви́деть (impf) (vee-dyet') to see
уви́деть (perf) (oo-vee-dyet') to see, to have seen
зе́ркало (zyer-kah-lah) mirror
маши́на (mah-shih-nah) car

Exercises

Exercise A

Put these 1st conjugation verbs into the correct form of the present tense.

1. Я (писа́ть) ....
2. Они́ (чита́ть) ....
3. Мы (петь) ....
4. Они́ (пить) ....
5. Вы (ждать) ....
6. Он (преподава́ть) ....
7. Я (знать) ....
8. Они́ (гуля́ть) ....
9. Она́ (понима́ть) ....
10. Вы (идти́) ....

11. Мы (е́хать) ....

12. Вы (де́лать) ....

13. Я (петь) ....

14. Они́ (отвеча́ть) ....

15. Я (слу́шать) ....

Exercise B

Put these 2nd conjugation verbs into the present tense.

1. Я (ходи́ть) ....

2. Оний (говори́ть) ....

3. Она́ (крича́ть) ....

4. Мы (ходи́ть) ....

5. Вы (говори́ть) ....

6. Они́ (крича́ть) ....

7. Я (смотре́ть) ....

8. Мы (сиде́ть) ....

9. Он (лете́ть) ....

10. Она́ (молча́ть) ....

11. Они́ (звони́ть) ....

12. Мы (покупа́ть) ....

13. Она́ (стоя́ть) ....

14. Я (ви́деть) ....

15. Я (води́ть) ....

Exercise C

Put the verb in parentheses into the correct form.

1. Мы (знать) .... , что у Ната́ши мно́го рабо́ты.

2. Вчера́ они́ (стоя́ть) .... в о́череди в магази́не, чтобы купи́ть проду́кты.

3. Сейча́с Воло́дя (говори́ть) .... с Ната́шей.

4. Когда́ Ната́ша была́ в магази́не, продаве́ц (показа́ть) ....

   ей красные перча́тки.

5. Вчера́ сапоги́ (сто́ить) четы́ре ты́сячи, сего́дня они́ (сто́ить) ....

   .... во́семь ты́сяч, а за́втра они́ (сто́ить) .... де́сять ты́сяч.

6. Сейча́с Ната́ша (смотре́ть) .... на перча́тки.

7. Воло́дя не (знать) .... , ско́лько сейча́с вре́мени.

8. Сейча́с Ната́ша (покупа́ть) ша́пку, сапоги́ и перча́тки, а продаве́ц (счита́ть) ....

.... , ско́лько всё (сто́ить) ....

9. Когда́ продаве́ц посчита́ла, Ната́ша (заплати́ть) .... в ка́ссу.

10. Хотя́ ша́пка сто́ила до́рого, Ната́ша (реши́ть) .... взять её.

Exercise D

On a separate piece of paper, translate the following text into English.

Бори́с рабо́тает недалеко́ от своего́ до́ма в Москве́. У него́ есть маши́на, но он хо́дит на рабо́ту пешко́м. Ка́ждое у́тро по пути́ в о́фис он покупа́ет газе́ту. Но вчера́ газе́т не́ было. Что он сде́лал? Он купи́л кни́гу. Он о́чень лю́бит чита́ть газе́ты, кни́ги и журна́лы. Он лю́бит кино́, но совсе́м не лю́бит смотре́ть телеви́зор: у него́ да́же телеви́зора нет.

Сейча́с зима́. На у́лице хо́лодно. Но Бори́су не хо́лодно, когда́ он хо́дит на рабо́ту. У него́ тёплое пальто́, ша́пка, шерстяны́е перча́тки и па́ра хоро́ших сапо́г.

Журна́л	(zhoor-_nahl_)	magazine
Чита́ть	(chee-_taht'_)	to read
Кино́	(kee-_noh_)	movie theater
да́же	(_dah_-zheh)	even
телеви́зор	(tee-lee-_vee_-zahr)	television
совсе́м	(sahf-_syem_)	completely, at all
Па́ра	(_pah_-rah)	pair
У́лица	(_oo_-lee-tsah)	street
на у́лице	(nah-_ool_-ee-tseh)	outside, on the street
Пальто́	(pahl'-_toh_)	coat
Пешко́м	(pyesh-_kom_)	on foot

Exercise E

Translate the following sentences into Russian.

1. **Every morning I buy a newspaper on my way to work.**

   ....

2. **Right now she is talking to Ivan.**

   ....

3. **Can I have a look at that hat, please?**

   ....

4. **I will take it even though it's expensive.**

   ....

5. **Show me those gloves, please.**

   ....

6. **Can I have a look at that coat, please?**

   ....

7. **Today we have a little free time.**

   ....

8. **Where is the cash register/till?**

   ....

9. **The cash register/till is over there, on the left.**

   ....

Exercise F

True or false?

1. У Наташи много работы.   T/F

2. Чёрные сапоги в углу стоят восемь тысяч рублей.   T/F

3. В России не очень холодно зимой.   T/F

4. Наташе хочется купить красные перчатки.   T/F

5. Наташа покупает чёрные перчатки.   T/F

6. Шапка стоит пять тысяч.   T/F

7. Наташа платит в кассу.   T/F

8. В России нужно иметь тёплые вещи, чтобы не замёрзнуть зимой.   T/F

9. The Weekend

Lesson 9 focuses on leisure activities and the vocabulary and verbs that you need to talk about what you like to do. You will also learn how to say things in the imperative and in the conditional tense.

ОБРА́ТНО В МОСКВУ́ ПО́ЕЗДОМ BACK TO MOSCOW BY TRAIN

Сего́дня пя́тница. Весь день прошёл в дела́х и спе́шке. А сейча́с рабо́та зако́нчена. Всё сде́лано. Пора́ е́хать домо́й!

(see-*vod*-nyah *pyaht*-nee-tsah. vyes' dyen' prah-*shol* vdee-*lahkh* ee *spyesh*-kyeh. ah seey-*chahs* rah-*boh*-tah zah-*kon*-chee-nah. fsyoh *zdyeh*-lah-nah. pah-*rah* yeh-*khaht'* dah-*moy*)

Today is Friday. The whole day was spent working and rushing around. But now work is finished. Everything is done. It's time to go home!

Ната́ша прилете́ла в Санкт-Петербу́рг самолётом. Но обра́тный биле́т на самолёт ей купи́ть не удало́сь. Не́ было мест. Поэ́тому она́ купи́ла биле́т на по́езд. Э́тот по́езд называ́ется "Кра́сная Стрела́". Он идёт из Санкт-Петербу́рга в Москву́ ка́ждую ночь.

(nah-*tah*-shah pree-lee-*tyeh*-lah fsahnkt-pee-teer-*boork* sah-mah-*lyoh*-tahm. noh ahb-*raht*-niy bee-*lyet* nah-sah-mah-*lyot* yey koo-*peet'* nyeh oo-dah-*los'*. nyeh-bih-lah myest. pah-*eh*-tah-moo ah-*nah* koo-*pee*-lah bee-*lyet* nah poh-yeest. eh-taht poh-yeest nah-zih-*vah*-yeh-tsah *krahs*-nah-yah stree-*lah*. on ee-*dyot* ees sahnkt-pee-teer-*boor*-gah vmahs-*kvoo* *kahzh*-doo-yoo noch')

Natasha flew to St. Petersburg (by plane). But she didn't manage to buy a return plane ticket. There were no seats. So she bought a ticket for the train. This train is called the "Red Arrow". It goes from St. Petersburg to Moscow every night.

В шесть часо́в ве́чера она́ хорошо́ пообе́дала с Воло́дей. Пото́м они́ немно́го гуля́ли по на́бережной Невы́. Зате́м Воло́дя проводи́л Ната́шу в гости́ницу. В гости́нице они́ попроща́лись.

(fshest' chah-<u>sof</u> <u>vyeh</u>-chee-rah ah-<u>nah</u> khah-rah-<u>shoh</u> pah-ah-<u>byeh</u>-dah-lah svah-<u>loh</u>-dyey. pah-<u>tom</u> ah-<u>nee</u> nee-<u>mnoh</u>-gah goo-<u>lyah</u>-lee pah <u>nah</u>-bee-reezh-nie nee-<u>vih</u>. zah-<u>tyem</u> vah-<u>loh</u>-dyah prah-vah-<u>deel</u> nah-tah-shoo vgahs-<u>tee</u>-nee-tsoo. vgahs-<u>tee</u>-nee-tseh ah-<u>nee</u> pah-prah-<u>shchah</u>-lees')

At six o'clock in the evening she had a nice meal with Volodya. Then they strolled for a while on the Neva embankment. After that, Volodya accompanied Natasha to the hotel. They said goodbye at the hotel.

Сейча́с де́вять часо́в ве́чера. Ната́ша уже́ в по́езде, в двухме́стном купе́. Она́ разгова́ривает со свои́м попу́тчиком.

(sey-<u>chahs</u> <u>dyeh</u>-vyat' chah-<u>sof</u> <u>vyeh</u>-chee-rah. nah-<u>tah</u>-shah oo-<u>zheh</u> <u>fpoh</u>-yeez-dyeh vdvookh-<u>myes</u>-nahm koo-<u>peh</u>. ah-<u>nah</u> rahz-gah-<u>vah</u>-ree-vah-yet sah-svah-<u>eem</u> pah-<u>poot</u>-chee-kahm)

It's now nine o'clock in the evening. Natasha is already on the train in a two-seat compartment. She is talking with her traveling companion.

Ната́ша	До́брый ве́чер!
	(<u>dob</u>-riy <u>vyeh</u>-cheer)
	Good evening.
Игорь	До́брый ве́чер! Нам е́хать вме́сте. Дава́йте знако́миться. Я – Игорь Григо́рьевич Милосла́вский.
	(<u>dob</u>-riy <u>vyeh</u>-cheer. nahm <u>yeh</u>-khaht' <u>vmyes</u>-tyeh. dah-<u>vie</u>-tyeh znah-<u>koh</u>-mee-tsah. yah ee-<u>gahr</u>' gree-<u>gor</u>'-yeh-veech mee-lah-<u>slahf</u>-skeey)
	Good evening. We are traveling together. Let's introduce ourselves. I am Igor Grigoryevich Miloslavsky.
Ната́ша	А я Ната́лья Петро́вна Ивано́ва . . . Вы мо́жете чуть-чуть откры́ть окно́?
	(ah yah nah-<u>tahl</u>'-yah peet-<u>rov</u>-nah ee-vah-<u>noh</u>-vah . . . vih <u>moh</u>-zheh-tyeh choot'-choot' aht-<u>kriht</u>' ahk-<u>noh</u>)
	And I am Natalya Petrovna Ivanova . . . Can you open the window just a little?
Игорь	Да, коне́чно. Здесь ужа́сно жа́рко . . . Вы живёте в Санкт-Петербу́рге?
	(dah kah-<u>nyesh</u>-nah. zdyes' oo-<u>zhas</u>-nah <u>zhahr</u>-kah. vih zhih-<u>vyoh</u>-tyeh fsahnkt-pee-teer-<u>boor</u>-gyeh)
	Yes, certainly. It's terribly hot in here. Do you live in St. Petersburg?
Ната́ша	Нет, я была́ здесь в командиро́вке то́лько три дня. Я живу́ в Москве́. А вы?
	(nyet yah bih-<u>lah</u> zdyes' fkah-mahn-dee-<u>rof</u>-kyeh <u>tol</u>'-kah tree dnyah. yah zhih-voo vmahs-<u>kvyeh</u>. ah vih)
	No, I was here on a business trip for just three days. I live in Moscow. And you?
Игорь	Я живу́ о́чень далеко́ отсю́да, в Ирку́тске. Я худо́жник и прие́хал посмотре́ть Эрмита́ж.
	(yah zhih-<u>voo</u> <u>oh</u>-chen' dah-lee-<u>koh</u> aht-<u>syoo</u>-dah vihr-<u>koots</u>-kyeh. yah

khoo-<u>dozh</u>-neek ee pree-<u>yeh</u>-khahl pah-smaht-<u>ryet'</u> er-mee-<u>tahsh)</u>
I live very far from here, in Irkutsk. I'm an artist, and I came to have a look at the Hermitage.

Ната́ша Я была́ там то́лько оди́н раз. Это великоле́пно! Я бы с удово́льствием провела́ там це́лую неде́лю. Но нет вре́мени!
(yah bih-<u>lah</u> tahm tol'-kah ah-<u>deen</u> rahs. <u>eh</u>-tah vee-lee-kah-<u>lyep</u>-nah. yah bih soo-dah-<u>vol'</u>-stvee-yem prah-vee-<u>lah</u> tahm <u>tseh</u>-loo-yoo nee-<u>dyeh</u>-lyoo. noh nyet <u>vryeh</u>-mee-nee)
I've been there only once. It's wonderful! I would gladly spend a whole week there. But there's no time!

Игорь Жаль! А я был там почти́ ка́ждый день в тече́ние це́лого ме́сяца. И всё равно́ бы́ло ма́ло – хоте́лось ещё бо́льше. Там так мно́го экспона́тов! И все шеде́вры!
(zhal'. ah yah bihl tahm pahch-<u>tee</u> <u>kahzh</u>-diy dyen' ftee-<u>cheh</u>-nee-ee <u>tseh</u>-lah-vah <u>myeh</u>-syah-tsah. ee fsyoh rahv-<u>noh</u> bih-lah mah-lah – khah-<u>tyeh</u>-lahs' yeh-<u>shchoh</u> <u>bol'</u>-sheh. tahm tahk <u>mnoh</u>-gah eks-pah-<u>nah</u>-tahf. ee fsyeh sheh-<u>dev</u>-rih)
What a pity! And I was there almost every day over the course of a whole month. All the same, it was too little – I wanted even more. There are so many things exhibited there. And they're all masterpieces!

Ната́ша Да, пра́вда . . . А как вы пое́дете домо́й?
(dah <u>prahv</u>-dah . . . ah kahk vih pah-<u>yeh</u>-dee-tyeh dah-<u>moy</u>)
Yes, that's true . . . And how will you get home?

Игорь Ох, э́то сло́жный вопро́с! Из Москвы́ вылета́ю самолётом в Ирку́тск. Пото́м из аэропо́рта пое́ду на авто́бусе в центр го́рода. Зате́м возьму́ такси́ и́ли ча́стную маши́ну до нача́ла мое́й о́чень дли́нной у́лицы. Там доро́га така́я плоха́я, что маши́не не прое́хать. Да́же ле́том. А сейча́с, когда́ снег . . .
(okh <u>eh</u>-tah <u>slozh</u>-niy vahp-<u>ros</u>. eez mahs-<u>kvih</u> vih-lee-<u>tah</u>-yoo sah-mah-<u>lyoh</u>-tahm vihr-<u>kootsk</u>. pah-<u>tom</u> eez-ah-eh-rah-<u>por</u>-tah pah-<u>yeh</u>-doo nah-ahf-<u>toh</u>-boo-syeh ftsentr <u>goh</u>-rah-dah. zah-<u>tyem</u> <u>vahz</u>'-moo tahk-<u>see</u> ee-lee chahs-noo-yoo mah-<u>shih</u>-noo dah nah-<u>chah</u>-lah mah-<u>yey</u> oh-chen' <u>dlee</u>-nie <u>oo</u>-lee-tsih. tahm dah-<u>roh</u>-gah tah-<u>kah</u>-yah plah-<u>khah</u>-yah shtoh mah-<u>shih</u>-nyeh nyeh prah-<u>yeh</u>-khaht'. <u>dah</u>-zheh <u>lyeh</u>-tahm. ah sey-<u>chahs</u> kahg-<u>dah</u> snyek . . .)
Oh, that's a complicated question! From Moscow, I'll fly to Irkutsk. Then from the airport, I'll go by bus to the center of town. Then I'll take a taxi or a private car just to the beginning of my very long street. The road there is so bad that a car can't get through. Even in summer. And now, when there's snow . . .

Ната́ша А что же вы бу́дете де́лать?
(ah <u>shtoh</u>-zheh vih <u>boo</u>-dee-tyeh <u>dyeh</u>-laht')
But what on earth will you do?

Игорь К сча́стью, Бог дал мне две ноги́. Это са́мый надёжный тра́нспорт. Я пойду́ пешко́м!

(kshchahs-tyoo, bog dahl mnyeh dvyeh nah-gee. eh-tah sah-miy nah-dyozh-niy trahns-pahrt. yah pie-doo peesh-kom)
Fortunately, God gave me two legs. That's
the most reliable transportation.
I'll walk.

Grammar

1. THE IMPERATIVE

In this lesson we have the imperative давáйте *(dah-vie-tyeh)* **let us**, **let's**. It is based on the verb давáть *(dah-vaht')*, which can be translated in a number of ways: **to give**, **to allow** and **to let**.

Давáйте is usually followed by another verb:

Давáйте знакóмиться. *(dah-vie-tyeh znah-koh-mee-tsah)*	Let's introduce ourselves.
Давáйте начнём наш урóк. *(dah-vie-tyeh nahch-nyom nahsh oo-rok)*	Let's start our lesson.8
Садúтесь, пожáлуйста. *(sah-dee-tyes' pah-zhahl-stah)*	Sit down, please.
Посмотрúте. *(pah-smah-tree-tyeh)*	Look.
Идúте сюдá. *(ee-dee-tyeh syoo-dah)*	Come here.
Извинúте. *(eez-vee-nee-tyeh)*	Excuse me/us.
Покажúте. *(pah-kah-zhih-tyeh)*	Show me/us.

All imperatives are in the **you** form which, in Russian as in English, can refer to one or more people. There is also an informal form, which you will find below.

THE FORMATION OF THE IMPERATIVE

When the stem of a 1st or 2nd conjugation verb ends in a vowel in the second person singular of the present tense, or future of the perfective, the singular (informal) imperative is formed by adding -й *(-y)*, and the plural (formal) form by adding -йте *(-ytyeh)* to that stem:

Stem	Imperative Singular	Imperative Plural
посчитá- ешь *(pah-shchee-tah-yesh)*	посчитáй add up *(pah-schee-tie)*	посчитáйте add up *(pah-schee-tie-tyeh)*
читá- ешь *(chee-tah-yesh)*	читáй read *(chee-tie)*	читáйте read *(chee-tie-tyeh)*
рабóта- ешь *(rah-boh-tah-yesh)*	рабóтай work *(rah-boh-tie)*	рабóтайте work *(rah-boh-tie-tyeh)*
дýма- ешь *(doo-mah- yesh)*	дýмай think *(doo-mie)*	дýмайте think *(doo-mie-tyeh)*
сто -йшь *(stah -eesh)*	стóй stand/halt *(stoy)*	стóйте stand/halt *(stoy-tyeh)*

When the stem ends in a consonant, -и *(-ee/ih)*/-ите *(ee-tyeh)* are added:

Stem	Imperative Singular	Imperative Plural
говор-и́шь *(gah-vahr-eesh)*	говори́ speak *(gah-vah-ree)*	говори́те speak *(gah-vah-ree-tyeh)*
скáж-ешь *(skahzh-esh)*	скажи́ say/tell *(skah-zhih)*	скажи́те say/tell *(skah-zhih-tyeh)*
кýп-ишь *(koop-eesh)*	купи́ buy *(koo-pee)*	купи́те buy *(koo-pee-tyeh)*
покáж-ешь *(poh-kahzh-esh)*	покажи́ show *(pah-kah-zhih)*	покажи́те show *(pah-kah-zhih-tyeh)*
реш -и́шь *(reesh-ihsh)*	реши́ decide *(ree-shih)*	реши́те decide *(ree-shih-tyeh)*

Reflexive and reciprocal verbs add -йся *(-ysyah)*, -йтесь *(-ytyes')*; -ись *(ees')*, -итесь *(-eetyes')*:

одевá -ешься *(ah-dee-vah-yesh-syah)*	одевáйся get dressed *(ah-dee-vie-syah)*	одевáйтесь get dressed *(ah-dee-vie-tyes')*
подпúш -ешься *(paht-peesh-esh-syah)*	подпишúсь sign *(paht-pee-shihs')*	подпишúтесь sign *(paht-pee-shih-tyes')*

2. ХОТЕТЬ *(khah-tyet')* / TO WANT/TO WISH

This is a 1st conjugation verb in the singular and a 2nd conjugation verb in the plural. This is a very useful verb to learn.

Present tense

Singular	Plural
я хочý *(yah khah-choo)* I want	мы хотúм *(mih khah-teem)* we want
ты хóчешь *(tih khoh-chesh)* you want	вы хотúте *(vih khah-tee-tyeh)* you want
он/онá/онó хóчет *(on/ah-nah/ah-noh khoh-chet)* he/she/it wants	они хотят *(ah-nee khah-tyat)* they want

You will already have seen these examples in earlier lessons:

Я поéду с вáми, éсли хотúте.
(yah pah-yeh-doo svah-mee yes-lee khah-tee-tyeh)

I will go with you if you wish.

Я хочý помóчь вам ...
(yah khah-choo pah-moch vahm ...)

I want to help you ...

Волóдя, я хочý спросúть ...
(vah-loh-dyah yah khah-choo sprah-seet' ...)

Volodya, I want to ask ...

Хотúте чáю?
(khah-tee-tyeh chah-yoo)

Would you like some tea?

The past tense of **хотéть** is regular:

Present tense

Singular

я хотéл *(yah khah-tyel)*
I wanted

ты хотéл *(tih khah-tyel)*
you wanted

он хотéл *(on khah-tyel)*
he wanted

онá хотéла *(ah-nah khah-tyeh-lah)*
she wanted

онó хотéло *(ah-noh khah-tyeh-lah)*
it wanted

Plural

мы хотéли *(mih khah-tyeh-lee)*
we wanted

вы хотéли *(vih khah-tyeh-lee)*
you wanted

онй *(хотéли ah-nee khah-tyeh-lee)*
they wanted

---

3. ХÓЧЕТСЯ (KHOH-CHEE-TSAH) / TO WANT/TO FEEL LIKE

Some reflexive verbs can be used in an **impersonal** sense to describe an inclination or desire when they follow the dative case of **я, ты, он, онá, онá мы, вы, онй**. A particularly useful expression is **хóчется** *(khoh-chee-tsah)*, which is derived from the imperfective verb **хотéться** *(khah-tyeh-tsah)* and expresses the idea of **feeling like** or **wanting** to do something.

Мне хóчется *(mnyeh khoh-chee-tsah)* means **to me it wants = I want, I feel like**.
In Lesson 4, Paul says:

Я óчень хочý побывáть в Санкт-Петербýрге.
(yah oh-chen' khah-choo pah-bih-vaht' fsahnkt-pee-teer-boor-gyeh)
I really want to spend some time in St. Petersburg.

Another way to say this is:

Мне óчень хóчется побывáть в Санкт-Петербýрге.
(mnyeh oh-chen' khoh-chee-tsah pah-bih-vaht' fsankt-pee-teer-boor-gyeh)
I really want to spend some time in St. Petersburg.

Similarly:

Мне хóчется есть.
(mnyeh khoh-chee-tsah yest')

I want to eat. = I am hungry.

Им хо́чется спать.
(eem khoh-chee-tsah spaht')
They want to sleep. = They are sleepy.

Нам хо́чется чита́ть.
(nahm khoh-chee-tsah chee-taht')
We feel like reading.

Note that the form **хо́чется** is the same for all persons in both the present tense and in the past tense (**хоте́лось** *(khah-tyeh-lahs')*):

Ему́ хоте́лось побыва́ть в ...
(ye-moo khah-tyeh-lahs' pah-bih-vaht' v ...)
He wanted to spend some time in ...

Ей хоте́лось купи́ть перча́тки.
(yey khah-tyeh-lahs' koo-peet' peer-chaht-kee)
She wanted to buy some gloves.

Нам хоте́лось пойти́ в кино́.
(nahm khah-tyeh-lahs' pie-tee fkee-noh)
We wanted to go to the movies.

Sometimes the person is omitted, as in this lesson, when Igor says:

И всё равно́ бы́ло ма́ло – хоте́лось ещё бо́льше.
(ee fsyoh rahv-noh bih-lah mah-lah – khah-tyeh-lahs' yeh-shchoh bohl'-sheh)
All the same it was too little – (I) wanted even more.

4. THE CONDITIONAL MOOD: WOULD /БЫ (BIH)

In Lesson 5, Natasha says:

Мы хоте́ли бы созда́ть совме́стное предприя́тие ...
(mih khah-tyeh-lee bih sahz-daht' sahv-myes-nah-yeh preet-pree-yah-tee-yeh ...)
We would like to set up a joint venture...

This is an example of the conditional **mood**, which has only one tense in Russian. It is formed by adding **бы** *(bih)* to the past tense of a perfective or imperfective verb and can have a present, future or past meaning, depending on the context.

In this lesson, Natasha says:

Я бы с удово́льствием провепа́ там це́лую неде́лю.
(yah bih soo-dah-vol'-stvee-yem prah-vee-lah tahm tseh-loo-yoo nee-dyeh-lyoo)

I would happily spend a whole week there.

5. ORDINAL NUMBERS 11TH–20TH

11th одиннадцатый *(ah-dee-nah-tsah-tiy)*

12th двенадцатый *(dvee-nah-tsah-tiy)*

13th тринадцатый *(tree-nah-tsah-tiy)*

14th четырнадцатый *(chee-tihr-nah-tsah-tiy)*

15th пятнадцатый *(pyaht-nah-tsah-tiy)*

16th шестнадцатый *(shes-nah-tsah-tiy)*

17th семнадцатый *(syem-nah-tsah-tiy)*

18th восемнадцатый *(vah-seem-nah-tsah-tiy)*

19th девятнадцатый *(dyeh-vyaht-nah-tsah-tiy)*

20th двадцатый *(dvah-tsah-tiy)*

The ordinal numbers above are formed by removing the soft sign from the end of cardinal numbers and adding the adjectival endings **-ый** *(-iy)*, **-ая** *(ah-yah)*, **-ое** *(ah-yeh)*.

For example: 20 **двадцать … двадцат** : (ь) + (ый) = 20th **двадцатый**

Note the shift in stress.

6. NOTE ON STRESS

In Lesson 1 we mentioned that the stress shifts in certain set expressions. In the dialogue, Natasha could not get a return ticket on the plane because **не было мест** *(neh bih-lah myest)* **there were no seats**. In this and in similar negative constructions, the stress shifts onto **не** from **был, была, было, были** and the pronunciation is *nyeh-bihl, nyeh-bih-lah*, etc.

Vocabulary

обра́тно *(ahb-raht-nah)* back (direction, movement)

проходи́ть *(impf)* *(prah-khah-deet')* to travel through, to pass (of time)

в дела́х *(v dyeh-lahkh)* on business, working

спе́шка *(spyesh-kah)* a rush

в спе́шке *(fspyesh-kyeh)* in a hurry, in a rush

зако́нчен *m.***/зако́нчена** *f.***/зако́нчено** *n.* *(zah-kon-cheen m./zah-kon-chee-nah f./ zah-kon-chee-nah n.)* finished *(short form adjective)*

сде́ланный *m.***/сде́ланная** *f.***/сде́ланное** *n.* *(zdeh-lah-niy m./zdeh-lah-nah-yah f./ zdeh-lah-nah-yeh n.)* done, finished

сде́лан *m.***/сде́лана** *f.***/сде́лано** *n.* *(zdeh-lahn m./zdeh-lah-nah f./zdeh-lah-nah n.)* *(short form)* done, finished

пора́ *(pah-rah)* it is time

прилета́ть *(impf)* *(pree-lee-taht')* to fly to, to arrive by air

ме́сто *(myes-tah)* place, seat

обе́дать *(impf)* *(ah-byeh-daht')* to dine, to have a meal/lunch (sometimes 'dinner')

пообе́дать *(perf)* *(pah-ah-byeh-daht')* to dine, to have dined

рестора́н *(rees-tah-rahn)* restaurant

бе́лый *m.***/бе́лая** *f.***/бе́лое** *n.* *(byeh-liy m./ byeh-lah-yah f./byeh-lah-yeh n.)* white

пото́м *(pah-tom)* then

на́бережная *(nah-bee-reezh-nah-yah)* embankment, wharf, waterfront

по на́бережной *(pah nah-bee-reezh-nie)* on/along the bank

зате́м *(zah-tyem)* after that

проводи́ть *(perf)* *(prah-vah-deet')* to accompany, to take (on foot), to see off

попроща́ться *(perf)* *(pah-prah-shchah-tsah)* to say goodbye

двухме́стный *(dvookh-myes-niy)* two-seat

купе́ *(koo-peh)* compartment

разгова́ривать *(impf)* *(rahz-gah-vah-ree-vaht')* to talk, to chat

попу́тчик *m.***/попу́тчица** *f.* *(pah-poot-cheek m./pah-poot-chee-tsah f.)* traveling companion

Дава́йте знако́миться. *(dah-vie-tyeh zhah-koh-mee-tsah)* Let's introduce ourselves.

чуть-чуть *(choot'-choot')* just a little, a tiny bit

откры́ть *(perf)* *(aht-kriht')* to open

ужа́сно *(oo-zhahs-nah)* terribly

жа́ркий *m.***/жа́ркая** *f.***/жа́ркое** *n.* *(zhahr-keey m./zhahr-kah-yah f./ zhahr-kah-yeh n.)* hot

даль *(dahl')* distance, expanse

далёкий *m.***/далёкая** *f.***/далёкое** *n.* *(dah-lyoh-keey m./dah-lyoh-kah-yah f./ dah-lyoh-kah-yeh n.)* distant, remote

худо́жник *m.***/худо́жница** *f.* *(khoo-dozh-neek m./khoo-dozh-nee-tsah f.)* artist

посмотре́ть *(perf)* *(pah-smah-tryet')* to look at, to see

оди́н раз *(ah-deen rahs)* one time, once

великоле́пный *m.***/великоле́пная** *f.***/ великоле́пное** *n.* *(vee-lee-kah-lyep-niy m./ vee-lee-kah-lyep-nah-yah f./vee-lee-kah-lyep-nah-yeh n.)* wonderful, splendid, magnificent

великоле́пно *(vee-lee-kah-lyep-nah)* *wonderfully, it's wonderful/ splendid/magnificent*

провести́ *(perf)* *(prah-vyes-tee) to spend (time)*

Жаль! *(zhal') What a pity!*

почти́ *(pahch-tee) almost*

тече́ние *(tee-cheh-nee-yeh) flow, course (of time); trend; current (river, etc.)*

в тече́ние *(ftee-cheh-nee-ee) during*

всё равно́ *(fsyoh rav-noh) all the same, in any case*

Мне всё равно́. *(mnyeh fsyoh rav-noh) It's all the same to me.*

ма́ло *(mah-lah) little*

экспона́т *(eks-pah-naht) exhibit item*

мно́го экспона́тов *(mnoh-gah eks-pah-nah-taf) a lot of exhibit items, many things on exhibit*

шеде́вр *(sheh-devr) masterpiece (from the French "chef-d'oeuvre")*

пра́вда *(prav-dah) truth; it is true*

сло́жный *m.*/**сло́жная** *f.*/**сло́жное** *n.* *(slozh-niy m./slozh-nah-yah f./ slozh-nah-yeh n.) difficult, complicated*

центр *(tsentr) center*

го́род *(goh-raht) town*

взять *(perf) (vzyat') to take*

Возьму́ такси́. *(vaz'-moo tahk-see) (I) will take a taxi.*

ча́стный *m.*/**ча́стная** *f.*/**ча́стное** *n.* *(chahs-niy m./chahs-nah-yah f./ chahs-nah-yeh n.) private*

маши́на *(mah-shih-nah) car*

нача́ло *(nah-chah-lah) beginning, start*

дли́нный *m.*/**дли́нная** *f.*/**дли́нное** *n.* *(dlee-niy m./dlee-nah-yah f./ dlee-nah-yeh n.) long*

плохо́й *m.*/**плоха́я** *f.*/**плохо́е** *n.* *(plah-khoy m./plah-khah-yah f./plah-khoh-yeh n.) bad*

тако́й *m.*/**така́я** *f.*/**тако́е** *n.* *(tah-koy m./ tah-kah-yah f./tah-koh-yeh n.) so, such*

прое́хать *(perf) (prah-yeh-khat') to go through (by transport)*

Маши́не не прое́хать. *(mah-shih-nyeh nyeh prah-yeh-khat') A car can't get through.*

ле́то *(lyeh-tah) summer*

ле́том *(lyeh-tahm) in summer*

снег *(snyek) snow*

сча́стье *(shchahs-tyeh) happiness, good fortune*

к сча́стью *(k shchahs-tyoo) fortunately, happily*

Бог *(bok) God*

нога́ *(nah-gah) leg, foot*

надёжный *m.*/**надёжная** *f.*/**надёжное** *n.* *(nah-dyozh-niy m./nah-dyozh-nah-yah f./ nah-dyozh-nah-yeh n.) reliable, trusty*

са́мый *m.*/**са́мая** *f.*/**са́мое** *n.* *(sah-miy m./ sah-mah-yah f./sah-mah-yeh n.) the most*

тра́нспорт *(trahns-pahrt) transport*

Exercises

Exercise A

Here are some more words that have been adopted into the Russian language. Translate them into English.

1. факс ....
2. калькуля́тор ....
3. бути́к ....
4. сноубо́рд ....
5. компью́тер ....
6. телефо́н ....
7. ксе́рокс ....

8. музыка́льный центр ....
9. при́нтер ....
10. ка́ртридж ....
11. пле́ер ....
12. ска́нер ....
13. да́йвинг ....
14. автомоби́ль ....

Exercise B

Put the following incomplete sentences into Russian and complete them with details about yourself where necessary.

1. **Good evening. Let's introduce ourselves.**

   ....

2. **I am (my name is)** ....

   And who are you? ....

3. **I'm a/an** .... (nationality).

4. **I was born in** .... (place of birth).

5. **I work** ....

6. **I like** ....

7. **I don't like** ....

8. **I am studying Russian** ....

Exercise C

Я хоте́л бы …/мне хоте́лось бы …

Translate the following sentences into English.

1. **Я хоте́л бы откры́ть окно́.**

   ....

2. **Мы хоте́ли бы созда́ть фи́рму в Ми́нске.**

   ....

3. **Ему́ хоте́лось бы быть там ка́ждый день.**

   ....

4. **Она́ хоте́ла бы купи́ть газе́ту.**

   ....

5. **Ей хоте́лось бы вы́пить минера́льной воды́.**

   ....

6. **Они́ хоте́ли бы пойти́ по магази́нам.**

   ....

7. **Им хоте́лось бы жить в Аме́рике.**

   ....

8. **Мне хоте́лось бы хорошо́ говори́ть по-ру́сски.**

   ....

9. **Я хоте́л бы пое́хать домо́й.**

   ....

10. **Хоте́ли бы вы рабо́тать в Москве́?**

   ....

Exercise D

Put the the following sentences into the present tense.

1. Он éхал домóй.

   ....

2. Онá покупáла билéт.

   ....

3. Онú гуляли по нáбережной Невы́.

   ....

4. Онú прощáлись в гостúнице.

   ....

5. Úгорь был в двухмéстном купé в пóезде.

   ....

6. Натáша и Úгорь разговáривали об Эрмитáже.

   ....

7. Úгорь жил в Иркýтске.

   ....

8. Мы обéдали в рестоáне.

   ....

9. Что вы бýдете дéлать?

   ....

Exercise E

True or false?

1. Ната́ша пое́хала в Санкт-Петербу́рг по́ездом.   T/F

2. Она́ купи́ла обра́тный биле́т на самолёт.   T/F

3. Ната́ша пое́дет домо́й в Москву́ на по́езде "Кра́сная Стрела́".   T/F

4. Ната́ша пообе́дала с Воло́дей в шесть часо́в ве́чера.   T/F

5. Ната́ша с Воло́дей пло́хо пообе́дали в рестора́не.   T/F

6. По́сле обе́да Ната́ша с Воло́дей погуля́ли по на́бережной Невы́.   T/F

7. И́горь Григо́рьевич живёт в Ми́нске.   T/F

8. В купе́ бы́ло хо́лодно.   T/F

9. Ната́ша откры́ла окно́.   T/F

10. И́горь бухга́лтер.   T/F

11. Ната́ша была́ в Эрмита́же то́лько оди́н раз.   T/F

12. И́горь никогда́ не был в Эрмита́же.   T/F

10. Communications

Lesson 10 focuses on written communications and you will learn how to write in Russian. Listen to the vocabulary audio as you go through the list and repeat it – this will help you to memorize the words and to perfect your pronunciation.

By the end of Lesson 10, you should be able to read and pronounce Russian without needing to refer to the phonetic transcription, so from Lesson 11 onwards, you will find just the Cyrillic text and the English translation. If you have any difficulty, take another look at the pronunciation guide in Lesson 1.

ПИСЬМО́ В АМЕ́РИКУ A LETTER TO AMERICA

Сейча́с Ната́ша нахо́дится в кабине́те своего́ нача́льника. Они́ обсужда́ют письмо́ к Ма́йку Ро́джерсу.
(sey-chahs nah-tah-shah nah-khoh-dee-tsah fkah-bee-nyeh-tyeh svah-yeh-voh nah-chahl'-nee-kah. ah-nee ahp-soozh-dah-yoot pees'-moh kmie-koo rod-zher-soo)
Right now, Natasha is in her boss's office. They are discussing a letter to Mike Rogers.

Ната́ша	Вот чернови́к письма́ к господи́ну Ро́джерсу.
	(vot cheer-nah-veek pees'-mah k gahs-pah-dee-noo rod-zher-soo)
	Here is a draft of the letter to Mr. Rogers.
Дмитрий	Посмо́трим. Хмм … Зна́чит, он прилета́ет к нам пе́рвого ма́рта?
	(pah-smot-reem. khmm … znah-cheet on pree-lee-tah-yet knahm pyer-vah-vah mahr-tah)

Let's have a look. Hmm . . . So, he's flying over (to us) on the first of March?

Ната́ша   Да, так мы договори́лись по телефо́ну.
(dah tahk mih dah-gah-vah-*ree*-lees' pah-tee-lee-*foh*-noo)
Yes, that's what we agreed on the phone.

Дмитрий   А ви́за у него́ уже́ есть?
(ah *vee*-zah oo-nee-*voh* oo-*zheh* yest')
And does he have a visa already?

Ната́ша   Пока́ нет, но я пошлю́ приглаше́ние с э́тим письмо́м.
(pah-*kah* nyet noh yah pahsh-*lyoo* pree-glah-*sheh*-nee-yeh *seh*-teem pees'-*mom*)
Not yet, but I'll send an invitation with this letter.

Дмитрий   Где он бу́дет жить?
(gdyeh on *boo*-deet zhiht')
Where will he stay?

Ната́ша   Он остано́вится в гости́нице "Звезда́". Для него́ уже́ заброни́рован но́мер.
(on ahs-tah-*noh*-vee-tsah vgahs-*tee*-nee-tseh zveez-*dah*. dlyah nee-*voh* oo-*zheh* zah-brah-*nee*-rah-vahn *noh*-meer)
He'll stay at the Zvezda [Star] Hotel. A room is already booked for him.

Дмитрий   Ско́лько он здесь пробу́дет?
(*skol*'-kah on zdyes' prah-*boo*-dyet)
How long will he stay here?

Ната́ша   Э́то бу́дет зави́сеть от того́, как пойду́т перегово́ры. Но, по-мо́ему, не ме́нее двух неде́ль.
(*eh*-tah *boo*-deet zah-*vee*-syet' aht-tah-*voh* kahk pie-*doot* pee-ree-gah-*voh*-rih. noh pah-*moh*-yeh-moo nyeh *myeh*-nee-yeh dvookh nee-*dyel*')
That will depend on how the negotiations go. But in my opinion, not less than two weeks.

Дмитрий   Ну, хорошо́. Спаси́бо. А! Оди́н вопро́с! Вы называ́ете его́ в письме́ "Майк". Вы с ним уже́ встреча́лись ра́ньше?
(noo khah-rah-*shoh*. spah-*see*-bah. ah. ah-*deen* vahp-*ros*. vih nah-zih-*vah*-yeh-tyeh yeh-*voh* fpees'-*myeh* miek. vih sneem oo-*zheh* fstree-*chah*-lees' *rahn*'-sheh)
Okay then. Thanks. Oh! One question! You call him "Mike" in the letter. Have you met him before?

Ната́ша   Да нет. Мы не́сколько раз говори́ли по телефо́ну. Но америка́нцы таки́е коммуника́бельные и просты́е! Он сра́зу же на́чал называ́ть меня́ "Ната́ша". А когда́ я обраща́юсь к нему́ "Ми́стер Ро́джерс", он всегда́ смеётся: "Я ещё не совсе́м ста́рый! Зови́те меня́ Майк!"
(dah nyet. mih *nyes*-kahl'-kah rahs gah-vah-*ree*-lee pah-tee-lee-*foh*-noo. noh ah-mee-ree-*kahn*-tsih tah-*kee*-yeh kah-moo-nee-*kah*-beel'-

nih-yeh ee prahs-<u>tih</u>-yeh. on <u>srah</u>-zoo-zheh <u>nah</u>-chahl nah-zih-<u>vaht'</u> mee-<u>nyah</u> nah-<u>tah</u>-shah. ah kahg-<u>dah</u> yah ah-brah-<u>shchah</u>-yoos' knee-<u>moo</u> <u>mees</u>-ter <u>rod</u>-zhers on fsee-<u>gdah</u> smee-<u>yoh</u>-tsah yah yeh-<u>shchoh</u> nyeh sahf-<u>syem</u> <u>stah</u>-riy. zah-<u>vee</u>-tyeh mee-<u>nyah</u> miek)

Oh, no. We spoke on the phone a few times. But Americans are so approachable and easy going! He right away started to call me "Natasha." And when I address him as "Mr. Rogers", he always laughs, "I'm not that old! Call me 'Mike'".

Дмитрий   **Ну, ла́дно. Спаси́бо, Ната́лья Петро́вна.**
(noo <u>lahd</u>-nah. spah-<u>see</u>-bah nah-<u>tahl'</u>-yah peet-<u>rov</u>-nah)
Okay then. Thank you, Natalya Petrovna.

ВОТ ПИСЬМО́ НАТА́ШИ МА́ЙКУ: *(vot pees'-moh nah-tah-shih mie-koo)*
HERE IS THE LETTER FROM NATASHA TO MIKE:

Московский Центральный Банк
Россия
115726 Москва
ул Ленина, 54

Дорого́й Майк,
(dah-rah-<u>goy</u> miek)
Dear Mike,
Я и мой колле́ги наде́емся, что Ваш визи́т состои́тся, как мы и договори́лись, 1-го ма́рта.
(yah ee mah-<u>ee</u> kah-<u>lyeh</u>-gee nah-<u>dyeh</u>-yem-syah shtoh vahsh vee-<u>zeet</u> sah-stah-<u>ee</u>-tsah kahk mih ee dah-gah-vah-<u>ree</u>-lees' <u>pyer</u>-vah-vah <u>mahr</u>-tah)
My colleagues and I hope that your visit will take place just as we agreed, on March 1st.
Я бу́ду встреча́ть Вас в аэропорту́ Шереме́тьево-2. В рука́х у меня́ бу́дет табли́чка с Ва́шим и́менем. Но́мер в гости́нице бу́дет зака́зан для Вас зара́нее.
(yah <u>boo</u>-doo fstree-<u>chaht'</u> vahs vah-eh-rah-pahr-<u>too</u> sheh-reeh-<u>myet'</u>-yeh-vah-dvah. vroo-<u>kahkh</u> oo-mee-<u>nyah</u> <u>boo</u>-deet tahb-<u>leech</u>-kah <u>svah</u>-shihm <u>ee</u>-mee-nyem. <u>noh</u>-meer vgahs-<u>tee</u>-nee-tseh <u>boo</u>-deet zah-<u>kah</u>-zahn dlyah vahs zah-<u>rah</u>-nee-yeh)
I will meet you at Sheremetyevo 2 airport. I will be holding a card with your name. A hotel room will be booked for you in advance.
Посыла́ю Вам официа́льное приглаше́ние. Оно́ необходи́мо для получе́ния ви́зы.
Вы должны́ обрати́ться за ви́зой в Росси́йское ко́нсульство. Там Вам вы́дадут две

анкéты, котóрые нáдо бýдет запóлнить (дáта и мéсто рождéния, домáшний áдрес, мéсто рабóты и т.п.).

(pah-sih-lah-yoo vahm ah-fee-tsih-al'-nah-yeh pree-glah-sheh-nee-yeh. ah-noh nee-ahp-khah-dee-mah dlyah pah-loo-cheh-nee-yah vee-zih. vih dalzh-nih ahb-rah-tee-tsah zah vee-zie vrah-seey-skah-yeh kon-sool'-stvah. tahm vahm vih-dah-doot dvyeh ahn-kyeh-tih kah-toh-rih-yeh nah-dah boo-deet zah-pol-neet' (dah-tah ee myes-tah rahzh-dyeh-nee-yah dah-mahsh-neey ahd-ryes myes-tah rah-boh-tih ee teh peh)

I am sending you an official invitation. It is essential for obtaining a visa. You must apply for the visa at the Russian Consulate. There, they will give you two forms that it will be necessary to complete (date and place of birth, home address, place of work, etc.).

Оформлéние вÍзы не должнó занÁть мнóго врéмени.

(ah-fahr-mlyeh-nee-yeh vee-zih nyeh dahlzh-noh zah-nyaht' mnoh-gah vryeh-mee-nee)

Processing the visa should not take long.

Ждём встрéчи с Вáми.

(zhdyom fstryeh-chee svah-mee)

Looking forward to seeing you.

С Íскренним уважéнием,

(sihs-kreen-neem oo-vah-zheh-nee-yem)

With sincere respect,

Натáша.

Grammar

1. RUSSIAN ADDRESSES

Here is the address of the bank again, this time with the stress marks. About the only place you will find stress marks in Russian texts for Russians is in dictionaries.

Москóвский Центрáльный Банк
Россúя
115726 Москвá
ул Лéнина, 54

Most Russians living in towns live in apartments. An apartment building is called a **дом** *(dom)*, which can mean **home**, **house** or **building**. An apartment, an office or even a shop is in a **дом**. Natasha lives in an apartment. Her address is:

Россúя,	Russia,
117192 Москвá,	117192 Moscow,
ул. Мира,	Street of Peace
дом 55, кóрпус 6, квартúра 15,	Building 55, Block 6, Apartment 15
Иванóвой Н. П.	(To) Ivanova N. P.

117192 is the postal code in Moscow. **ул.** is short for **ýлица** *(oo-lee-tsah)*, street. **Дом 55** is the building in which Natasha lives. However, there may be several buildings on Peace Street with the same number! So the address contains the **ко́рпус** _(kor-poos)_ or block number, **6**. This is followed by the apartment number, **15**. Then Natasha's family name, **Ивано́ва**, is given in the dative case, **Ивано́вой**, as the letter is being sent to her.

Note: in letters, **Вы** is usually written with a capital.

2. MONTHS

The months of the year are all masculine and only start with a capital letter at the beginning of a sentence.

янва́рь _(yahn-<u>vahr</u>')_ January	апре́ль _(ahp-<u>ryel</u>')_ April	Ию́ль _(ee-<u>yool</u>')_ July	октя́брь _(ahk-<u>tyahbr</u>')_ October
февра́ль _(feev-<u>rahl</u>')_ February	Ма́й _(mie)_ May	а́вгуст _(<u>ahv</u>-goost)_ August	ноя́брь _(nah-<u>yahbr</u>')_ November
март _(mahrt)_ March	Ию́нь _(ee-<u>yoon</u>')_ June	сентя́брь _(seen-<u>tyahbr</u>')_ September	дека́брь _(dee-<u>kahbr</u>')_ December

Note how the stress shifts when these months are in the prepositional case:

в январе́ _(vyahn-vah-<u>ryeh</u>)_	в феврале́ _(f feev-rah-<u>lyeh</u>)_	в ма́рте _(<u>vmahr</u>-tyeh)_	в апре́ле _(vahp-<u>ryeh</u>-lyeh)_
в ма́е _(<u>vmah</u>-yeh)_	в ию́не _(vih-<u>yoo</u>-nyeh)_	в ию́ле _(vih-yoo-lyeh)_	в а́вгусте _(<u>vahv</u>-goos-tyeh)_
в сентябре́ _(fseen-tyahb-<u>ryeh</u>)_	в октябре́ _(vahk-tyahb-<u>ryeh</u>)_	в ноябре́ _(vnah-yahb-<u>ryeh</u>)_	в декабре́ _(vdyeh-kahb-<u>ryeh</u>)_

3. DATES

When stating the current date, Russians use the neuter form of the ordinal number, followed by the name of the month **in the genitive**. This is because the neuter word число *(chees-loh)* – date – is understood: **пе́рвое (число́) января́** the first (date) of January.

Here are some examples:

пе́рвое января́   the first of January
(pyer-vah-yeh yahn-vah-ryah)

второ́е февраля́   the second of February
(ftah-roh-yeh feev-rah-lyah)

третье ма́рта the third of March
(tryeh-tyeh mahr-tah)

четвёртое апре́ля   the fourth of April
(cheet-vyor-tah-yeh ahp-ryeh-lyah)

деся́тое октября́   the tenth of October
(dee-syah-tah-yeh ahk-tyah-bryah)

To indicate the date on which something will or did take place (**on the first of ...**, etc.), the genitive of the ordinal is used, followed by the genitive of the month. In this lesson, Natasha asks:

... он прилета́ет к нам пе́рвого ма́рта?   ... he is flying in on the first of March?
(... on pree-lee-tah-yet knahm pyer-vah-vah mahr-tah)

пе́рвого is the genitive of **пе́рвое**.

Here are some examples:

пя́того ма́я   on the fifth of May
(pyah-tah-vah mah-yah)

седьмо́го ию́ля   on the seventh of July
(seed'-moh-vah ee-yoo-lyah)

девя́того сентября́   on the ninth of September
(dee-vyah-tah-vah seen-tyahb-ryah)

двена́дцатого декабря́   on the twelfth of December
(dvee-nah-tsah-tah-vah dee-kahb-ryah)

обсужда́ть *(impf) (ahp-soozh-<u>daht'</u>) to discuss*

чернови́к *(cheer-nah-<u>veek</u>) a draft*

е́сли *(<u>yes</u>-lee) if*

вноси́ть *(impf) (vnah-<u>seet'</u>) to enter, register*

измене́ние *(eez-mee-<u>nyeh</u>-nee-yeh) a change*

компью́тер *(kahm-<u>pyoo</u>-ter) computer*

догова́риваться *(impf) (dah-gah-<u>vah</u>-ree-vah-tsah) to agree*

договори́ться *(perf) (dah-gah-vah-<u>ree</u>-tsah) to agree*

телефо́н *(tee-lee-<u>fon</u>) telephone*

по телефо́ну *(pah tee-lee-<u>foh</u>-noo) on the phone, by phone*

ви́за *(<u>vee</u>-zah) visa*

пока́ *(pah-<u>kah</u>) until*

пока́ нет *(pah-<u>kah</u> nyet) not yet*

посыла́ть *(impf) (pah-sih-<u>laht'</u>) to send*

приглаше́ние *(pree-glah-<u>sheh</u>-nee-yeh) invitation*

остана́вливать *(impf) (ah-stah-<u>nahv</u>-lee-vaht') to stop (somebody/thing)*

останови́ть *(perf) (ah-stah-nah-<u>veet'</u>) to stop (somebody/thing)*

остана́вливаться *(impf) (ah-stah-<u>nahv</u>-lee-vah-tsah) to stop, to stay*

останови́ться *(perf) (ah-stah-nah-<u>vee</u>-tsah) to stop, to stay*

звезда́ *(zveez-<u>dah</u>) star*

брони́ровать *(impf) (brah-<u>nee</u>-rah-vaht') to reserve, to book*

заброни́ровать *(perf) (zah-brah-<u>nee</u>-rah-vaht') to reserve, to book*

Ско́лько? *(<u>skol'</u>-kah) How much/many/long?*

пробы́ть *(perf) (prah-<u>biht'</u>) to stay, to live*

through (for a certain amount of time)

Ско́лько вре́мени он здесь пробу́дет? *(<u>skol'</u>-kah <u>vryeh</u>-mee-nee on zdyes' prah-<u>boo</u>-deet) How long will he be here?*

зави́сеть *(impf) (zah-<u>vee</u>-syet') to depend (on)*

зави́сеть от того́, как ... *(zah-<u>vee</u>-syet' aht tah-<u>voh</u> kahk ...) to depend on how ...*

перегово́ры *(pee-ree-gah-<u>voh</u>-rih) negotiations, talks*

иду́т перегово́ры *(ee-<u>doot</u> pee-ree-gah-<u>voh</u>-rih) negotiations are going on/taking place*

по-мо́ему *(pah-<u>moh</u>-yeh-moo) in my opinion*

не ме́нее *(nee-<u>myeh</u>-nee-yeh) not less*

называ́ть *(nah-zih-<u>vaht'</u>) to call, to address (someone)*

Да нет. *(dah nyet) Oh, no.*

не́сколько *(<u>nyes</u>-kal'-kah) a few, several*

не́сколько раз *(<u>nyes</u>-kal'-kah rahs) several times*

коммуника́бельный *m./* **коммуника́бельная** *f./* **коммуника́бельное** *n. (kah-moo-nee-<u>kah</u>-beel'-niy m./kah-moo-nee-<u>kah</u>-beel'-nah-yah f./kah-moo-nee-<u>kah</u>-beel'-nah-yeh n.) approachable*

просто́й *m./***проста́я** *f./***просто́е** *n. (prahs-<u>toy</u> n./prahs-<u>tah</u>-yah f./prahs-<u>toh</u>-yeh n.) simple, straightforward, easygoing*

сра́зу *(<u>srah</u>-zoo) at once, right away, immediately*

же *(zheh) no specific meaning: it serves to emphasize another word*

обраща́ться *(impf) (ahb-rah-<u>shchah</u>-tsah) to address (someone)*

обрати́ться *(perf) (ahb-rah-<u>tee</u>-tsah) to*

address (someone)

совсéм (sahf-<u>syem</u>) completely

звать (zvaht') to call (use a name)

зовúте (zah-<u>vee</u>-tyeh) call, address (imperative)

лáдно (<u>lahd</u>-nah) right, all right, okay, fine

коллéга (kah-<u>lyeh</u>-gah) colleague (male or female)

надéяться (impf) (nah-<u>dyeh</u>-yah-tsah) to hope

визúт (vee-<u>zeet</u>) a visit

состоя́ться (perf) (sah-stah-<u>yah</u>-tsah) to take place

встрéча (<u>fstryeh</u>-chah) meeting, get together

встречáть (impf) (fstree-<u>chaht'</u>) to meet

встрéтить (perf) (<u>fstryeh</u>-teet') to meet

в рукáх (v roo-<u>kahkh</u>) in (one's) hands

таблúчка (tahb-<u>leech</u>-kah) a card, small poster

с úменем (<u>sih</u>-mee-nyem) with the first name

закáз (zah-<u>kahs</u>) an order

закáзан (zah-<u>kah</u>-zahn) booked, reserved

закáзывать (impf) (zah-<u>kah</u>-zih-vaht') to book, to reserve

заказáть (perf) (zah-kah-<u>zaht'</u>) to book, to reserve, to order

рáно (<u>rah</u>-nah) early

зарáнее (zah-<u>rah</u>-nee-yeh) in advance, earlier

официáльный m./**официáльная** f./**официáльное** n. (ah-fee-tsih-<u>ahl'</u>-niy m./ ah-fee-tsih-<u>ahl'</u>-nah-yah f./ah-fee-tsih-<u>ahl'</u>-nah-yeh n.) official

необходúмый m./**необходúмая** f./**необходúмое** n. (nee-ahp-khah-<u>dee</u>-miy m./ nee-ahp-khah-<u>dee</u>-mah-yah f./nee-ahp-khah-<u>dee</u>-mah-yeh n.) unavoidable, necessary

необходúмо (nee-ahp-khah-<u>dee</u>-mah) unavoidable, necessary (short form)

получéние (pah-loo-<u>cheh</u>-nee-yeh) acquisition, obtaining

россúйский m./**россúйская** f./**россúйское** n. (rah-<u>seey</u>-skeey m./rah-<u>seey</u>-skah-yah f./ rah-<u>seey</u>-skah-yeh n.) Russian (pertaining to the Russian state)

кóнсульство (<u>kon</u>-sool'-stvah) consulate

выдавáть (impf) (vih-dah-<u>vaht'</u>) to hand out, to give, to issue

вы́дать (perf) (<u>vih</u>-daht') to hand out, to give, to issue

анкéта (ahn-<u>kyeh</u>-tah) form, questionnaire

заполня́ть (impf) (zah-pahl-<u>nyaht'</u>) to fill, to fill in, to complete (a form)

запóлнить (perf) (zah-<u>pol</u>-neet') to fill, to fill in, to complete (a form)

дáта (<u>dah</u>-tah) date

рождéние (rahzh-<u>dyeh</u>-nee-yeh) birth

домáшний m./**домáшняя** f./**домáшнее** n. (dah-<u>mahsh</u>-neey m./dah-<u>mahsh</u>-nyah-yah f./ dah-<u>mahsh</u>-nyeh-yeh n.) home

мéсто рабóты (<u>myes</u>-tah rah-<u>boh</u>-tih) place of work

оформлéние (ah-fahr-<u>mlyeh</u>-nee-yeh) preparation, processing

занимáть (impf) (zah-nee-<u>maht'</u>) to take up, to occupy

заня́ть (perf) (zah-<u>nyaht'</u>) to take up, to occupy

ждать (impf) (zhdaht') to wait, to await

úскренний m./**úскренняя** f./**úскреннее** n. (<u>ees</u>-kreen-neey m./<u>ees</u>-kreen-nyah-yah f./ <u>ees</u>-kreen-nyeh-yeh n.) sincere

уважéние (oo-vah-<u>zheh</u>-nee-yeh) respect

Exercises

Exercise A

Translate the following sentences into English.

1. Сего́дня воскресе́нье, вчера́ была́ суббо́та, а за́втра бу́дет понеде́льник.

   ....

2. Рабо́та зако́нчена. Иди́те домо́й.

   ....

3. Вчера́ ве́чером Ива́н прилете́л в Москву́ самолётом.

   ....

4. Мне не удало́сь купи́ть перча́тки.

   ....

5. Как называ́ется э́тот по́езд?

   ....

6. В де́сять часо́в утра́ я пил ко́фе в рестора́не с Ната́шей.

   ....

7. Мо́жно закры́ть дверь? Здесь ужа́сно хо́лодно.

   ....

8. Влади́мир ходи́л в Эрмита́ж почти́ ка́ждый день в тече́ние це́лой неде́ли.

   ....

9. Вино́ бы́ло хоро́шее – хоте́лось ещё бо́льше.

   ....

10. У меня́ нет свое́й маши́ны, но у меня́ есть своя́ отде́льная кварти́ра.

   ....

11. **Майк живёт óчень далекó от Москвы́ – в Амéрике.**

....

12. **Я бы с удовóльствием жил в Филадéльфии.**

....

13. **Как они поéдут домóй?**

....

14. **Что вы бýдете дéлать зáвтра вéчером?**

....

15. **Вчерá мы купи́ли нóвую маши́ну.**

....

Exercise B

Translate the following imperatives into Russian, complete with stress marks.

1. **Come here** ....

2. **Sit down** ....

3. **Excuse me** ....

4. **Show me** ....

5. **Think** ....

6. **Decide** ....

7. **Get dressed** ....

8. **Don't smoke** ....

9. **Don't sign** ....

10. **Read** ....

11. **Work** ....

12. Don't buy ....

13. Don't shout ....

14. Don't wear ....

15. Don't pay ....

Exercise C

Put the appropriate form of the present tense of **хоте́ть**, **to want**, with stress marks, on the dotted line.

1. Я .... купи́ть маши́ну.

2. Мой оте́ц и мать .... купи́ть отде́льную кварти́ру.

3. Майк .... прие́хать к нам в Москву́.

4. Мы .... пообе́дать с ва́ми.

5. Воло́дя и Ната́ша .... подписа́ть контра́кт с америка́нской фи́рмой.

6. Ты .... пить?

7. Она́ .... поговори́ть с ва́ми.

8. Они́ .... гуля́ть по на́бережной Невы́.

Exercise D

Give the masculine form of the ordinal equivalents of these cardinal numbers.

For example: оди́н: пе́рвый

1. два ....

2. три ....

3. четы́ре ....

4. четы́рнадцать ....

5. пять ....

6. пятна́дцать ....

7. шесть ....

8. семь ....

9. во́семь ....

10. де́вять ....

Exercise E

True or false?

1. Ната́ша с Ники́той обсужда́ли письмо́ к господи́ну Ро́джерсу. T/F

2. У них не́ было черновика́ письма́. T/F

3. Майк прилета́ет к ним пе́рвого ма́рта. T/F

4. У Майка ви́за уже́ есть. T/F

5. В Москве́ Майк бу́дет жить у Ната́ши. T/F

6. Ната́ша сказа́ла, что Майк бу́дет жить в Москве́ не ме́нее двух неде́ль. T/F

7. Ната́ша называ́ет Ма́йка в письме́ "Господи́н Ро́джерс". T/F

8. Ната́ша уже́ встреча́лась с Ма́йком ра́ньше. T/F

9. Ната́ша бу́дет встреча́ть Ма́йка в аэропорту́. T/F

10. Она́ посыла́ет Ма́йку официа́льное приглаше́ние. T/F

11. Review: Lessons 7–10

This review section is a revision of what you have learnt so far. Take the time to listen to the audio dialogues again and see how much you can understand without turning back to the English versions in the previous chapters! Don't forget to do the short exercise section too!

DIALOGUE 7: НА РАБО́ТЕ

Воло́дя рабо́тает недалеко́ от гости́ницы "Нева́". Ната́ша идёт к нему́ на рабо́ту пешко́м. По пути́ она́ покупа́ет газе́ту. Она́ прихо́дит то́чно в полпя́того ...

Воло́дя	Здра́вствуйте, Ната́ша!
Ната́ша	Здра́вствуйте, Воло́дя! Как дела́?
Воло́дя	Норма́льно. А что но́вого у вас?
Ната́ша	У меня́ всё по-ста́рому. Как всегда́ мно́го рабо́ты.
Воло́дя	Хоти́те ча́ю? Йли ко́фе?
Ната́ша	Нет, спаси́бо. Я о́чень мно́го пила́ ко́фе сего́дня. Мо́жно минера́льную во́ду?
Воло́дя	Коне́чно! Вот минера́льная во́да, а вот ко́пии рекла́мных проспе́ктов из Аме́рики.
Ната́ша	Спаси́бо. Хмм ... Интере́сно. Я ду́маю, э́то как раз то, что нам ну́жно ... Здесь жа́рко. Мо́жно откры́ть окно́?
Воло́дя	Коне́чно. Я откро́ю.
Ната́ша	Когда́ вы смо́жете прие́хать к нам в Москву́? Мы с ва́ми должны́ обсуди́ть вопро́с о совме́стном предприя́тии с мои́м но́вым нача́льником Ники́той Серге́евичем Кали́ниным.
Воло́дя	Како́е сего́дня число́? Два́дцать пе́рвое?

Ната́ша	Два́дцать пе́рвое ноября́, вто́рник.
Воло́дя	Я смог прие́хать к вам че́рез неде́лю. Ска́жем, в сре́ду, два́дцать девя́того.
Ната́ша	Отли́чно! Я зна́ю, что Ники́та Сергéевич бдет свобóден в срéду.

DIALOGUE 8: НАТА́ША ДÉЛАЕТ ПОКУ́ ПКИ

Как мы уже́ зна́ем, у Ната́ши мно́го рабо́ты. Коне́чно, в Москве́ она́ покупа́ет продкты в магази́нах. Но у неё почти́ нет врéмени ходи́ть по магазнам, что́бы купть одéжду, óбувь и другe вéщи.

Сегóдня она́ всё ещё в Санкт-Петербрге. У неё есть немнóго свобóдного врéмени. Поэтому она́ реши́ла пойт по магазнам и купть себé тёплую ша́пку, перча́тки и сапог. У нас в Росси хóлодно зимóй! Нжно имéть тёплые вéщи, что́бы не замёрзнуть.

Сейча́с Ната́ша в магази́не "Гостный Двор". Она́ говорт с продавцóм . . .

Ната́ша	Пожа́луйста, покажи́те мне э́ти сапог.
Продаве́ц	Каке?
Ната́ша	Вот те чёрные, в угл.
Продаве́ц	Вот э́ти?
Ната́ша	Да, спаси́бо. Скóлько он стóят?
Продаве́ц	Восемь ты́сяч.
Ната́ша	Ой, дóрого! У вас есть подеше́вле?
Продаве́ц	Да. Вот э́ти стóят четы́ре тсячи.
Ната́ша	Хорошó. А мóжно посмотрéть э́ти перча́тки?
Продаве́ц	Чёрные?
Ната́ша	Нет, кра́сные, пожа́луйста.
Продаве́ц	Пожа́луйста.
Ната́ша	Спаси́бо. Дмаю, э́ти мне подойдт. И ещё покажи́те мне, пожа́луйста, ша́пку.
Продаве́ц	Меховю ли шерстяню?
Ната́ша	Кра́сную шерстяню. Скóлько она́ стóит?
Продаве́ц	Две тсячи.
Ната́ша	Я возьм её, хоть и дóрого. Она́ така́я красвая и тёплая! И, конéчно, сапог и перча́тки. Посчита́йте, пожа́луйста, всё вмéсте.
Продаве́ц	Ша́пка – двтсячи, перча́тки – одна́ тсяча и четре тсячи за сапог. Всегó семь тсяч.
Ната́ша	Платть вам?
Продаве́ц	Нет, в ка́ссу.
Ната́ша	А где ка́сса?

| Продавец | Вон там, нале́во. |
| Ната́ша | Спасбо. |

DIALOGUE 9: ОБРАА́ТНО В МОСКВУ́ ПО́ЕЗДОМ

Сего́дня птница. Весь день прошёл в дела́х и спе́шке. А сейча́с рабо́та зако́нчена. Всё сде́лано. Пора́ е́хать домо́й!
Ната́ша прилете́ла в Санкт-Петербрг самолётом. Но обра́тный биле́т на самолёт ей купть не удало́сь. Не́ было мест. Потому она́ купа биле́т на по́езд. Этот по́езд называ́ется "Кра́сная Стрела́". Он идёт из Санкт-Петербрга в Москв ка́ждую ночь. В шесть часо́в ве́чера она́ хорошо́ пообе́дала с Воло́дей. Пото́м он немно́го гулли по на́бережной Нев. Зате́м Воло́дя проводл Ната́шу в гостницу. В гостнице он попроща́лись.
Сейча́с де́вять часо́в ве́чера. Ната́ша уже́ в по́езде, в двухме́стном купе́. Она́ разгова́ривает со свом поптчиком.

Ната́ша	До́брый ве́чер!
горь	До́брый ве́чер! Нам е́хать вме́сте. Дава́йте знако́миться. Я – горь Григо́рьевич Милосла́вский.
Ната́ша	А я Ната́лья Петро́вна Ивано́ва ... Вы мо́жете чуть-чуть открть окно́?
горь	Да, коне́чно. Здесь ужа́сно жа́рко ... Вы живёте в Санкт-Петербрге?
Ната́ша	Нет, я была́ здесь в командиро́вке то́лько три дня. Я жив в Москве́. А вы?
горь	Я жив о́чень далеко́ отсю́да, в Ирктске. Я худо́жник и прие́хал посмотре́ть Эрмита́ж.
Ната́ша	Я была́ там то́лько одн раз. Это великоле́пно! Я бы с удово́льствием провела́ там це́лую неде́лю. Но нет вре́мени!
горь	Жаль! А я был там почт ка́ждый день в тече́ние це́лого ме́сяца. И всё равно́ бло ма́ло – хоте́лось ещё бо́льше. Там так мно́го экспона́тов! И все – шеде́вры!
Ната́ша	Да, пра́вда ... А как вы пое́дете домо́й?
горь	Ох, то сло́жный вопро́с! Из Москв вылета́ю самолётом в Ирктск. Пото́м из аэропо́рта пое́ду на авто́бусе в центр го́рода. Зате́м возьм такс ли ча́стную машну до нача́ла мое́й о́чень длнной лицы. Там доро́га така́я плоха́я, что машне не прое́хать. Да́же ле́том. А сейча́с, когда́ снег ...
Ната́ша	А что же вы бдете де́лать?
горь	К сча́стью, Бог дал мне две ног. Это са́мый надёжный тра́нспорт. Я пойд пешко́м!

DIALOGUE 10: ПИСЬМО́ В АМЕ́РИКУ

Сейча́с Ната́ша нахо́дится в кабине́те своего́ нача́льника. Он обсужда́ют письмо́ к Ма́йку Ро́джерсу.

Ната́ша	Вот черновк письма́ к господну Ро́джерсу.
Дмитрий	Посмо́трим. Хмм . . . Зна́чит, он прилета́ет к нам пе́рвого ма́рта?
Ната́ша	Да, так мы договорлись по телефо́ну.
Дмитрий	А вза у него́ уже́ есть?
Ната́ша	Пока́ нет, но я пошлю́ приглаше́ние с тим письмо́м.
Дмитрий	Где он бдет жить?
Ната́ша	Он остано́вится в гостнице "Звезда́". Для него́ уже́ забронрован но́мер.
Дмитрий	Ско́лько он здесь пробдет?
Ната́ша	Это бдет завсеть от того́, как пойдт перегово́ры. Но, по-мо́ему, не ме́нее двух неде́ль.
Дмитрий	Ну, хорошо́. Спасбо. А! Один вопро́с! Вы называ́ете его́ в письме́ "Майк". Вы с ним уже́ встреча́лись ра́ньше?
Ната́ша	Да нет. Мы не́сколько раз говорли по телефо́ну. Но америка́нцы таке коммуника́бельные и просте! Он сра́зу же на́чал называ́ть мен "Ната́ша". А когда́ я обраща́юсь к нем "Мстер Ро́джерс", он всегда́ смеётся: "Я ещё не совсе́м ста́рый! Зовте мен 'Майк'!"
Дмитрий	Ну, ла́дно. Спасбо, Ната́лья Петро́вна.

Exercises

Exercise A

Listen again to the dialogue from Lesson 7 and repeat.

Exercise B

Translate the dialogue in Lesson 7 into English. Then check your translation against ours on pages

88–90.

Exercise C

Listen again to the dialogue from Lesson 8 and repeat.

Exercise D

Translate the dialogue from Lesson 8 and check your translation against that on pages 103–106.

Exercise E

Listen again to the dialogue from Lesson 9 and repeat.

Exercise F

Translate the dialogue in Lesson 9 into English and check your translation against ours on pages 119–122.

Exercise G

Listen again to the dialogue from Lesson 10 and repeat.

Exercise H

Read Natasha's letter out loud.
ВОТ ПИСЬМÓ НАТÁШИ МÁЙКУ:

Московский Центральный Банк
Россия
115726 Москва
ул Ленина, 54

Дорогóй Майк,
Я и мо коллéги надéемся, что Ваш визт состотся, как мы и договорлись, 1-го мáрта.
Я бду встречáть Вас в аэропорт Шеремéтьево-2. В рукáх у мен бдет таблчка с Вáшим
менем. Нóмер в гостнице бдет закáзан для Вас зарáнее.
Посылáю Вам официáльное приглашéние. Онó необходмо для получéния взы. Вы
должн обратться за взой в Россйское кóнсульство. Там Вам вдадут две анкéты,
котóрые нáдо бдет запóлнить (дáта и мéсто рождéния, домáшний áдрес, мéсто
рабóты и т.п.).

Оформле́ние взы не должно́ занть мно́го вре́мени.

Ждём встре́чи с Ва́ми.

С скренним уваже́нием,

Ната́ша.

Exercise I

Translate the letter and check your version against ours on pages 136–137.

Exercise J

Write out the correct form of the words given in parentheses:

1. Воло́дя (рабо́тать) .... о́чень далеко́ от (гостница)

   .... "Нева́".

2. Пол пшет (кнга) ....

3. Ра́ньше Борс (пить) .... ча́й по (тро) .... , а тепе́рь

   он (пить) .... ко́фе.

4. Хотте (ча́й) .... , (ко́фе), (во́дка) .... ли

   (минера́льная вода́) .... ?

5. У мен нет (вре́мя) .... стоть в (о́чередь) ....

6. Я о́чень рад познако́миться с (вы) ....

7. Он (быть) .... ждать (вы) .... в (гостница)

   ....

8. Я возьм (та газе́та) .... с (себ) ....

9. Я бы с (удово́льствие) .... провела́ (це́лая неде́ля)

   .... в (Эрмита́ж) ....

12. A Visit to Moscow

Lesson 12 takes you on a visit to Moscow. You will learn and expand your knoweledge of adverbs related to time, movement and place. You will also further build your vocabulary and you should be feeling more at ease with the language.

МАЙК Е́ДЕТ В РОССИ́Ю MIKE GOES TO RUSSIA

Майк прилете́л из Нью-Йо́рка в Москву́ ночны́м ре́йсом. Самолёт приземли́лся в три часа́ дня по моско́вскому вре́мени.
Mike flew from New York to Moscow on a night flight. The plane landed at three o'clock in the afternoon, Moscow time.

Майк прошёл че́рез порани́чный контро́ль и тамо́женный осмо́тр. В за́ле прибы́тия бы́ло о́чень мно́го наро́ду. Пассажи́ры с трудо́м протскивались сквозь толпу́. Майк сра́зу увдел табли́чку со свом менем ...
Mike went through the immigration checkpoint and the customs inspection. In the arrivals hall there were a lot of people. Passengers squeezed through the crowd with difficulty. Mike saw the sign with his name right away ...

Майк	Ната́ша?
	Natasha?
Ната́ша	Да. А вы, наве́рное, Майк? Добро́ пожа́ловать в Москву́!
	Yes. And you must be Mike? Welcome to Moscow!
Майк	Я о́чень рад встре́титься с ва́ми.
	I'm very glad to meet you.
Ната́ша	Мы так мно́го говорли по телефо́ну! И, наконе́ц, мы

встре́тились лчно. А э́то для вас!
We've talked so much on the phone! At last we've met in person. And this is for you!

Она́ даёт ему́ буке́т цвето́в.
She gives him a bouquet of flowers.

| Майк | Цветы́? Как прия́тно! Большо́е спаси́бо.
Flowers? How nice! Thank you very much. |
| Ната́ша | Здесь так мно́го люде́й и так шмно. Мы лчше поговорм в машне.
There are so many people here and it's so noisy. We'll speak more easily in the car. |

Он выхо́дят из аэропо́рта и садя́тся в машну.
They come out of the airport and get in a car.

| Ната́ша | Как вы долете́ли?
How was your flight? |
| Майк | Прекра́сно! Я о́чень хорошо́ пообе́дал, впил два стака́на джна с то́ником, и всё остально́е вре́мя спал.
Great! I had a very good meal, drank two glasses of gin and tonic, and all the rest of the time I slept. |
| Ната́ша | Зна́чит, вы не о́чень уста́ли?
So, you're not very tired? |
| Майк | Совсе́м не уста́л. Но я бы хоте́л приня́ть душ. Я немно́го вспоте́л. В аэропо́рт бло о́чень жа́рко.
I'm not tired at all. But I would like to take a shower. I'm a little sticky (*lit.* I perspired a bit). It was very hot in the airport. |
| Ната́ша | Я предлага́ю пое́хать пря́мо в гости́ницу, что́бы вы смогл освежться, распакова́ть чемода́ны и устро́иться. А о́коло 7 часо́в ве́чера мы зае́дем за ва́ми и пое́дем обе́дать.
I suggest we go straight to the hotel, so that you can freshen up, unpack (your) suitcases and settle in. And around 7 o'clock this evening we'll come for you (in the car) and we'll go out for dinner. |
| Майк | Мы?
We? |
| Ната́ша | Я прие́ду с мом нача́льником. Он о́чень хо́чет встре́титься с ва́ми.
I'll come with my boss. He very much wants to meet you. |
| Майк | Э́то но́вый нача́льник?
Is that the new boss? |
| Ната́ша | Да. Он рабо́тал в отделе́нии на́шего ба́нка в Варша́ве. Он прие́хал к нам приме́рно шесть ме́сяцев наза́д. |

Yes. He used to work at the bank's Warsaw branch. He came to us about six months ago.

Маш́на бстро мч́алась по Тверсќой – бвшей лице Ѓорького. Вдруг Майк спросл:
The car was racing fast along Tverskaya (street) – formerly Gorky Street. Suddenly Mike asked:

Майк	Что́ э́то? What's that?
Нат́аша	Э́то мосќовский Кремль. Мы недалеќо от Кр́асной пл́ощади. А вот и в́аша гост́ница. It's the Moscow Kremlin. We're not far from Red Square. And here's your hotel.

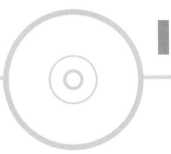

Grammar

1. RUSSIAN ADVERBS

TIME-RELATED ADVERBS

You already know some Russian adverbs:

дн́ём	by day, in the daytime	весн́ой	in spring, from весн́а
́утром	in the morning	л́етом	in summer, from л́ето
в́ечером	in the evening	́осенью	in autumn, from ́осень
н́очью	at night	зим́ой	in winter, from зим́а

TIME-RELATED ADVERBS CONTINUED

Take the time to learn these time-related adverbs below, you will use these regulary.

сего́дня	today		пото́м	then
когда́	when;		сейча́с	now, just now
когда́-нибудь	some time (or other)		ско́ро	quickly
			сра́зу	all at once, right away
никогда́	never		тепе́рь	now
иногда́	sometimes		тогда́	then
давно́	long ago		снача́ла	at first
до́лго	long, a long time		сно́ва	once more
ра́но	early		уже́	already
по́здно	late		вчера́	yesterday
обы́чно	usually		за́втра	tomorrow
опя́ть	again			

PLACE-RELATED ADVERBS

You will notice that Russian uses **preserved directional adverbs** that have almost died out in English (whither, whence, etc.). **Where?** can be expressed by где (static location) and куда́ (direction toward something).

где	where	там	there, over there
нигде́	nowhere	тут	here
где́-нибудь	somewhere or other, somewhere	нале́во	on the left
		напра́во	on the right
бли́зко	close, near	до́ма	at home
далеко́	far, far away		
		внизу́	downstairs
здесь	here	наверху́	upstairs

MOVEMENT-RELATED ADVERBS

домо́й	home, to home	отту́да	from there
куда́	where to	сюда́	here, to here
никуда́	to nowhere	отсю́да	from here
куда́-нибудь	to somewhere or other	вперёд	in front, forward
		наза́д	behind, backwards
отку́да	where from	вниз	down, downwards
туда́	to there	вверх	up, upwards

2. ADVERBS AND THE SHORT FORM OF ADJECTIVES

In Lesson 7 there was an example of the short form of the adjective **free**:

Я зна́ю, что Ники́та Серге́евич бу́дет свобо́ден в сре́ду.
I know that Nikita Sergeyevich will be free on Wednesday.

свобо́ден *m.*/свобо́дна *f.*/свобо́дно *n.* are the short forms of свобо́дный *m.*/свобо́дная *f.*/ свобо́дное *n.*

We shall be looking at the short form of adjectives in Lesson 14. Many Russian adverbs are the same as the neuter form of short adjectives, for example:

пло́хо badly, from плохо́й
ско́ро quickly, from ско́рый

The short form of adjectives is frequently used in impersonal sentences as the predicate (the part of a sentence that says something about the subject):

В Росси́и хо́лодно.	It is cold in Russia.
В Аме́рике хорошо́.	It's good in America.

3. NEGATIVE ADVERBS

The negative adverbs не́когда, не́куда, не́где have a very different meaning from никогда́, никуда́, нигде́, and convey the idea of the absolute impossibility of something. Sentences using these adverbs are constructed differently: не́когда, не́куда, не́где are used with a dative and infinitive, while никода́, никуда́, нигде́ are used with не and a verb. Compare the following examples:

Мне не́когда гуля́ть.	I have no time for walking and looking around.
Я никогда́ не гуля́ю.	I never walk and look around.
Ему́ не́куда идти́.	He has nowhere to go.
Он никуда́ не идёт.	He is not going anywhere.
Им не́где жить.	They have nowhere to live.
Они́ нигде́ не живу́т.	They don't live anywhere.

Here are a few useful sentences that contain adverbs.

У меня́ всё хорошо́.	I'm fine.
Иди́те сюда́.	Come here.
Я лечу́ туда́ самолётом.	I will go there by plane.

Вы до́лго бу́дете в Санкт-Петербу́рге?	Will you stay long in St. Petersburg?
У меня́ то́лько оди́н чемода́н.	I only have one suitcase.
Я роди́лся в Аме́рике, но сейча́с живу́ в Росси́и.	I was born in America, but I now live in Russia.
У меня́, как всегда́, мно́го рабо́ты.	I have a lot of work, as always.

Vocabulary

ночно́й *m.*/**ночна́я** *f.*/**ночно́е** *n. night*

рейс *flight*

благополу́чно *safely*

приземли́ться *(perf) to land*

по моско́вскому вре́мени *(by/according to) Moscow time*

грани́ца frontier/border *(noun)*

пограни́чный *frontier/border (adjective)*

контро́ль *m. control/checkpoint/monitoring*

тамо́женный досмо́тр *customs* **inspection** *(тамо́жня customs)*

зал *hall*

прибы́тие *arrival*

наро́д *people, the people*

мно́го наро́ду *a lot of people*

прибыва́ть *(impf) to arrive*

прибы́вший *m.*/**прибы́вшая** *f.*/**прибы́вшее** *n. arrived (in English, often "arriving")*

пассажи́р *passenger*

труд *work, exertion*

с трудо́м *with difficulty*

проти́скиваться *(impf) to push one's way through/squeeze through*

сквозь *through*

толпа́ *crowd*

сра́зу *immediately*

табли́чка a board, sign or card *(like the ones held up in airports with the name of a passenger)*

наве́рное *surely, certainly*

добро́ пожа́ловать *welcome*

ли́чно *personally, in person*

буке́т *bouquet*

цвето́к *flower*

лю́ди *people*

шум *noise*

Шу́мно. *It is noisy.*

лу́чше *better*

зда́ние *building*

аэровокза́л *air terminal*

сади́ться *(impf) to sit down*

сади́ться в маши́ну *to get in a car*

ожида́ть *(impf) to wait*

долете́ть *(perf) to fly to, to fly here*

стака́н *a glass*

джин *gin*

то́ник *tonic*

остально́й *m.*/**остальна́я** *f.*/**остально́е** *n. remaining*

спать *(impf) to sleep*

устава́ть *(impf) to be tired*

уста́ть *(perf) to get tired*

совсе́м не *not at all*

душ *shower*
приня́ть душ *(perf) to take a shower*
немно́го *not much, a little*
вспоте́ть *(perf) to perspire, to get sweaty*
жа́рко *hot*
предлага́ть *(impf) to suggest*
пря́мо *straight, directly*
освежи́ться *(perf) to freshen (oneself) up*
распакова́ть *(perf) to unpack*
устра́иваться *(impf) to arrange, settle in, get organized*
устро́иться *(perf) to arrange, settle in, get organized*
заезжа́ть *(impf) to call on, come round, pick up*
зае́хать за *(perf) to call on; to stop by for, to collect*
приезжа́ть *(impf) to arrive*
прие́хать *(perf) to arrive*

неда́вно *not long ago, recently*
переводи́ть *(impf) to translate, to transfer*
перевести́ *(perf) to translate, to transfer*
отделе́ние *section, division, branch*
приме́рно *approximately, about*
бы́стро *quickly (the name of a bistro or small restaurant comes from this word)*
мча́ться *(impf) to hurry along, to zip*
Тверска́я *a famous street in Moscow (from Tver, a city on the road to St. Petersburg)*
по Тверско́й *along Tverskaya (street)*
бы́вший *m./*бы́вшая *f./*бы́вшее *n. former*
вдруг *suddenly*
спра́шивать *(impf) to ask*
спроси́ть *(perf) to ask*
кремль *m. castle, fort, kremlin (many towns have one)*
Кра́сная пло́щадь *Red Square*

Exercises

Exercise A

Translate the following words into English. Note that English words beginning with "**h**" often begin with the letter "г" in Russian.

1. венде́тта ....
2. вентиля́ция ....
3. газ ....
4. га́мбургер ....
5. га́нгстер ....
6. гандика́п ....
7. гара́ж ....
8. мегалома́ния ....
9. раси́зм ....

Exercise B

Translate the following sentences into English.

1. **В России хо́лодно зимо́й, а жа́рко ле́том.**

   ....

2. **Я рабо́таю днём, а сплю но́чью.**

   ....

3. **Вчера́ они́ бы́ли в Нью-Йо́рке, а за́втра бу́дут в Москве́.**

   ....

4. **Я никогда́ не́ был в Аме́рике, но хочу́ пое́хать туда́ когда́-нибу́дь.**

   ....

5. **Здесь хорошо́, а там лу́чше.**

   ....

6. **Банк напра́во, а гости́ница нале́во.**

   ....

7. **Сейча́с я иду́ домо́й. До́ма я бу́ду смотре́ть телеви́зор.**

   ....

8. **Куда́ вы?**

   ....

9. **Отку́да вы?**

   ....

Exercise C

Put the words in parentheses into the correct form.

1. (День) .... я рабо́таю, а (ночь) .... я сплю.

2. В (зал) .... бы́ло мно́го (наро́д) ....

3. Она́ не ви́дела (табли́чка) .... со (своё и́мя)

   ....

4. Он был о́чень рад встре́титься с (она́) ....

5. Она́ была́ о́чень ра́да встре́титься с (он) ....

6. Я бы (хоте́ть) .... приня́ть душ.

7. Он вы́пил два (стака́н джин) .... с (то́ник)

   ....

8. Они́ бы́стро е́хали по (Тверска́я у́лица) ....

9. Я живу́ недалеко́ от (Кра́сная пло́щадь) ....

Exercise D

Translate the following sentences into Russian.

1. **Excuse me, but what is that?**

   ....

2. **There are a lot of people here.**

   ....

3. **I'm not at all tired.**

   ....

4. **Are you very tired, Natasha?**

   ....

5. Is that our new (female) student?

....

6. I very much want to meet you.

....

7. She works in our branch in Washington.

....

8. She came to us about five months ago.

....

9. He flew into New York from Moscow on a night flight.

....

Exercise E

True or false?

1. Майк приéхал в Москвý ночны́м пóездом.   T/F

2. В зáле прибы́тия нé было мнóго нарóду.   T/F

3. Натáша встрéтила Мáйка в зáле.   T/F

4. Майк был не рад встрéтиться с Натáшей.   T/F

5. Натáша далá Мáйку букéт цветóв.   T/F

6. В зáле прибы́тия бы́ло шýмно.   T/F

7. Майк не óчень хорошó пообéдал в самолёте.   T/F

8. Пóсле обéда Майк хорошó спал.   T/F

9. Майк óчень устáл. Емý хóчется спать.   T/F

13. Reservations

Lesson 13 covers hotel reservations. Again, listen to the audio to immerse yourself in the language so that you become accustomed to forming sentences – this will also help you to absorb the grammar easily. Finally, you will learn some new verbs and vocabulary.

В ГОСТИ́НИЦЕ IN THE HOTEL

Гости́ница "Звезда́" нахо́дится недалеко́ от Кра́сной пло́щади. Это но́вая ча́стная гости́ница. Она́ небольша́я: в ней всего́ со́рок номеро́в. Майк с Ната́шей подхо́дят к столу́ регистра́ции …

The Zvezda [Star] Hotel is situated not far from Red Square. I's a new, private hotel. It's small: it has forty rooms in all. Mike and Natasha go up to the registration desk …

Администра́тор	Здра́вствуйте. Вы зака́зывали но́мер?
	Good afternoon. Do you have a reservation? (lit. Have you booked a room?)
Майк	Да, заказа́л. Вот ко́пия электро́нного письма́, в кото́ром вы подтвержда́ете, что зака́з при́нят.
	Yes, I have a reservation. Here's a copy of the e-mail in which you confirm that the booking is accepted.
Администра́тор	Хорошо́. Ваш па́спорт, пожа́луйста.
	Okay. Your passport, please.
Майк	Во́т он.
	Here it is.
Администра́тор	Спаси́бо. Вы смо́жете получи́ть его́ за́втра у́тром.
	Thank you. You can have it back tomorrow morning.

Майк	Скажи́те, пожа́луйста, в но́мере есть телеви́зор?
	Tell me, please, is there a television in the room?
Администра́тор	Коне́чно. Мно́го кана́лов на ру́сском языке́. И есть не́сколько на англи́йском, наприме́р, Си-Эн-Эн. Они́ передаю́т це́лый день по-англи́йски.
	Of course. There are a lot of channels in Russian. And there are some in English, CNN, for example. They broadcast in English the whole day.
Майк	Зна́ете ли вы, когда́ передаю́т но́вости?
	Do you know when they broadcast the news?
Администра́тор	Извини́те меня́, то́чно не по́мню. Но вся информа́ция есть в но́мере на ру́сском и на англи́йском языка́х.
	Sorry, I don't remember exactly. But all the information is in the room in both Russian and English.
Майк	Спаси́бо. А как здесь мо́жно постира́ть ве́щи? И есть ли тут химчи́стка?
	Thank you. And how can I get laundry done here? And is there dry cleaning here?
Администра́тор	Е́сли вы отдади́те нам те ве́щи, кото́рые ну́жно постира́ть и почи́стить, до 12 часо́в дня, они́ бу́дут гото́вы к 8 часа́м утра́ на сле́дующий день.
	If you give us those things that need washing and cleaning before 12 noon, they will be ready by 8 a.m. the following day.
Майк	Прекра́сно! Что ещё? Да! Чуть не забы́л! Есть ли у вас каки́е-нибу́дь англи́йские и́ли америка́нские газе́ты?
	Great! What else? Yes! I nearly forgot! Do you have any English or American newspapers?
Администра́тор	Да, мы получа́ем англи́йскую "Та́ймс" и "Интернэшнл Гера́льд Трибью́н".
	Yes, we get the English *Times* and the *International Herald Tribune*.
Майк	Как рабо́тает ваш рестора́н? Когда́ он откры́т?
	How does your restaurant operate? When is it open?
Администра́тор	У нас нет рестора́на. Но здесь за угло́м, совсе́м бли́зко, есть рестора́н.
	We don't have a restaurant. But there is one just around the corner, very close by.
Майк	А где мо́жно поза́втракать?
	And where can I have breakfast?
Администра́тор	У нас есть буфе́т с лёгкими заку́сками и пи́ццей на второ́м этаже́. Меню́ есть в ва́шем но́мере. Вы мо́жете позвони́ть го́рничной и заказа́ть за́втрак пря́мо в но́мер, е́сли хоти́те.
	We have a buffet with light snacks and pizzas on the second floor. The menu is in your room. You can call room service and order breakfast (to be delivered) straight to (your) room, if you wish.
Майк	Спаси́бо. Вы о́чень помогли́ мне.
	Thank you. You've been a great help.

Grammar

1. QUESTIONS WITH ЛИ

You already know that a statement can be changed into a question by changing the intonation (Lesson 2). Questions can also be formed by using the particle **ли**.

In the dialogue, Mike asks: **И есть ли тут химчи́стка?**   And is there dry cleaning here?

In questions with ли, the subject and the verb are frequently inverted and ли put between them:

Тут есть химчи́стка. (statement)	There is dry cleaning here.
Тут есть химчи́стка? (interrogatory intonation)	There is dry cleaning here?
Есть ли тут химчи́стка? (question with ли)	Is there dry cleaning here?

Similarly:

У вас есть америка́нские газе́ты.	You have American newspapers.
У вас е́сть америка́нские газе́ты?	You have American newspapers?
Есть ли у вас америка́нские газе́ты?	Do you have American newspapers?

If a particular point needs to be emphasized, this can be achieved through intonation or, using **ли**, by putting the thing to be emphasized at the beginning of the sentence. Compare the meanings conveyed in the following:

Майк дал па́спорт администра́тору.
Mike gave (his) passport to the receptionist.

Майк дал па́спорт администра́тору?
Did Mike give (his) passport to the receptionist?

Свой ли па́спорт Майк дал администра́тору?
Was it his passport that Mike gave to the receptionist? (as opposed to that of somebody else)

Майк дал па́спорт администра́тору вчера́.
Mike gave (his) passport to the receptionist yesterday.

Майк дал па́спорт администра́тору вчера́?
Did Mike give (his) passport to the receptionist yesterday?

Вчера́ ли Майк дал па́спорт администра́тору?
Was it yesterday that Mike gave his passport to the receptionist? (as opposed to some other time)

2. THE PERFECTIVE AND IMPERFECTIVE: ЗАКАЗА́ТЬ, ЗАКА́ЗЫВАТЬ/ TO BOOK, TO ORDER

At the beginning of this lesson, the администра́тор asked: Вы зака́зывали но́мер? **Did you book a room?/Have you booked a room?** This is a useful example of the use of the imperfective verb.

The imperfective is used here because it is not clear to the администра́тор whether the process of booking was successful (complete), or not as yet successful (incomplete).

So, when Mike replies: Да, заказа́л (using the perfective), he confirms that the process has been completed.

If, however, the confirmation had not been received and the reservation was still in question, Mike would have replied: Да, я зака́зывал номер, or simply Зака́зывал, because he knew that the process of booking a room had been started, but was unaware of the outcome.

3. NOUNS WITH NUMERALS AND THE DECLENSION OF CARDINAL NUMBERS 1–4

In Russian, all cardinal numbers decline.

ОДИ́Н *m.*/ОДНА́ *f.*/ОДНО́ *n.*

There are three forms of the number **one** in Russian:

Оди́н is the masculine form: оди́н вопро́с, оди́н стол, оди́н студе́нт.
Одна́ is the feminine form: одна́ кни́га, одна́ газе́та, одна́ студе́нтка.
Одно́ is the neuter form: одно́ окно́, одно́ сло́во, одно́ по́ле.

Оди́н *m.*/одна́ *f.*/одно́ *n.* agree with the noun that they qualify both in gender and in case. They are declined as follows:

	masculine	feminine	neuter
Nom.	оди́н вопро́с	одна́ кни́га	одно́ сло́во
Acc.	оди́н вопро́с	одну́ кни́гу	одно́ сло́во
Gen.	одного́ вопро́са	одно́й кни́ги	одного́ сло́ва
Dat.	одно́му вопро́су	одно́й кни́ге	одному́ сло́ву
Instr.	одни́м вопро́сом	одно́й кни́гой	одни́м сло́вом
Prep.	одно́м вопро́се	одно́й кни́ге	одно́м сло́ве

There is a plural form of **оди́н**, which is used with nouns that only occur in a plural form, such as **часы́** (**clock/watch**) or **очки́** (**eyeglasses**).

Another plural form of **оди́н** is worth looking at. Sometimes **оди́н** can mean **alone** in both singular and plural:

Она́ была́ одна́.	She was alone.
Он оди́н.	He is alone.
Мы бы́ли одни́.	We were alone.
Они́ прие́хали домо́й одни́.	They came home alone.

два *m.*/две́ *f.*/два́ *n.*

Nouns following **два** (masculine and neuter) or **две** (feminine) are in the genitive singular:
два вопро́са, два стола́, два студе́нта
две кни́ги, две газе́ты, две студе́нтки
два сло́ва, два окна́, два по́ля

три, четы́ре

The numbers three and four are the same for all genders. Like two, they are also followed by nouns in the genitive singular:
три вопро́са, три стола́, четы́ре студе́нта
три кни́ги, четы́ре газе́ты, три студе́нтки
четы́ре сло́ва, три окна́, четы́ре по́ля

The numerals 2, 3 and 4 are declined as follows:

Nom.	два	две	три	четы́ре
*Acc.**	двух	двух	трёх	четырёх
Acc.	два	две	три	четы́ре
Gen.	двух	двух	трёх	четырёх
Dat.	двум	двум	трём	четырём
Instr.	двумя́	двумя́	тремя́	четырьмя́
Prep.	двух	двух	трёх	четырёх

* when denoting human beings

Vocabulary

администра́тор *receptionist; administrator*

пло́щадь *f.* **square**

ча́стный *m.*/**ча́стная** *f.*/**ча́стное** *n. private, personal*

небольшо́й *m.*/**небольша́я** *f.*/
небольшо́е *n. small, little*

всего́ *in all, total*

подходи́ть *(impf) to approach, to go up to*

регистра́ция *registration*

стол регистра́ции *reception desk*

зака́зывать *(impf) to order*

заказа́ть *(perf) to order*

ко́пия *a copy*

электро́нное письмо́ *e-mail*

подтвержда́ть *(impf) to confirm*

подтверди́ть *(perf) to confirm*

зака́з *an order*

принима́ть *(impf) to accept*

приня́ть *(perf) to accept*

получа́ть *(impf) to receive*

получи́ть *(perf) to receive*

телеви́зор *television set*

кана́л *channel*

переда́ча *transmission, broadcast*

смотре́ть переда́чу *to watch a program*

передава́ть *(impf) to broadcast, transmit*

но́вости *the news*

то́чно *exactly*

по́мнить *(impf) to remember*

информа́ция *information*

стира́ть *(impf) to wash (clothes)*

постира́ть *(perf) to wash (clothes)*

химчи́стка *dry cleaning*

пробы́ть *(perf) to stay, to remain*

отда́ть *(perf) to hand in, to give back, to return*

чи́стить *(impf) to clean*

почи́стить *(perf) to clean*

до 12 часо́в дня *before 12 noon*

гото́вый *m.*/**гото́вая** *f.*/**гото́вое** *n. ready*

гото́в *m.*/**гото́ва** *f.*/**гото́во** *n. ready (short form of the adjective)*

сле́дующий *m.*/**сле́дующая** *f.*/
сле́дующее *n. next*

Что ещё? *What else?*

забыва́ть *(impf) to forget*

забы́ть *(perf) to forget*

Чуть не забы́л! *I almost forgot!*

како́й-нибудь *m.*/**кака́я-нибудь** *f.*/
како́е-нибудь *n. some or other, any*

приходи́ть *(impf) to come*

за угло́м *around the corner*

бли́зко *close (adjective)*

за́втракать *(impf) to have breakfast*

поза́втракать *(perf) to have breakfast*

обе́д *lunch/dinner, meal*

за́втрак *breakfast*

буфе́т *buffet*

заку́ска *snack*

лёгкие заку́ски *light snacks*

пи́цца *pizza*

меню́ *menu*

звони́ть *(impf) to phone, to call*

позвони́ть *(perf) to phone, to call*

го́рничная maid, cleaner *(room service)*

Мо́жно? *Is it possible?/can one?*

Exercises

Exercise A

Translate the following sentences into English:

1. **Мой дом нахо́дится недалеко́ от гости́ницы "Звезда́".**

   ....

2. **Скажи́те, пожа́луйста, где регистра́ция?**

   ....

3. **Я заказа́л но́мер по электронной почте.**

   ....

4. **Вы подтверди́ли, что зака́з при́нят.**

   ....

5. **Вот мой па́спорт. Когда́ я смогу́ получи́ть его?**

   ....

6. **В но́мере е́сть ра́дио, телеви́зор и телефо́н?**

   ....

7. **Когда́ передаю́т но́вости по-англи́йски?**

   ....

8. **Я хочу́ купи́ть и англи́йские, и америка́нские газе́ты.**

   ....

9. **Я хочу́ за́втракать в но́мере.**

   ....

Exercise B

Put the words in parentheses into the correct form.

1. Вот ко́пия (письмо́) .... , в кото́ром вы подтвержда́ете, что зака́з

   при́нят.

2. В (но́мер) .... есть телеви́зор?

3. Есть кана́л, по (кото́рый) .... мо́жно смотре́ть переда́чи по-

   англи́йски.

4. Вся информа́ция есть в (но́мер) .... на (ру́сский)

   .... и на (англи́йский) .... языка́х.

5. Сейча́с они́ (получа́ть) .... америка́нские (газе́та)

   .... ка́ждый день. ,

6. У них нет (рестора́н) .... , но у них есть хоро́ший буфе́т.

7. Меню́ есть в (ваш) .... но́мере.

8. (Знать) .... ли вы когда́ (передава́ть) .... но́вости?

Exercise C

Translate the following into Russian:

1. The Hotel Zvezda is not far from my home.

   ....

2. I have a big new car.

   ....

3. Is there a television in the (hotel) room?

   ....

4. Is the booking (reservation) accepted?

....

5. Is it possible to watch programs in English? [use ли]

....

6. We will be here three to four days.

....

7. I am there two days every month.

....

8. Is there dry cleaning in the hotel?

....

Exercise D

Look at the price list below. How much will you have to pay the hotel? You will stay for seven nights, have six dinners and seven breakfasts. The word обéд is difficult to translate. It is the midday meal, but also usually the most significant meal of the day, so neither "**lunch**" nor "**dinner**" quite captures its meaning.

ГОСТИ́НИЦА ПЛАНÉТА (planet)

нóмер (однá ночь) .... четы́ре ты́сячи рублéй

обéд .... пятьсóт рублéй

зáвтрак (+ чáй или кóфе) .... двéсти рублéй

....

Exercise E

True or false?

1. Гости́ница "Звезда́" нахо́дится далеко́ от Кра́сной пло́щади.   T/F

2. "Звезда́" – но́вая ча́стная гости́ница.   T/F

3. Майк дал па́спорт администра́тору.   T/F

4. У Ма́йка в но́мере нет телеви́зора.   T/F

5. Администра́тор не зна́ет, когда́ передаю́т но́вости по-англи́йски.   T/F

6. В гости́нице мо́жно получа́ть америка́нские и англи́йские газе́ты.   T/F

7. В Москве́ мо́жно смотре́ть переда́чи Си-Эн-Эн.   T/F

8. В гости́нице то́лько оди́н кана́л рабо́тает на англи́йском языке́.   T/F

9. Недалеко́ от гости́ницы есть рестора́н.   T/F

10. Мо́жно купи́ть лёгкие заку́ски и пи́ццу в буфе́те гости́ницы.   T/F

14. Making Plans

Lesson 14 will further develop your command of natural speech as this chapter revolves around making plans. You will also learn how to use the short form of adjectives. Don't forget that you can be listening to your vocabulary audio downloads even when you're not using the book.

ЭКСКУ́РСИЯ ПО МОСКВЕ́ A TRIP AROUND MOSCOW

В Росси́и хо́лодно зимо́й. Но в после́дние пять-семь лет зи́мы бы́ли не о́чень холо́дные. Скоре́е да́же о́чень нехоло́дные, с температу́рой ча́сто вы́ше нуля́.
In Russia it is cold in winter. But in the last five to seven years, the winters were not very cold. Actually not even very cold at all, with the temperature often above 0°C (32°F).

Но никто́ не рад э́тому теплу́; ча́сто быва́ет си́льный ве́тер, идёт снег с дождём … А когда́ температу́ра, ска́жем, ми́нус 20 гра́дусов, и не́бо безо́блачное и голубо́е, и со́лнце сия́ет, и снег искри́тся – здесь чуде́сно!
But nobody is happy with this warmth; there is often a strong wind, and sleet … But when the temperature is, say, -20°C (-4°F), and the sky is cloudless and blue, and the sun is shining, and the snow sparkles – it is wonderful here!

А в нача́ле ма́рта пого́да о́чень неусто́йчива. Но́чью – ми́нус 18, а днём – плюс 4! На у́лице сля́коть под нога́ми.
But at the beginning of March, the weather is very variable. At night it is -18°C (-0.4°F), but during the day it is +4°C (39.2°F)! On the streets there is slush underfoot.

Майк прие́хал в Москву́ в са́мом нача́ле весны́. Сия́ет со́лнце; по голубо́му не́бу плыву́т ма́ленькие бе́лые облака́. День так чуде́сен, что про́сто невозмо́жно сиде́ть в ко́мнате, и они́ с Ната́шей реши́ли отпра́виться на экску́рсию по Москве́.

Mike came to Moscow at the very beginning of spring. The sun is shining; small, white clouds are floating in a blue sky. The day is so lovely that it is simply not possible to sit indoors, and Mike and Natasha decide to set off on a trip around Moscow.

Ната́ша	Э́то Кра́сная пло́щадь.
	That's Red Square.
Майк	А э́то что за зда́ние? Це́рковь?
	And what is that building? A church?
Ната́ша	Да, э́то собо́р Васи́лия Блаже́нного. Соверше́нно уника́льное зда́ние. Бы́ло постро́ено при Ива́не Гро́зном. Говоря́т, что, когда́ строи́тельство бы́ло зако́нчено, архите́кторов ослепи́ли.
	Yes, it's Saint Basil's Cathedral . It's an absolutely unique building. It was built under Ivan the Terrible. They say that when the building was finished they blinded the architects.
Майк	Ослепи́ли? Но почему́?
	Blinded (them)? But why?
Ната́ша	Что́бы они́ не могли́ постро́ить ещё что-нибу́дь, бо́лее краси́вое.
	So that they wouldn't be able to build anything else more beautiful.
Майк	Ужа́сно!
	How awful!
Ната́ша	Да. В э́той стране́ бы́ли тира́ны: Ива́н Гро́зный, Ста́лин … И, в то же вре́мя, э́то страна́ ру́сской интеллиге́нции и вели́ких писа́телей, таки́х как Пу́шкин, Толсто́й, Достое́вский …
	Yes. There were some tyrants in this country: Ivan the Terrible, Stalin… And at the same time it's the country of the Russian intelligentsia and of great writers such as Pushkin, Tolstoy, Dostoyevsky…
Майк	Посмотри́те! Как здо́рово игра́ет со́лнце на тех золоты́х купола́х!
	Look! How beautifully the sun sparkles on those golden domes!
Ната́ша	Да. Э́то Кремль. Он был постро́ен ещё в 12-ом ве́ке. Но дава́йте вернёмся в маши́ну. Я хочу́, что́бы мы пое́хали посмотре́ть Новоде́вичий.
	Yes. That's the Kremlin. It was built as early as the 12th century. But let's go back to the car. I want us to go and look at Novodevichy.
Майк	Что э́то тако́е?
	What is that?
Ната́ша	Э́то монасты́рь на берегу́ Москва́-реки, постро́енный ещё до Петра́ Пе́рвого.
	It's a monastery on the bank of the Moscow River, built even before Peter the Great.

Grammar

1. TOGETHER WITH

Look at the following sentence:

Они́ с Ната́шей реши́ли отпра́виться на экску́рсию.

Literally, this means **They with Natasha decided to…** . It can also mean that one or more persons, together with Natasha, decided to do something. In the text, however, it means **Mike and Natasha decided to…** .

A common mistake that Russians, even Russians with good English, make is to say things like: **We with father…** and **We with Mike…** , instead of **My father and I…** and **Mike and I…** This is because they are translating directly from the Russian.

мы с отцо́м	I with father; we with father (My father and I)
мы с бра́том	I with brother; we with brother (My brother and I)
мы с сестро́й	I with sister; we with sister (My sister and I)
они́ с Ива́ном	he with Ivan; she with Ivan; they with Ivan
они́ с Ната́шей	he with Natasha; she with Natasha; they with Natasha

Since more than one person is involved, the verb that follows is in the plural:

Они́ с Ната́шей реши́ли …

мы с отцо́м пое́хали …

мы с сестро́й лю́бим …

они́ с Ива́ном иду́т …

Just who is with father, sister, Ivan, etc. is usually clear from the context.

2. THE SHORT FORM OF ADJECTIVES

Many adjectives have a **short** form, which can serve as the predicate (the part of a sentence that says something about the subject).

In Lesson 7 there was an example of the short form of the adjective **free**:

Ники́та Серге́евич бу́дет свобо́ден в сре́ду.
Nikita Sergeyevich will be free on Wednesday.

Свобо́ден *m.*/свобо́дна *f.*/свобо́дно *n.* are the short forms of свобо́дный *m.*/свобо́дная *f.*/свобо́дное *n.*

Other examples from the dialogue are:

Пого́да о́чень неусто́йчива. (неусто́йчивый *m.*/неусто́йчивая *f.*/неусто́йчивое *n.*)
День так чуде́сен. (чуде́сный *m.*/чуде́сная *f.*/чуде́сное *n.*)

The short form of the masculine singular is made by dropping the ending **-ый**, **-ой**, **-ий** from the long form, leaving only the stem:

краси́вый – крас´в   beautiful
молодо́й – мо́лод   young
хоро́ший – хоро́ш   good

If the stem of the adjective ends in two or more consonants, as in the case of **свобо́дный** and **чуде́сный** above, **-о-** or **-е-** is usually inserted.
The short form of the feminine singular is made by adding **-а** to the stem:

краси́вая – краси́ва   молода́я – молода́   хоро́шая – хороша́

The short form of the neuter singular is made by adding **-о** to the stem:

краси́вое – краси́во   молодо́е – мо́лодо   хоро́ший – хорошо́

The short form of the plural for all three genders is made by adding **-ы** to the stem (or **-и** if the stem ends in **г**, **к**, **х**, **ж**, **ч**, **ш**, or **щ**):

краси́вы   мо́лоды   хороши́

Here are some short forms that are worth learning. Note the change in position of the stress.

Full form	Short form			
Masculine	Masculine	Feminine	Neuter	Plural
больно́й sick	бо́лен	больна́	больно́	больны́
вели́кий great	вели́к	велика́	велико́	велики́
дли́нный long	дли́нен	длинна́	длинно́	длинны́

Full form	Short form			
Masculine	Masculine	Feminine	Neuter	Plural
Поле́зный useful	Поле́зен	поле́зна	поле́зно	поле́зны
По́лный full	По́лон	Полна́	полно́	полны́
пра́вый right	прав	права́	пра́во	пра́вы
Прекра́сный splendid, beautiful	Прекра́сен	прекра́сна	прекра́сно	прекра́сны
Прия́тный pleasant	Прия́тен	прия́тна	прия́тно	прия́тны
Ску́чный boring	Ску́чен	скучна́	ску́чно	скучны́
Слы́шный audible, heard	Слы́шен	слышна́	слы́шно	слышны́
Стра́шный awful, terrible	Стра́шен	страшна́	стра́шно	страшны́
тру́дный difficult, hard	тру́ден	трудна́	тру́дно	трудны́
удо́бный convenient, comfortable	удо́бен	удо́бна	удо́бно	удо́бны
у́мный clever, wise	Умён	Умна́	умно́	умны́
холо́дный cold	хо́лоден	холодна́	хо́лодно	холодны́
Широ́кий broad, wide	Широ́к	широка́	широко́	широки́

It is important to note that the **short adjective** is only used to **form the predicate** in a sentence, whereas the **full adjective** can be used attributively or **for emphasis**:

дли́нная доро́га	a long road
Доро́га дли́нная.	The road is a long one.
Доро́га длинна́.	The road is long.
по́лные стака́ны	full glasses
Стака́ны по́лные.	The glasses are full to the brim.
Стака́ны полны́.	The glasses are full.
прекра́сный го́род	a beautiful town
Го́род прекра́сный.	The town is a beautiful one.
Го́род прекра́сен.	The town is beautiful.

The short form is used much more often in the predicate than the long form:

Путеше́ствие бы́ло прия́тно.	The journey was pleasant.
Уро́ки бы́ли скучны́.	The lessons were boring.
Пти́цы слышны́ по утра́м.	The birds are heard in the mornings.
Рабо́та была́ трудна́.	The work was difficult.
Маши́на о́чень удо́бна.	The car is very comfortable.
Моя́ мама о́чень умна́.	My mother is very clever.

3. RUSSIAN LETTERS

In order to ask people how something is spelt, you need to know how to phrase the question and also how to recognize the letters of the alphabet.

First, learn to say:

Как э́то пи́шется?	How is it written?/How do you spell it?

Letter	Sound	Pronunciation
А а	[a] in car	ah
Б б	[b] in bed	beh
В в	[v] in vodka	veh
Г г	[g] in gold	geh
Д д	[d] in dot	deh
Е е	[ye] in yet	yeh
Ё ё	[yo] in yogurt	yoh
Ж ж	[s] in measure	zheh
З з	[s] in please	zeh
И и	[ee] in street	ee
Й й	[y] in young	И кра́ткое *(ee kraht-kah-yeh)*
К к	[c] in cover	kah
Л л	[l] in low	el
М м	[m] in mad	em
Н н	[n] in not	en
О о	[o] in north (when stressed)	oh
П п	[p] in plot	peh
Р р	[r] in grey	er
С с	[s] in salt	es
Т т	[t] in town	teh
У у	[oo] in cool	oo
Ф ф	[f] in fee	ef
Х х	[h] in hurry	khah
Ц ц	[tz] in quartz	tseh
Ч ч	[ch] in chunk	cheh
Ш ш	[sh] in shawl	shah
Щ щ	[shch] in hush child	shchah
Ъ ъ	No sound.	Твёрдый знак *(tvyor-diy znahk)*
Ы ы	[i] in thing	ih
Ь ь	No sound.	Мя́гкий знак *(myahkh-keey znahk)*
Э э	[e] in every	eh
Ю ю	[u] in union	yoo
Я я	[ya] in Yankee	yah

4. ASKING FOR DIRECTIONS

Different verbs are used to say that you are for traveling on foot or going by transportation. This applies to driving and other modes of transportation.

How to get to? on foot is **Как пройти́?**

How to get to? by transportation is **Как прое́хать?**

When approaching somebody to ask for directions, start by saying: **Извини́те** (**excuse me**), followed by: **Вы не ска́жете ...** (literally, **Won't you say**, but used to mean **Can you tell me?**).

So, to ask the way to the American Embassy on foot, you say:

Извини́те, вы не ска́жете, как пройти́ к Америка́нскому посо́льству?

If you are driving a car, you say:

Извини́те, вы не ска́жете, как прое́хать к Америка́нскому посо́льству?

Here are some more examples of ways to ask for directions when you are walking:

Извини́те, вы не ска́жете, как пройти́ ...

... к гости́нице Метропо́ль?	... to the Hotel Metropol?
... к Большо́му Теа́тру?	... to the Bolshoi Theater?
... к Кра́сной Пло́щади?	... to Red Square?
... к ближа́йшему ба́нку?	... to the nearest bank?

You may have to ask where something is:

Извини́те, вы не ска́жете ...

... где здесь нахо́дится ближа́йший туале́т?
... .where the nearest toilet is (here)?

... где здесь нахо́дится ближа́йший телефо́н-автома́т?
... where the nearest public telephone is?

Here are some common directions:

turn	поверни́те (or, more colloquial сверни́те)
turn left	поверни́те нале́во
turn right	поверни́те напра́во
... at the next corner	на сле́дующем поворо́те
... at the traffic lights	у светофо́ра
opposite	напро́тив
It is opposite the post office.	Э́то напро́тив по́чты.

in front of	пе́ред
It is in front of the church.	Э́то пе́ред це́рковью.
behind	за
It is behind the Hotel Metropol.	Э́то за гости́ницей Метропо́ль.
straight	пря́мо
Go straight ahead.	Иди́те пря́мо.

Vocabulary

экску́рсия *trip, excursion*
после́дний *m.*/после́дняя *f.*/после́днее *n. last*
скоре́е *faster, rather, more likely*
температу́ра *temperature*
высоко́ *high*
вы́ше *higher*
нульт *zero*
Никто́ не рад. *Nobody is happy.*
Тепло́. *It is warm.*
тепло́ *(neuter noun) warmth*
си́льный *m.*/си́льная *f.*/си́льное *n. strong*
ве́тер *wind*
Идёт снег. *It is snowing.*
дождьт *rain*
идёт дождь *it is raining*
ми́нус *minus, negative*
гра́дус *degree (temperature)*
не́бо *sky*
о́блако *cloud*
о́блачный *m.*/о́блачная *f.*/о́блачное *n. cloudy*
безо́блачный *m.*/безо́блачная *f.*/

безо́блачное *n. cloudless*
голубо́й *m.*/голуба́я *f.*/голубо́е *n. blue*
со́лнце *sun*
сия́ть *(impf) to shine*
искри́ться *(impf) to sparkle*
так *so*
неусто́йчивый *m.*/неусто́йчивая *f.*/неусто́йчивое *n. variable*
сля́коть *f. slush*
под нога́ми *under the feet*
плыть *(impf) to swim, to float*
бе́лый *m.*/бе́лая *f.*/бе́лое *n. white*
чуде́сный *m.*/чуде́сная *f.*/чуде́сное *n. wonderful, marvelous*
чуде́сен *m.*/чуде́сна *f.*/чуде́сно *n. wonderful, marvelous (short form of adj.)*
Невозмо́жно. *It is impossible.*
ко́мната *room*
реша́ть *(impf) to decide*
реши́ть *(perf) to decide*
отпра́виться *(perf) to set off*
зда́ние *building*
це́рковь *f. church*

собо́р *cathedral*

соверше́нно *completely, absolutely*

уника́льный *m.*/уника́льная *f.*/
уника́льное *n. unique*

стро́ить *(impf) to build*

постро́ить *(perf) to build*

при Ива́не Гро́зном *under/during the reign
of Ivan The Terrible*

строи́тельство *building, construction*

зако́нчено *finished*

архите́ктор *architect*

ослепи́ть *(perf) to blind, to put out
someone's eyes*

бо́лее *more*

ужа́сный *m.*/ужа́сная *f.*/ужа́сное *n. awful,
horrible*

страна́ *country*

прекра́сный *m.*/прекра́сная *f.*/
прекра́сное *n. beautiful, pretty*

смесь *f.*/ *mixture*

интеллиге́нция *intelligentsia*

вели́кий *m.*/вели́кая *f.*/вели́кое *n. great*

писа́тельм *writer*

тира́н *tyrant*

игра́ть *to play*

золото́й *m.*/золота́я *f.*/золото́е *n.* **golden**

ку́пол *dome*

век *century*

возврати́ться *(perf) to return, come back*

верну́ться *(perf) to return, go back*

монасты́рь *m. monastery, convent*

бе́рег **bank** *(of a river, lake)*

река́ *river*

Exercises

Exercise A

Translate the following sentences into English.

1. В Росси́и хо́лодно зимо́й, но в после́дние пять-семь лет зи́мы бы́ли не о́чень
   холо́дные.

   ....

   ....

2. Зимо́й в Росси́и температу́ра ча́сто вы́ше нуля́.

   ....

   ....

3. Ча́сто быва́ет си́льный ве́тер, и идёт снег с дождём.

....

4. Когда́ не́бо безо́блачное и голубо́е, и со́лнце сия́ет, и снег искри́тся – в Росси́и чуде́сно.

....

....

5. В нача́ле ма́рта пого́да о́чень неусто́йчива в Нью-Йо́рке.

....

....

6. Ма́йк прие́хал в Москву́ в са́мом нача́ле весны́.

....

7. Мы реши́ли отпра́виться на экску́рсию по Москве́.

....

8. Э́то что за зда́ние?

....

9. Собо́р Васи́лия Блаже́нного – соверше́нно уника́льное зда́ние.

....

....

10. Пу́шкин, Толсто́й и Достое́вский бы́ли вели́кие писа́тели.

....

11. Дава́йте вернёмся в маши́ну.

....

12. Новоде́вичий – монасты́рь на берегу́ Москва́-реки.

....

Exercise B

You are going around Moscow. Ask the way to the following places:

1. **(by car) the Tretyakov Gallery** Третьяко́вская галлере́я

....

2. **(on foot) the nearest subway** метро́

....

3. **(on foot) the nearest department store** универма́г

....

4. **(on foot) the nearest church** це́рковь

....

5. **(by car) the nearest hospital** больни́ца

....

6. **(on foot) the nearest pharmacy** апте́ка

....

7. **(on foot) the Lenin Mausoleum** Мавзоле́й Ле́нина

....

8. **(by car) Tver Street** Тверска́я у́лица

....

9. **(by car) the university** университе́т

....

10. **(by car) the Hotel Ukraine** гости́ница "Украи́на"

....

Exercise C

Translate the following sentences into Russian.

1. **As you already know, in Russia it is cold in winter.**

   ....

   2. **The temperature is often above zero.**

      ....

3. **Often there is a strong wind.**

   ....

4. **It is snowing.**

   ....

5. **The temperature is minus 10 degrees.**

   ....

6. **The sky is blue, and the sun is shining.**

   ....

7. **It is wonderful here!**

   ....

8. **At the beginning of March, the weather is very variable.**

   ....

9. **The temperature quickly changes.**

   ....

10. **At night it is minus 20, but by day it is 10 above.**

    ....

11. Mike came to Moscow at the very beginning of spring.

....

12. The day is so nice that it is simply not possible to sit in the hotel.

....

13. The cathedral was constructed under Ivan the Terrible.

....

14. It's a beautiful country

....

15. Tolstoy was a great writer.

....

Exercise D

True or false?

1. В последние пять-семь лет зимы в России были очень холодные.　　T/F

2. В последние пять-семь лет температура зимой в России никогда не
　былá выше нуля.　　T/F

3. Никто не рад этому теплу.　　T/F

4. В начале марта в России ночью бывает плюс 18, а днём – минус 18.　　T/F

5. Собор Василия Блаженного – совершенно уникальное здание.　　T/F

6. Собор Василия Блаженного был построен при Иване Грозном.　　T/F

7. Новодевичий – это гостиница на берегу Москва-реки.　　T/F

15. Daily Life

Lesson 15 follows Mike as he begins some Russian classes. You will learn how to talk about some general daily activities and you will also learn the time. Remember that much of the vocabulary you learn is transferrable and can apply to many other situations too.

МАЙК У́ЧИТ РУ́ССКИЙ ЯЗЫ́ MIKE STUDIES RUSSIAN

Майк наме́рен приезжа́ть в Росси́ю дово́льно ча́сто. Е́сли дела́ по созда́нию совме́стного предприя́тия с ба́нком пойду́т хорошо́, он мог бы проводи́ть в Москве́ от шести́ ме́сяцев до го́да. Поэ́тому он реши́л всерьёз заня́ться ру́сским языко́м.

Mike intends to come to Russia fairly often. If things go well with setting up a joint venture with the bank, he could spend from six months to a year in Moscow. Therefore, he has decided to study the Russian language seriously.

Ната́ша познако́мила его́ с А́нной Ива́новной Смирно́вой, кото́рая согласи́лась дава́ть Ма́йку ча́стные уро́ки. Сейча́с Майк пришёл к ней домо́й и звони́т в дверь ...

Natasha has introduced him to Anna Ivanovna Smirnova, who has agreed to give Mike private lessons. Mike has just arrived at her home and rings the doorbell ...

А́нна Ива́новна	До́брый ве́чер! Входи́те, пожа́луйста.
	Good evening. Please come in.
Майк	До́брый ве́чер!
	Good evening!
А́нна Ива́новна	Где вы изуча́ли ру́сский?

Where did you learn Russian?

Майк
Я учи́лся в Аме́рике, но тепе́рь, когда́ я бу́ду подо́лгу жить в Москве́, мне на́до лу́чше знать ру́сский.

I learned it in America, but now that I will be spending a long time in Moscow, I need to know Russian better.

А́нна Ива́новна
Чем и́менно вы хоте́ли бы заня́ться?

What exactly would you like to study?

Майк
Пре́жде всего́ мне на́до расши́рить запа́с слов. Когда́ я смотрю́ телеви́зор, я понима́ю дово́льно мно́го. А пото́м вдруг попада́ются одно́-два незнако́мых сло́ва, и я перестаю́ понима́ть, теря́ю смысл.

First of all, I need to increase my vocabulary. When I watch television, I understand quite a lot. But then suddenly one or two unknown words turn up, and I stop understanding and lose the meaning.

А́нна Ива́новна
У вас хоро́шее ру́сское произноше́ние. И вы уже́ сейча́с непло́хо говори́те по-ру́сски. Я уве́рена, что мы смо́жем расши́рить ваш слова́рный запа́с.

Your Russian pronunciation is good. And you already speak Russian quite well. I'm sure that we can broaden your vocabulary.

Майк
Да, я наде́юсь … И ещё одна́ пробле́ма – э́то когда́ лю́ди говоря́т бы́стро. По телеви́зору я ещё бо́лее-ме́нее понима́ю но́вости, но по ра́дио, когда́ нет изображе́ния, почти́ ничего́ не понима́ю.

Yes, I hope so … And another problem is when people speak quickly. On television I still more or less understand the news, but on the radio, when there are no images, I understand almost nothing.

А́нна Ива́новна
Я ду́маю, что смогу́ вам помо́чь и в э́том то́же. Ната́ша мне немно́го рассказа́ла о ва́ших тру́дностях, и я пригото́вила програ́мму, кото́рая, я наде́юсь, бу́дет вам поле́зна.

I think I can help you with that, too. Natasha told me a little about your difficulties, and I have prepared a program which, I hope, will be helpful to you.

Майк
Пре́жде чем нача́ть, я хоте́л бы вы́яснить всё насчёт опла́ты.

Before starting, I would like to clarify everything regarding payment.

А́нна Ива́новна
Опла́ты? Никако́й опла́ты! Вы друг мое́й хоро́шей знако́мой. Я хочу́ помо́чь вам. Друзья́ для э́того и существу́ют.

Payment? No payment at all! You are a friend of a good friend of mine. I want to help you. That's what friends are for.

Майк
Прости́те, но я так не могу́. Я наста́иваю.

Excuse me, but I can't do that. I insist.

А́нна Ива́новна
Ну, спаси́бо. Но вы уж тогда́ учи́тесь хорошо́, что́бы я не зря их получа́ла!

Well, thank you. But you'll really have to study hard, so that I don't get paid for nothing.

Grammar

1. THE PREPOSITION ПРИ

При takes the prepositional case. It can be translated into English in a number of ways, depending on the context:

1. attached to
   Гара́ж при до́ме.   The garage is attached to the house.

2. in the presence of, before, in front of
   Они́ сказа́ли э́то при мне.   They said that in my presence.

3. during, in the time of, under (a ruler, government, etc.)
   при Коммуни́зме   under Communism

4. with, on
   У них все де́ньги при себе́.   They have all the money on/with them.
   Она́ нахо́дится при ма́тери.   She is with her mother.
   При по́мощи друзе́й всё бу́дет   With the help of friends, everything will be okay.
   хорошо́.

2. VERBS: ПРИЕЗЖА́ТЬ AND ПРИÉХАТЬ

Приезжа́ть (impf) and **прие́хать** (perf) mean **to arrive, to come**. In the narrative at the beginning of this lesson, you saw: **Майк наме́рен приезжа́ть в Росси́ю дово́льно ча́сто.** Here, the imperfective приезжа́ть is used because Mike intends to visit Russia frequently on an indefinite basis.

Compare this with: **Майк наме́рен прие́хать в Росси́ю в суббо́ту.** Here Mike intends to complete the process of coming to Russia on Saturday. So **прие́хать** is used.

Try to memorize the conjugation of these verbs:

Present tense		
	приезжа́ть (impf)	прие́хать (perf)
Я	Приезжа́ю	THE
Ты	Приезжа́ешь	PERFECTIVE
он, она́, оно́	Приезжа́ет	HAS
Мы	Приезжа́ем	NO
Вы	Приезжа́ете	PRESENT
Они́	Приезжа́ют	TENSE

	Future tense	
	приезжа́ть *(impf)*	прие́хать *(perf)*
Я	бу́ду приезжа́ть	прие́ду
Ты	бу́дешь приезжа́ть	прие́дешь
он, она́, оно́	бу́дет приезжа́ть	прие́дет
Мы	бу́дем приезжа́ть	прие́дем
вы	бу́дете приезжа́ть	прие́дете
Они́	бу́дут приезжа́ть	прие́дут

3. КАК AND КАКО́Й WITH ADJECTIVES

Как (**how**) has only one form and is used with the short form of the adjective; како́й *m.*/кака́я *f.*/ како́е *n.* are used with the full form:

Как я глупт/Как я глупа́f!	How stupid I am!
(from глу́пый *m.*/глу́пая *f.*/глу́пое *n.* **stupid**)	
Кака́я я глу́пая!	How stupid I am!
Как ты бле́ден!	How pale you are!
Како́й ты бле́дный!	How pale you are!
Как она́ умна́!	How clever she is!
Кака́я она у́мная!	How clever she is!
Как оно́ широко́!	How wide it is!
Како́е оно́ широ́кое!	How wide it is!
Как мы бедны́!	How poor we are!
Каки́е мы бе́дные!	How poor we are!

4. TIME

one o'clock	час *(nom.)*
two o'clock	два часа́ *(gen. sing.)*
three o'clock	три часа́ *(gen. sing.)*
four o'clock	четы́ре часа́ *(gen. sing.)*
five o'clock	пять часо́в *(gen. pl.)*
six o'clock	шесть часо́в *(gen. pl.)*
seven through twelve o'clock	7–12 часо́в *(gen. pl.)*
twelve o'clock midnight	По́лночь
twelve o'clock midday	по́лдень

To express "**at**", i.e. at X time, **в** is used, followed by the accusative case of the number (this is the same as the nominative). Two, three and four are followed by the genitive singular of **час**: **часá**. Five through twelve are followed by the genitive plural of **час**: **часóв**.

at one o'clock	в час (no number is needed)
at two o'clock	в два часá
at three o'clock	в три часá
at four o'clock	в четы́ре часá
at five o'clock	в пять часóв
at six o'clock	в шесть часóв
at seven through twelve o'clock	в 7–12 часóв
at twelve o'clock midnight	в пóлночь
at twelve o'clock midday	в пóлдень

In Russia, as elsewhere, the 24-hour clock is used in official contexts. In order to distinguish times of day, the genitive singular of the words for day and night is used: **ýтро** becomes **утрá**; **день** becomes **дня**; **вéчер** becomes **вéчера** and **ночь** becomes **нóчи.** In Russian, **ночь** is used for the hours immediately after midnight. So:

at one o'clock in the morning	в час нóчи
at two o'clock in the afternoon	в два часá дня
at three o'clock in the morning	в три часá утрá
at four o'clock in the afternoon	в четы́ре часá дня
at five o'clock in the evening	в пять часóв вéчера
at six o'clock in the morning	в шесть часóв утрá
at ten o'clock in the evening	в дéсять часóв вéчера

Russians tend to have their lunch/(dinner) – **обéд** – at their workplace, between one and three in the afternoon, when many shops and offices are closed. So the expression **пóсле обéда** –**after lunch/ (dinner)** – usually tends to mean **after two o'clock**.

In the evening, Russians tend to have a lighter meal **ýжин** – **dinner/supper** – at about seven o'clock. So the expression **пóсле ýжина** – **after dinner/supper** – tends to mean **after seven o'clock**.

HOURS AND MINUTES

Russians think of time a little differently than we do. They think of the hour between noon and 1 o'clock as the first hour, the hour between two and three as the second hour, etc. So whereas we express time in terms of minutes past the hour, Russians refer to the minutes of the following hour.

One minute past six is literally **one minute of the seventh (hour)**:
однá минýта седьмóго.

Two minutes past six is **two minutes of the seventh (hour)**:
две мину́ты седьмо́го.

Ten minutes past six is **ten minutes of the seventh (hour)**:
де́сять мину́т седьмо́го.

The formula is as follows:

With **one**, the feminine nominative одна́ (cardinal number), the nominative мину́та + седьмо́го (ordinal number, gen., masc., sing.) are used.

The same applies to compound numbers ending in **one**: **twenty-one**, etc.:
два́дцать одна́ мину́та седьмо́го

With **two**, the feminine nominative of the cardinal number, две, and the genitive singular мину́ты + седьмо́го (ordinal number, gen., masc., sing.) are used.

The same applies to compound numbers ending in **two**: **twenty-two**, **thirty-two**, etc.:
три́дцать две мину́ты седьмо́го

With **three** and **four**, the nominative of the number, три, четы́ре and the genitive singular мину́ты + седьмо́го (ordinal number, gen., masc., sing.) are used.

With other numbers, the nominative of the number and the genitive plural мину́т + the hour (ordinal number, gen., masc., sing.) are used.

де́сять (cardinal number) мину́т (gen., pl. of мину́та) седьмо́го (gen., masc., sing.).

Here are some examples:

two minutes past twelve	две мину́ты пе́рвого
at two minutes past twelve	в две мину́ты пе́рвого
five past one	пять мину́т второ́го
at five past one	в пять мину́т второ́го
twelve minutes past three	двена́дцать мину́т четвёртого
at twelve minutes past three	в двена́дцать мину́т четвёртого
ten past four	де́сять мину́т пя́того
at ten past four	в де́сять мину́т пя́того
twenty-eight minutes past six	два́дцать во́семь мину́т седьмо́го
at twenty-eight minutes past six	в два́дцать во́семь мину́т седьмо́го

A QUARTER PAST ЧЕ́ТВЕРТЬ, HALF PAST ПОЛОВИ́НА

a quarter past four	че́тверть пя́того
at a quarter past four	в че́тверть пя́того
half past five	полови́на шесто́го
at half past five	в полови́не (prepositional) шесто́го

For **to** the hour, Russians use **без** – **less** – with the minutes in the genitive. Мину́т is frequently omitted. The hour is a cardinal number, in the nominative.

two minutes to twelve ('twelve less two minutes')	без двух (мину́т) двена́дцать
at two minutes to twelve	без двух (мину́т) двена́дцать

Note that with **без в** is not used to indicate **at**.

Here are a few more examples:

(at) five to one	без пяти́ (мину́т) час
(at) twelve minutes to three	без двена́дцати (мину́т) три
(at) ten to four	без десяти́ (мину́т) четы́ре
(at) twenty-eight minutes to six	без двадцати́ восьми́ (мину́т) шесть
(at) a quarter to one	без че́тверти час
(at) a quarter to three	без че́тверти три

Vocabulary

намерева́ться to intend
он наме́рен he intends
приезжа́ть (impf) to come
прие́хать (perf) to come
дово́льно rather, fairly
созда́ние establishing, setting up
проводи́ть (impf) to accompany; to spend(time)
провести́ (perf) to accompany; to spend(time)
реша́ть (impf) to decide
реши́ть (perf) to decide
всерьёз seriously, in earnest
занима́ться (impf) to engage in; to deal with; to study
заня́ться (perf) to engage in; to deal with; to study

заня́ться языко́м to study a language
соглаша́ться (impf) to agree
согласи́ться (perf) to agree
дава́ть ча́стные уро́ки to give private lessons
звони́ть в дверь to ring the doorbell
подо́лгу a long time
жить (impf) to live, to be alive; to stay or spend time somewhere
мне на́до I must, it is necessary for me; I need
знать to know
лу́чше better
и́менно precisely, specially
Чем вы хоте́ли бы …? What would you like to … ?
пре́жде всего́ first of all

расширя́ть *(impf) to broaden, to widen*
расши́рить *(perf) to broaden, to widen*
запа́с *store, stock*
смотре́ть телеви́зор *to watch television*
попада́ться *(perf) to be caught*
незнако́мый *m./*незнако́мая *f./*
незнако́мое *n. unknown*
переставáть *(impf) to cease, to stop*
перестáть *(perf) to cease, to stop*
понимáть *(impf) to understand, to comprehend*
поня́ть *(perf) to understand, to comprehend*
теря́ть *(impf) to lose*
потеря́ть *(perf) to lose*
смысл *sense, meaning*
произноше́ние *pronunciation*
уве́рен *m./*уве́рена *f./*уве́рено *n. convinced*
надéяться *(impf) to hope*
по телеви́зору *on television*
бóлее-мéнее *more or less*
по рáдио *by radio, on the radio*
изображéние *image, picture*

трýдность *difficulty, hardship*
готóвить *(impf) to prepare, get ready, make*
приготóвить *(perf) to prepare, get ready, make*
прогрáмма *program*
полéзный *m./*полéзная *f./*полéзное *n. useful, beneficial*
прéжде чем *before*
начинáть *(impf) to start, to begin*
начáть *(perf) to start, to begin*
выясня́ть *(impf) to clear up, find out*
вы́яснить *(perf) to clear up, find out*
насчёт *concerning, with regard to, about*
оплáта *payment, settlement*
никакóй *m./*никакáя *f./*никакóе *n. none, not any*
знакóмый *m./*знакóмаяf *acquaintance*
существовáть *(impf) to exist*
прощáть *(impf) to pardon, forgive*
прости́ть *(perf) to pardon, forgive*
настáивать *(impf) to insist, to stick by*
настоя́ть *(perf) to insist, to stick by*
зря *for nothing, in vain*

Exercises

Exercise A

Translate the following sentences into English.

1. Я намéрен жить в Москвé.

....

2. Я реши́л всерьёз заня́ться рýсским языкóм.

....

3. Профе́ссор согласи́лся дава́ть мне ча́стные уро́ки.

....

4. Сейча́с Ната́ша пришла́ к нему́ домо́й и звони́т в дверь.

....

5. Входи́те, пожа́луйста.

....

6. Где Майк изуча́л ру́сский? В Аме́рике?

....

7. Да, но тепе́рь ему́ на́до лу́чше знать ру́сский.

....

8. Ей на́до расши́рить запа́с слов.

....

9. Когда́ она́ смо́трит телеви́зор, она́ понима́ет дово́льно мно́го.

....

10. У него́ хоро́шее ру́сское произноше́ние.

....

11. Она́ пло́хо говори́т по-ру́сски.

....

12. У меня́ одна́ пробле́ма.

....

13. Когда́ лю́ди говоря́т бы́стро, я не понима́ю.

....

14. Ната́ша пригото́вила обе́д.

....

15. Кни́га бу́дет вам поле́зна.

....

Exercise B

Translate the following sentences into Russian.

1. **Mike could spend from six months to a year in Moscow.**

....

2. **I decided to study the Russian language seriously.**

....

3. **Anna agreed to give Mike private lessons.**

....

4. **Where did you learn English?**

....

5. **I will not stay in Moscow for a long time.**

....

6. **We have to know Russian better.**

....

7. **When I watch television, I understand quite a lot.**

....

8. **I think that I can help you.**

....

Exercise C

Кото́рый час? What time is it? Answer in Russian.

1. 0:00 ....

2. 12:00 ....

   ....

3. 15:05 (2 ways) ....

   ....

4. 4:10 ....

5. 17:15 (2 ways)...

   ....

6. 6:20 ....

7. 12:30 (2 ways) ....

   ....

8. 7:40 ....

9. 20:45 (2 ways) ....

   ....

10. 9:57 (2 ways) ....

    ....

Exercise D

True or false?

1. Майк не наме́рен приезжа́ть ча́сто в Росси́ю.   T/F

2. Ната́ша познако́мила Ма́йка с А́нной Ива́новной Смирно́вой.   T/F

3. А́нна Ива́новна согласи́лась дава́ть Ма́йку ча́стные уро́ки.   T/F

4. Майк пришёл к А́нне домо́й и позвони́л в дверь.   T/F

5. А́нна спроси́ла, где Майк изуча́л ру́сский.

6. Тепе́рь, когда́ Майк бу́дет подо́лгу жить в Москве́, ему́ на́до лу́чше

   знать ру́сский.   T/F

7. А́нна не спроси́ла Ма́йка, чем и́менно он хоте́л бы заня́ться.   T/F

8. Пре́жде всего́ Ма́йку на́до расши́рить свой запа́с слов.   T/F

9. Когда́ Майк смо́трит телеви́зор, он понима́ет дово́льно мно́го.   T/F

10. Когда́ попада́ются одно́-два незнако́мых сло́ва, Майк совсе́м перестаёт

    понима́ть и теря́ет смысл.   T/F

11. У Ма́йка хоро́шее ру́сское произноше́ние, и он уже́ непло́хо говори́т

    по-ру́сски.   T/F

12. А́нна уве́рена, что они́ смо́гут расши́рить слова́рный запа́с Ма́йка.   T/F

13. Когда́ лю́ди говоря́т бы́стро по ра́дио, Майк не понима́ет.   T/F

14. По телеви́зору Майк бо́лее-ме́нее понима́ет но́вости, но по ра́дио,

    когда́ нет изображе́ния, он почти́ ничего́ не понима́ет.   T/F

15. Ната́ша ничего́ не расска́зывала А́нне о тру́дностях Ма́йка.   T/F

16. Review: Lessons 12-15

This review section is a revision of what you have learnt so far. Take the time to listen to the audio dialogues again and see how much you can understand without turning back to the English versions in the previous chapters! Don't forget to do the short exercise section too!

DIALOGUE 12: МАЙК Е́ДЕТ В РОССИ́Ю

Майк прилете́л из Нью-Йо́рка в Москву́ ночны́м ре́йсом. Самолёт приземли́лся в три часа́ дня по моско́вскому вре́мени. Майк прошёл че́рез пограни́чный контро́ль и тамо́женный досмо́тр. В за́ле прибы́тия бы́ло о́чень мно́го наро́ду. Пассажи́ры с трудо́м проти́скивались сквозь толпу́. Майк сра́зу уви́дел табли́чку со свои́м и́менем …

Майк	Ната́ша?
Ната́ша	Да. А вы, наве́рное, Майк? Добро́ пожа́ловать в Москву́!
Майк	Я о́чень рад встре́титься с ва́ми.
Ната́ша	Мы так мно́го говори́ли по телефо́ну! И, наконе́ц, мы встре́тились ли́чно. А э́то для вас!

Она́ даёт ему́ буке́т цвето́в.

| Майк | Цветы́? Как прия́тно! Большо́е спаси́бо. |
| Ната́ша | Здесь так мно́го люде́й и так шу́мно. Мы лу́чше поговори́м в маши́не. |

Они́ выхо́дят из аэропо́рта и садя́тся в маши́ну.

| Ната́ша | Как вы долете́ли? |
| Майк | Прекра́сно! Я о́чень хорошо́ пообе́дал, вы́пил два стака́на джи́на с то́ником и всё остально́е вре́мя спал. |

Наташа	Значит, вы не очень устали.
Майк	Совсем не устал. Но я бы хотел принять душ. Я немного вспотел. В аэропорту было очень жарко.
Наташа	Я предлагаю поехать прямо в гостиницу, чтобы вы смогли освежиться, распаковать чемоданы и устроиться. А около 7 часов вечера мы заедем за вами и поедем обедать.
Майк	Мы?
Наташа	Я приеду с моим начальником. Он очень хочет встретиться с вами.
Майк	Это новый начальник?
Наташа	Да. Он работал в отделении нашего банка в Варшаве. Он приехал к нам примерно шесть месяцев назад.

Машина быстро мчалась по Тверской – бывшей улице Горького. Вдруг Майк спросил:

Майк	Что это?
Наташа	Это московский Кремль. Мы недалеко от Красной площади. А вот и ваша гостиница.

DIALOGUE 13: В ГОСТИНИЦЕ

Гостиница "Звезда" находится недалеко от Красной площади. Это новая частная гостиница. Она небольшая: в ней всего сорок номеров. Майк с Наташей подходят к столу регистрации …

Администратор	Здравствуйте. Вы заказывали номер?
Майк	Да, заказал. Вот копия электронного письма, в котором вы подтверждаете, что заказ принят.
Администратор	Хорошо. Ваш паспорт, пожалуйста.
Майк	Вот он.
Администратор	Спасибо. Вы сможете получить его завтра утром.
Майк	Скажите, пожалуйста, в номере есть телевизор?
Администратор	Конечно. Много каналов на русском языке. И есть несколько на английском, например, Си-Эн-Эн. Они передают целый день по-английски.
Майк	Знаете ли вы, когда передают новости?
Администратор	Извините меня, точно не помню. Но вся информация есть в номере на русском и на английском языках.
Майк	Спасибо. А как здесь можно постирать вещи? И есть ли тут химчистка?
Администратор	Если вы отдадите нам те вещи, которые нужно постирать и почистить, до 12 часов дня, они будут готовы к 8 часам утра

	на сле́дующий день.
Майк	Прекра́сно! Что ещё? Да! Чуть не забы́л! Есть ли у вас каки́е-нибу́дь англи́йские и́ли америка́нские газе́ты?
Администра́тор	Да, мы получа́ем англи́йскую "Та́ймс" и "Интернэ́шнл Гера́льд Трибью́н".
Майк	Как рабо́тает ваш рестора́н? Когда́ он откры́т?
Администра́тор	У нас нет рестора́на. Но здесь за угло́м, совсе́м бли́зко, есть рестора́н.
Майк	А где мо́жно поза́втракать?
Администра́тор	У нас есть буфе́т с лёгкими заку́сками и пи́ццей на второ́м этаже́. Меню́ есть в ва́шем но́мере. Вы мо́жете позвони́ть го́рничной и заказа́ть за́втрак пря́мо в но́мер, е́сли хоти́те.
Майк	Спаси́бо. Вы о́чень помогли́ мне.

DIALOGUE 14: ЭКСКУ́РСИЯ ПО МОСКВЕ́

В Росси́и хо́лодно зимо́й. Но в после́дние пять-семь лет зи́мы бы́ли не о́чень холо́дные. Скоре́е да́же о́чень не холо́дные, с температу́рой ча́сто вы́ше нуля́. Но никто́ не рад э́тому теплу́: ча́сто быва́ет си́льный ве́тер, идёт снег с дождём … А когда́ температу́ра, ска́жем, ми́нус 20 гра́дусов, и не́бо безо́блачное и голубо́е, и со́лнце сия́ет, и снег искри́тся – здесь чуде́сно!

А в нача́ле ма́рта пого́да о́чень неусто́йчива. Но́чью – ми́нус 18, а днём – плюс 4! На у́лице сля́коть под нога́ми.

Майк прие́хал в Москву́ в са́мом нача́ле весны́. Сия́ет со́лнце: по голубо́му не́бу плыву́т ма́ленькие бе́лые облака́. День так чуде́сен, что про́сто невозмо́жно сиде́ть в ко́мнате, и они́ с Ната́шей реши́ли отпра́виться на экску́рсию по Москве́.

Ната́ша	Э́то Кра́сная пло́щадь.
Майк	А э́то что за зда́ние? Це́рковь?
Ната́ша	Да, э́то собо́р Васи́лия Блаже́нного. Соверше́нно уника́льное зда́ние. Бы́ло постро́ено при Ива́не Гро́зном. Говоря́т, что, когда́ строи́тельство бы́ло зако́нчено, архите́кторов ослепи́ли.
Майк	Ослепи́ли? Но почему́?
Ната́ша	Что́бы они́ не могли́ постро́ить ещё что-нибу́дь, бо́лее краси́вое.
Майк	Ужа́сно!
Ната́ша	Да. В э́той стране́ бы́ли тира́ны: Ива́н Гро́зный, Ста́лин … И, в то же вре́мя, э́то страна́ ру́сской интеллиге́нции и вели́ких писа́телей, таки́х как Пу́шкин, Толсто́й, Достое́вский …
Майк	Посмотри́те! Как здо́рово игра́ет со́лнце на тех золоты́х купола́х!
Ната́ша	Да. Э́то Кремль. Он был постро́ен ещё в 12-ом ве́ке. Но дава́йте вернёмся в маши́ну. Я хочу́, что́бы мы пое́хали посмотре́ть Новоде́вичий.

Майк	Что это такое?
Наташа	Это монастырь на берегу Москва-реки, построенный ещё до Петра Первого.

DIALOGUE 15: МАЙК УЧИТ РУССКИЙ ЯЗЫК.

Майк намерен приезжать в Россию довольно часто. Если дела по созданию совместного предприятия с банком пойдут хорошо, он мог бы проводить в Москве от шести месяцев до года. Поэтому он решил всерьёз заняться русским языком. Наташа познакомила его с Анной Ивановной Смирновой, которая согласилась давать Майку частные уроки. Сейчас Майк пришёл к ней домой и звонит в дверь ...

Анна Ивановна	Добрый вечер! Входите, пожалуйста.
Майк	Добрый вечер!
Анна Ивановна	Где вы изучали русский?
Майк	Я учился в Америке, но теперь, когда я буду подолгу жить в Москве, мне надо лучше знать русский.
Анна Ивановна	Чем именно вы хотели бы заняться?
Майк	Прежде всего мне надо расширить запас слов. Когда я смотрю телевизор, я понимаю довольно много. А потом вдруг попадаются одно-два незнакомых слова, и я перестаю понимать, теряю смысл.
Анна Ивановна	У вас хорошее русское произношение. И вы уже сейчас неплохо говорите по-русски. Я уверена, что мы сможем расширить ваш словарный запас.
Майк	Да, я надеюсь ... И ещё одна проблема – это когда люди говорят быстро. По телевизору я ещё более-менее понимаю новости, но по радио, когда нет изображения, почти ничего не понимаю.
Анна Ивановна	Я думаю, что смогу вам помочь и в этом тоже. Наташа мне немного рассказала о ваших трудностях, и я приготовила программу, которая, я надеюсь, будет вам полезна.
Майк	Прежде чем начать, я хотел бы выяснить всё насчёт оплаты.
Анна Ивановна	Оплаты? Никакой оплаты! Вы друг моей хорошей знакомой. Я хочу помочь вам. Друзья для этого и существуют.
Майк	Простите, но я так не могу. Я настаиваю.
Анна Ивановна	Ну, что ж, спасибо. Но вы уж тогда учитесь хорошо, чтобы я не зря их получала!

Exercises

Exercise A

Listen again to the dialogue from Lesson 12 and repeat.

Exercise B

Translate the dialogue from Lesson 12 into English and check your translation against ours on pages 152–154.

Exercise C

Listen again to the dialogue from Lesson 13 and repeat.

Exercise D

Now translate the dialogue from Lesson 13 and check your version against ours on pages 163–165.

Exercise E

Listen again to the dialogue from Lesson 14 and repeat.

Exercise F

Now translate the dialogue from Lesson 14 and check your version against ours on pages 173–175.

Exercise G

Listen again to the dialogue from Lesson 15 and repeat.

Exercise H

Translate the dialogue from Lesson 15 and check your version against ours on pages 186–188.

Exercise I

Put the words in parentheses into the correct form.

1. Сейча́с он (находи́ться) .... в (кабине́т) .... своего́

    (нача́льник) ....

2. Мы бу́дем говори́ть по (телефо́н) ....

3. Вчера́ (ве́чер) .... мы (гуля́ть) .... по (у́лицы)

    .... в (це́нтр) .... (Москва́) ....

4. Воло́дя с (Ната́ша) .... обсужда́ли письмо́ к (господи́н Ро́джерс)

    ....

5. В де́сять (час) .... (ве́чер) .... я пил (во́дка)

    .... в (рестора́н) .... с (Ива́н) ....

6. Извини́те, вы не (сказа́ть) .... , как пройти́ к (Америка́нское

    посо́льство) .... ?

7. Извини́те, вы не (сказа́ть) .... , как прое́хать к (Кра́сная Пло́щадь)

    .... ?

8. Извини́те, вы не (сказа́ть) .... , как пройти́ к (ближа́йший банк)

    .... ?

9. Извини́те, вы не (сказа́ть) .... , где здесь нахо́дится (ближа́йщий

    туале́т) .... ?

10. Поверни́те напра́во на (сле́дующий поворо́т) .... Э́то пе́ред

    (це́рковь) ....

17. Dining In & Out

Lesson 7 is all about food! Learn how to order food and drinks out and about and the vocabulary you need to talk about it at home. You will also learn prepositions of time, more pronouns and verbs, and you will further develop your language skills.

В РЕСТОРА́НЕ IN THE RESTAURANT

Майк про́был в Москве́ уже́ о́коло двух неде́ль. Че́рез пять-шесть дней он возврати́тся в Соединённые Шта́ты. Сего́дня ве́чером он пригласи́л Ната́шу пообе́дать с ним ...

Mike has already been in Moscow for about two weeks. He will return to the United States in five or six days. This evening he has invited Natasha to have dinner with him.

Ната́ша	Большо́е спаси́бо за приглаше́ние, Майк!
	Many thanks for the invitation, Mike!
Майк	Я уже́ два́жды был здесь. Они́ вку́сно гото́вят. Обе́д из пяти́ блюд с во́дкой, вино́м, шампа́нским и коньяко́м. Что вы хоти́те на заку́ски?
	I have been here twice already. The food's tasty. The dinner is five courses with vodka, wine, champagne and cognac. What would you like for starters?
Ната́ша	Дава́йте посмо́трим меню́.
	Let's have a look at the menu.
Майк	Есть ры́ба, икра́, колбаса́, сала́ты ...
	(They) have fish, caviar, sausage, salads ...

Наташа	Я бы хотёла всего – понемнóжку.
	I'd like a little of everything.
Майк	А пéрвое? У них здесь óчень вкýсная соля́нка по-москóвски.
	And for the first course? They have a very tasty Moscow style solyanka soup here.
Наташа	Я люблю́ соля́нку.
	I like solyanka.
Майк	Хорошó, две соля́нки. А что на горя́чее? Ры́ба или мя́со?
	Good. Two solyankas. And what for the main (hot) course? Fish or meat?
Наташа	А что вы посовéтуете?
	What do you recommend?
Майк	У них сегóдня осетри́на – э́то óчень вкýсно!
	Today they have sturgeon – it's very tasty.
Наташа	Осетри́на мне подхóдит. А что вы реши́ли, Майк?
	Sturgeon suits me. And what have you decided, Mike?
Майк	Я, пожáлуй, возьмý мя́со. Здесь óчень хорошó готóвят котлéты по-ки́евски … Хотя́ нет. Сегóдня я попрóбую беф-стрóганов. Говоря́т, он счита́ется лýчшим в Москвé.
	I think I'll have meat. They make very delicious Chicken Kievs here … Actually – no. Today I'll try the Beef Stroganoff. They say it's considered the best in Moscow.
Наташа	Э́то впечатля́ет.
	That's impressive.
Майк	А на десéрт …
	And dessert …
Наташа	Нет, нет, не сейча́с! Посмóтрим, чегó нам захóчется к концý обéда. Вот тогдá и реши́м.
	No, no, not now! Let's see what we feel like towards the end of the meal. And then we'll decide.
Майк	Что бýдем пить? Шампáнское? Конéчно! А тáкже бокáл бéлого вина́ к рыбе и бокáл крáсного к мя́су.
	What shall we drink? Champagne? Of course! And also a glass of white wine with the fish and a glass of red wine with the meat.
Наташа	Замеча́тельно!
	Wonderful!
Майк	Официа́нт! Мы готóвы сдéлать закáз.
	Waiter! We are ready to order.

Grammar

1. ЕСТЬ AND ПИТЬ

Two commonly used verbs you will need to learn are **есть to eat** and **пить to drink** in the imperfective, and **съесть** and **вы́пить** in the perfective. Their conjugations are shown in the table below.

Note: students of Russian frequently confuse the present tense of **есть** with that of **éхать to go** (Lesson 4). Compare the two conjugations and familiarize yourself with them!

	Imperfective		Perfective	
	есть	пить	съесть	вы́пить
PRESENT TENSE				
я	ем	пью	THE	
ты	ешь	пьёшь	PERFECTIVE	
он, она́, оно́	ест	пьёт	HAS	
мы	еди́м	пьём	NO	
вы	еди́те	пьёте	PRESENT	
они́	едя́т	пьют	TENSE	
PAST TENSE				
я, ты *m.*	ел	пил	съел	вы́пил
я, ты *f.*	éла	пила́	съéла	вы́пила
он	ел	пил	съел	вы́пил
она́	éла	пила́	съéла	вы́пила
оно́	éло	пи́ло	съéло	вы́пило
мы, вы, они́	éли	пи́ли	съéли	вы́пили
FUTURE TENSE				
я	бу́ду есть	бу́ду пить	съем	вы́пью
ты	бу́дешь есть	бу́дешь пить	съешь	вы́пьешь
он, она́, оно́	бу́дет есть	бу́дет пить	съест съесть	вы́пьет вы́пить
мы	бу́дем есть	бу́дем пить	съеди́м	вы́пьем
вы	бу́дете есть	бу́дете пить	съеди́те	вы́пьете
они́	бу́дут есть	бу́дут пить	съедя́т	вы́пьют

	Imperfective		Perfective	
	есть	пить	съесть	вы́пить
	IMPERATIVE			
	ешь	пей	съешь	вы́пей
	éшьте	пéйте	съéшьте	вы́пейте

2. БРАТЬ AND КЛАСТЬ

The imperfective verbs **брать to take** and **класть to put**, **to place** have perfective forms that are derived from different roots: **взять** and **положи́ть**.

	Imperfective		Perfective	
	брать	класть	взять	положи́ть
	PRESENT TENSE			
я	беру́	кладу́	THE	
ты	берёшь	кладёшь	PERFECTIVE	
он, она́, оно́	берёт	кладёт	HAS	
мы	берём	кладём	NO	
вы	берёте	кладёте	PRESENT	
они́	беру́т	кладу́т	TENSE	
	PAST TENSE			
я, тыm	брал	клал	взял	положи́л
я, тыf	брала́	клала́	взяла́	положи́ла
он	брал	клал	взял	положи́л
она́	брала́	клала́	взяла́	положи́ла
оно́	бра́ло	кла́ло	взяло́	положи́ло
мы	бра́ли	кла́ли	взя́ли	положи́ли
вы	бра́ли	кла́ли	взя́ли	положи́ли
они́	бра́ли	кла́ли	взя́ли	положи́ли
	FUTURE TENSE			
я	бу́ду брать	бу́ду класть	возьму́	положу́
ты	бу́дешь брать	бу́дешь класть	возьмёшь	поло́жишь
он, она́, оно́	бу́дет брать	бу́дет класть	возьмёт	поло́жит
мы	бу́дем брать	бу́дем класть	возьмём	поло́жим

	Imperfective		Perfective	
	есть	пить	съесть	вы́пить
	FUTURE TENSE (cont.)			
вы	бу́дете брать	бу́дете класть	возьмёте	поло́жите
они́	бу́дут брать	бу́дут класть	возьму́т	поло́жат
	IMPERATIVE			
	бери́	клади́	возьми́	положи́
	бери́те	клади́те	возьми́те	положи́те

3. THE INTERROGATIVE PRONOUN

The interrogative pronoun **чей? whose?** has three gender forms in the singular.

	Singular			Plural
	Masculine	Feminine	Neuter	All genders
Nom.	чей	чья	чьё	чьи
Acc.	чей/чьего́	чью	чьё	чьи/чьих
Gen.	чьего́	чьей	чьего́	чьих
Dat.	чьему́	чьей	чьему́	чьим
Instr.	чьим	чьей/чье́ю	чьим	чьи́ми
Prep.	чьём	чьей	чьём	чьих

Here are some examples. Note that **чей** here is accompanied by **э́то**:

чей	Чей э́то дом?	Whose house is that?
чья	Чья э́то руба́шка?	Whose shirt is that?
чьё	Чьё э́то я́блоко?	Whose apple is that?
чьи	Чьи э́то кни́ги?	Whose books are these?

4. THE PREPOSITIONS ÓКОЛО AND ЧЕРЕЗ

The preposition óколо means **around**, **about**, **approximately**, or **almost**. It is frequently used in time-related expressions, as in the dialogue for this lesson:

Майк пробыл в Москве уже около двух недель.
Mike has already been in Moscow for about two weeks.

The preposition через takes the accusative and is used in expressions of **location** (**across**, **through**, **via**, **over**) and **time** (**in**, **within**, **after**):

Location:

Мы прилетели в Москву через Лондон.
We flew to Moscow via London.

Я поеду домой через мост.
I am going home across the bridge.

Time:

Она будет дома через час.
She will be home in an hour.

Через пять-шесть дней он возвратится в Соединённые Штаты.
He will return to the United States in five to six days.

5. NOUNS WITH CARDINAL AND COMPOUND NUMBERS

As described in Lesson 13, in Russian all cardinal numbers decline. Nouns following один *m.*/одна *f.*/одно *n.* **one** stay in the nominative form. Nouns following два *m*/*n.* or две *f.* **two** are in the genitive singular.

The numbers три **three** and четыре **four** take the same form for nouns of all genders. Like два or две, they are also followed by nouns in the genitive singular.

With the exception of compound numbers, all other cardinals from five onwards are followed by a noun in the genitive plural. Thus: пять часов; шестьдесят рублей

Compound numbers (**twenty-one**, **thirty-three**, **fifty-six**, etc.) are followed by a noun governed by the last number:

двадцать один стол
тридцать два стола
тридцать две книги
сорок три рубля
сорок три книги

пятьдесят четыре рубля
пятьдесят четыре книги
шестьдесят пять рублей
шестьдесят шесть копий

6. ЖЕ FOR EMPHASIS

Же can be placed after a word in order to emphasize it:

он же	the very same man
онá же	the very same woman
сегóдня же	this very day
И что же э́то такóе?	And just what is that?, And what on earth is that?

Vocabulary

пробы́ть (perf) to stay, to spend time, to stop (for a time)

возвраща́ться (impf) to return

возврати́ться (perf) to return

Спаси́бо за приглаше́ние. Thanks for the invitation.

два́жды twice

вку́сно tasty

вку́сно гото́вить to cook well (lit. to prepare deliciously)

блю́до dish, course in a meal

обед из пятти́ блюд a five course meal

шампáнское champagne

конья́к cognac

затó but, however

ры́ба fish

икрá caviar

колбасá sausage

салáт salad

всегó понемнóжку a little of everything

соля́нка по-москóвски solyanka soup, Moscow style

горя́чий m./**горя́чая** f./**горя́чее** n. hot

горя́чее блю́до main course

мя́со meat

совéтовать (impf) to advise

посовéтовать (perf) to advise, to recommend

осетрти́на sturgeon

Мне (ему́, им, etc.**) подхóдит.** It suits me (him, them, etc.).

пожáлуй perhaps, very likely, "I dare say".

брать (impf) to take

взять (perf) to take

котлéты cutlets

котлéты по-кти́евски Chicken Kiev (breaded chicken with butter)

рекомендовáть (impf) to recommend

порекомендовáть (perf) to recommend

беф-стрóганов Beef Stroganoff

счита́ться (impf) to be considered, to consider

впечатля́ть (impf) to impress

десéрт dessert

захотéться (perf) to desire, to want

вы́пить (perf) to drink up

буты́лка bottle

тост toast (when drinking)

дру́жба friendship

за дру́жбу "to friendship"

класть (impf) to put, to place

положи́ть (perf) to put, to place

Exercises

Exercise A

Translate the following sentences into English.

1. Мы про́были в Ми́нске уже́ о́коло пяти́ неде́ль.

....

2. Че́рез три дня я возвраща́юсь в Росси́ю.

....

3. Вчера́ я пригласи́л его́ пообе́дать со мно́й.

....

4. У них сего́дня о́чень вку́сное мя́со.

....

5. Что вы мне сего́дня посове́туете?

....

6. Я возьму́ буты́лку кра́сного вина́.

....

7. Че́рез неде́лю мы возврати́мся в Росси́ю.

....

8. Сего́дня ве́чером мы пригласи́ли Ива́на пообе́дать с на́ми.

....

9. Большо́е спаси́бо за приглаше́ние.

....

10. Мы никогда́ там не́ были.

....

11. Мо́жно посмотре́ть меню́?

....

12. Я о́чень люблю́ ры́бу и мя́со.

....

13. Осетри́на - ры́ба. Э́то о́чень вку́сно!

....

14. На́ши котле́ты по-ки́евски счита́ются лу́чшими в Москве́.

....

15. Я хочу́ буты́лку кра́сного вина́ к мя́су и буты́лку бе́лого – к ры́бе.

....

Exercise B

Translate these sentences into Russian.

1. In six days they will return to the United States.

....

2. I invited my friends to have dinner with me this evening.

....

3. Many thanks for the invitation.

....

4. The dinner is five courses, with vodka, wine, champagne and cognac.

....

5. We were here yesterday.

....

6. I've never been there.

....

7. Is it possible to look at the menu?

....

8. Do you have fish?

....

9. Do you have meat?

....

10. I like red wine.

....

11. What do you recommend?

....

12. To our friendship!

....

Exercise C

Put the words in parenthesis into the correct form.

1. Она́ пробыла́ в (Москва́) .... уже́ о́коло (две неде́ли)

....

2. Вчера́ (ве́чер) .... мы (пригласи́ть) .... (Ната́ша)

.... пообе́дать с (мы) ....

3. Обе́д из (четы́ре) .... блюд с (во́дка, вино́, шампа́нское и

коньяк). ....

4. Ната́ша никогда́ там не (быть) ....

5. У нас нет (ры́ба, икра́, колбаса́, сала́ты). ....

6. У (они́) .... сего́дня хоро́шая осетри́на, но их беф-стро́ганов

счита́ется (лу́чший) .... в (Москва́) .... ,

7. Мы посмо́трим, (что) .... нам захо́чется к (коне́ц)

.... (обе́д) ....

8. Мы (быть) .... пить (буты́лка) .... (кра́сное вино́)

....

Exercise D

True or false?

1. Майк про́был в Москве́ уже́ о́коло шести́ неде́ль.   T/F

2. Че́рез пять-шесть дней Майк возврати́тся в Соединённые Шта́ты.   T/F

3. Сего́дня ве́чером Ната́ша пригласи́ла Майка пообе́дать с ней.   T/F

4. Майк уже́ был в рестора́не.   T/F

5. В рестора́не есть ры́ба, икра́, колбаса́ и сала́ты.   T/F

6. Ната́ша лю́бит соля́нку.   T/F

7. Осетри́на Ната́ше не подхо́дит.   T/F

8. Беф-стро́ганов счита́ется лу́чшим в Санкт-Петербу́рге.   T/F

18. Culture

Lesson 18 is about cultural activities. You will learn how to speak casually among friends. You will also learn how to make comparisons in Russian and how to use the present continuous tense to talk about actions that are ongoing. Don't forget to listen to the vocabulary section online.

ВÉЧЕР В ТЕÁТРЕ AN EVENING AT THE THEATER

Натáша приглаcи́ла Мáйка в Моско́вский Худо́жественный Теа́тр. Там они́ посмотрéли дрáму Анто́на Чéхова "Вишнёвый Сад" в но́вой постано́вке. Спектáкль был великолéпный.
Natasha invited Mike to the Moscow Art Theater. There, they saw a new production of Anton Chekhov's *The Cherry Orchard*. The performance was magnificent.

Натáша	Вам понрáвилась пьéса?
	Did you like the play?
Майк	Ещё бы! Это было́ замечáтельно! Актёры о́чень хорошо́ игрáли. А как в Москвé с билéтами? Трýдно достáть?
	I should say so! It was remarkable! The actors performed very well. But what's it like getting tickets in Moscow? Are they difficult to get?
Натáша	По-рáзному. У нас пьéсы Чéхова о́чень лю́бят и чáсто прихо́дится стоя́ть в о́череди. Обы́чно все билéты бывáют распро́даны за нéсколько дней до спектáкля и остаю́тся то́лько стоя́чие местá.
	It depends. Chekhov's plays are very popular here and you often have to stand in line. All the tickets are usually sold out several days before the

performance and only standing room is left.

Майк А вы ча́сто хо́дите в теа́тр?

And do you often go to the theater?

Ната́ша Да, но мне бо́льше нра́вится бале́т. Бале́т – мо́ё люби́мое иску́сство. О́чень люблю́ и кино́. Но смотре́ть телеви́зор, по-мо́ему, поте́ря вре́мени.

Yes, but I prefer ballet. Ballet is my favorite art form. I also love the movies. But watching television, in my opinion, is a waste of time.

Майк По пра́вде сказа́ть, бале́т не о́чень люблю́. По-мо́ему, кино́ интере́снее, чем теа́тр. Что сейча́с идёт в кинотеа́трах? Не могли́ бы вы посове́товать, како́й хоро́ший ру́сский фильм я могу́ посмотре́ть?

To tell the truth, I don't like ballet much. In my opinion, the movies are more interesting than the theater. What's on at the cinema now? Could you recommend a good Russian movie I can go and see?

Ната́ша Мой люби́мый ру́сский фильм – э́то "Война́ и Мир" Бондарчука́. Вы смотре́ли?

My favorite Russian movie is Bondarchuk's *War and Peace*. Have you seen it?

Майк Да. Зна́ете, мно́го лет наза́д я посмотре́л америка́нскую инсцениро́вку рома́на Толсто́го "Война́ и Мир", но ду́маю что ру́сский фильм лу́чше.

Yes. You know, many years ago I saw the American film version of Tolstoy's novel *War and Peace*, but I think that the Russian movie is better.

Ната́ша Я по́лностью согла́сна с ва́ми. Мы одина́ково ду́маем о мно́гих веща́х, Майк. А сейча́с, ча́ю хоти́те?

I agree with you entirely. We think the same way about a lot of things, Mike. And now, would you like some tea?

Майк Ну что́ вы! Я угощу́ вас бока́лом шампа́нского! Пошли́!

Oh, come on! I'll treat you to a glass of champagne! Let's go!

Grammar

1. THE PRESENT PERFECT CONTINUOUS

The present tense can be used for an action that has been taking place for some time and that is still continuing. Compare:

Ната́ша уже́ пять лет живёт в Москве́.
Natasha has been living in Moscow for five years already. (She still does.)

Ива́н жил пять лет в Москве́.
Ivan lived in Moscow for five years. (He no longer lives there.)

2. ГОД AND ЛЕТ WITH NUMBERS

The word for **year** is **год**. It is not used in the genitive plural (with rare exceptions). Instead, the genitive plural of the word for **summer** (**ле́то**) is used: **лет**. **Лет** is used to mean **years** after:

- numbers that require the genitive plural (five, six, etc.) when they are in the nominative or genitive case;

- numbers two, three and four when in the genitive case.

Here are some examples:

оди́н год	Он про́жил здесь то́лько оди́н год. He lived here for only one year.
два го́да	Она́ изуча́ла ру́сский язы́к два го́да. She studied Russian for two years.
три го́да	Я не́ был в Ми́нске три го́да. I haven't been to Minsk for three years.
четы́ре го́да	Э́тот дом стро́или четы́ре го́да. They were building this house for four years.
пять лет	В Моско́вском университе́те у́чатся пять лет. At Moscow State University, they study for five years.
шесть лет	Они́ встре́тились то́лько че́рез шесть лет. They met only after six years.

3. THE PARTITIVE GENITIVE, SOME

Compare the following pairs of sentences:

Да́йте мне хлеб, пожа́луйста.	Give me the bread, please.
Да́йте мне хле́ба, пожа́луйста.	Give me some bread, please.
Переда́й мне соль, пожа́луйста!	Pass me the salt, please!
Доба́вь со́ли в суп.	Add some salt to the soup.
Вы хоти́те чай или ко́фе?	Would you like tea or coffee?
Хоти́те ча́ю?	Would you like some tea?

The genitive case is used when the word **some** is understood in the sentence.

4. THE COMPARATIVE

Similarly to how English pairs the adverb **more** with an adjective to create a comparative form, Russian uses the invariable adverb **бо́лее**:

бо́лее интере́сный фильм	a more interesting movie
в бо́лее интере́сном фи́льме	in a more interesting movie
бо́лее краси́вая страна́	a more beautiful country
в бо́лее краси́вой стране́	in a more beautiful country
бо́лее краси́вое о́зеро	a more beautiful lake
на берегу́ бо́лее краси́вого о́зера	on the banks of a more beautiful lake

The Russian for **less** is **ме́нее**. It can be used in exactly the same way:

ме́нее интере́сный фильм	a less interesting movie
ме́нее интере́сная кни́га	a less interesting book
ме́нее интере́сное собы́тие	a less interesting event

Russian also has one-word comparatives (similar to **-er** forms, such as **stronger**, **longer**) that add -ee or -ée to the stem of the adjective. If the resulting word has only two syllables, the ending is stressed (-ée). If it has three or more syllables, the stem stress usually is maintained.

длѝнный	long	длиннѐе	longer
сѝльный	strong	сильнѐе	stronger
красѝвый	beautiful	красѝвее	more beautiful

Exceptions are **горячѐе (hotter)**, and **холоднѐе (colder)**.

This form is also invariable (i.e., it does not decline):

Э́тот фильм интерѐснее.	This movie is more interesting.
Э́та дорóга длиннѐе.	This road is longer.
Э́то óзеро красѝвее.	This lake is more beautiful.

Note that if the comparative comes before the noun, the **бóлее** form must be used:

| Э́то бóлее интерѐсный фильм. | It is a more interesting movie. |

After the noun, both forms can be used:

| Э́тот фильм интерѐснее. | This movie is more interesting. |
| Э́тот фильм бóлее интерѐсный. | This movie is more interesting. |

Some irregular forms to remember are:

большóй	big	бóльше	bigger
мáленький	small	мéньше	smaller
хорóший	good	лýчше	better
плохóй	bad	хýже	worse

Than, чем

Э́тот фильм мéнее интерѐсный, чем "Войнá и Мир".
This movie is less interesting than *War and Peace*.

Э́та кнѝга интерѐснее, чем другáя.
This book is more interesting than the other.

Это о́зеро ме́нее интере́сное, чем Байка́л.
This lake is less interesting than Lake Baikal.

much (more), гора́здо/намно́го

Этот фильм гора́здо интере́снее, чем "Война́ и Мир".
This movie is much more interesting than *War and Peace*.

Эта кни́га намно́го интере́снее, чем друга́я.
This book is much more interesting than the other.

Это о́зеро гора́здо краси́вее, чем Байка́л.
This lake is much more beautiful than Lake Baikal.

Пить минера́льную во́ду намно́го лу́чше, чем пить во́дку.
To drink mineral water is much better than to drink vodka.

5. THE SUPERLATIVE

A simple way to form the superlative is to use the invariable adverb **наибо́лее the most**:

Это наибо́лее интере́сный фильм.   It is the most interesting movie.

Это наибо́лее краси́вая страна́.   It is the most beautiful country.

Это наибо́лее ску́чное ме́сто.   It is the most boring place.

However, a more common way to form the superlative is to use **са́мый the most**.
Са́мый declines like an adjective, and agrees in gender, number and case with the adjective it precedes:

Это са́мый интере́сный фильм.   It is the most interesting film.

Это са́мая интере́сная страна́.   It is the most interesting country.

Это са́мое ску́чное ме́сто.   It is the most boring place.

Compare:

В наибо́лее ску́чных места́х в э́той кни́ге …
In the most boring places in this book …

В са́мых ску́чных места́х в э́той кни́ге …
In the most boring places in this book …

Yet another way of forming the superlative is to use the comparative followed by the genitive singular or plural of **всё**: **всего́, всех.**

Я бо́льше всего́ люблю́ бале́т.
I like ballet most of all.

Бо́льше всех компози́торов я люблю́ Чайко́вского.
Of all composers, I love Tchaikovsky the most.

Vocabulary

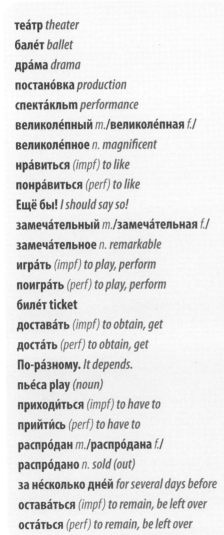

теа́тр *theater*

бале́т *ballet*

дра́ма *drama*

постано́вка *production*

спекта́кльт *performance*

великоле́пный *m.*/великоле́пная *f.*/
великоле́пное *n. magnificent*

нра́виться *(impf) to like*

понра́виться *(perf) to like*

Ещё бы! *I should say so!*

замеча́тельный *m.*/замеча́тельная *f.*/
замеча́тельное *n. remarkable*

игра́ть *(impf) to play, perform*

поигра́ть *(perf) to play, perform*

биле́т *ticket*

достава́ть *(impf) to obtain, get*

доста́ть *(perf) to obtain, get*

По-ра́зному. *It depends.*

пье́са *play (noun)*

приходи́ться *(impf) to have to*

прийти́сь *(perf) to have to*

распро́дан *m.*/распро́дана *f.*/
распро́дано *n. sold (out)*

за не́сколько дне́й *for several days before*

остава́ться *(impf) to remain, be left over*

оста́ться *(perf) to remain, be left over*

стоя́чее ме́сто *standing room*

люби́мый *m.*/люби́мая *f.*/люби́мое *n.*
favorite

иску́сство *art*

кино́, кинотеа́тр *movies, film, movie
theater, cinema*

поте́ря вре́мени *a waste of time*

по пра́вде сказа́ть *to tell the truth*

о́пера *opera*

пока́зывать *(impf) to show, to stage*

показа́ть *(perf) to show, to stage*

инсцениро́вка *dramatization, adaptation*

рома́н *novel*

по́лностью *completely*

одина́ково *the same way*

Ну что́ вы! *Oh, come on!*

угоща́ть *(impf) to treat*

угости́ть *(perf) to treat*

бока́л *glass*

бо́лее *more*

ме́нее *less*

гора́здо *much (more)*

намно́го *much (more)*

бо́льше *more*

о́зеро *lake*

страна́ *country*

Exercises

Exercise A

Translate the following sentences into English.

1. Я бу́ду приглаша́ть Ната́шу в Большо́й теа́тр на бале́т ка́ждую неде́лю.

   ....

2. Вчера́ ве́чером спекта́кль в теа́тре был великоле́пный.

   ....

3. Мно́го лет наза́д я жил в А́фрике.

   ....

4. Я о́чень хочу́ посмотре́ть фильм "Война́ и Мир".

   ....

5. Э́тот фильм интере́снее/бо́лее интере́сный, чем друго́й.

   ....

6. Эта кни́га бо́лее интере́сная, чем друга́я.

   ....

7. Моя́ жизнь стано́вится всё ху́же и ху́же.

   ....

8. Жизнь моего́ отца́ станови́лась всё лу́чше и лу́чше, когда́ он жил в Аме́рике.

   ....

9. Что вам бо́льше нра́вится, кино́ и́ли телеви́дение?

   ....

Exercise B

Put the words in parentheses into the correct form.

1. Вчера́ ве́чером мы (пригласи́ть) .... её в теа́тр на (пье́са)

   ....

2. Мно́го (год) .... наза́д я (смотре́ть) .... фильм

   Бондарчука́ "Война́ и мир".

3. Они́ (ви́деть) .... э́тот фильм вчера́, и он (они́) ....

   о́чень (понра́виться) ....

4. У (мы) .... пье́сы (Че́хов) .... о́чень (люби́ть)

   ....

5. Вчера́ (ве́чер) .... они́ (угоща́ть) .... (я)

   .... бока́лом (шампа́нское) ....

6. Скажи́те (я) .... , что (вы) .... бо́льше нра́вится,

   мя́со и́ли ры́ба?

7. По (пра́вда) .... сказа́ть, я не о́чень люблю́ (ры́ба)

   ....

8. Мы всегда́ одина́ково (ду́мать) .... о (мно́гие) ....

   веща́х. Смотре́ть телеви́зор, по-моему, потеря́ (вре́мя) ....

Exercise C

Translate the following sentences into Russian.

1. Ivan invited me to the theater, to a ballet.

   ....

2. The opera was magnificent.

....

3. That is remarkable!

....

4. Many years ago, I lived in Russia.

....

5. I saw that film too.

....

6. I like to watch television very much.

....

7. The theater is more interesting than opera and ballet.

....

8. Could you recommend a good Russian play?

....

Exercise D

True or false?

1. Ната́ша пригласи́ла Ма́йка в Большо́й теа́тр на бале́т.   T/F

2. Майк сказа́л, что спекта́кль был замеча́тельный.   T/F

3. Мно́го лет наза́д Майк смотре́л фильм "Война́ и мир".   T/F

4. Ната́ша не ви́дела э́тот фильм.   T/F

5. Ната́ша ча́сто хо́дит в теа́тр.   T/F

6. Ната́ше бо́льше нра́вится о́пера.   T/F

7. Ната́ша о́чень лю́бит телеви́дение, и ду́мает, что кино́ – э́то поте́ря вре́мени.   T/F

8. Майк ду́мает, что ру́сский фильм лу́чше.   T/F

19. Family & Friends

Lesson 19 is about forging friendships for the future. You will look at possessive pronouns and really perfect your Russian. Listen carefullly to the audio and compare it with your own pronunciation before continuing on to the final lesson.

МАЙК ВОЗВРАЩА́ЕТСЯ В АМЕ́РИКУ MIKE GOES BACK TO AMERICA

Майк с Ната́шей сидя́т в рестора́не, располо́женном над за́лом вы́лета в Шереме́тьево-2. Они́ прие́хали туда́ о́чень ра́но, и у них доста́точно вре́мени, чтоы вы́пить ко́фе и поовори́ть …

Mike and Natasha are sitting in the restaurant situated above the departure hall of Sheremetyevo-2. They arrived there very early, and they have enough time to drink coffee and to talk …

Майк	*Мы одина́ково ду́маем о мно́гих веща́х, Ната́ша. Мы о́чень хорошо́ ла́дим друг с дру́гом, и мне прия́тно рао́тать с ва́ми. Но я почти́ ничего́ не зна́ю о вас.*
	We think identically about many things, Natasha. We get along with each other very well, and for me it's a pleasure to work with you. But I know almost nothing about you.
Ната́ша	*Да почти́ и не́чего знать, Майк. Я родила́сь в Новосии́рске, учи́лась здесь, в Москве́, в Моско́вском госуда́рственном университе́те. Пото́м получи́ла рабо́ту в ба́нке.*
	Well, there's almost nothing to know, Mike. I was born in Novosibirsk, studied here in Moscow, at Moscow State University. Then I got a job in

	the bank.
Майк	Вы о́чень ми́лая и обая́тельная же́нщина, Ната́ша. Мне о́чень прия́тно быть в ва́шем о́бществе. You're a very sweet and charming woman, Natasha. It's very pleasant to be in your company.
Ната́ша	И мне то́же легко́ с ва́ми. С ва́ми я могу́ говори́ть о чём-уго́дно. Жаль, что вам на́до возвраща́ться в Аме́рику. And I'm comfortable with you too. With you, I can talk about anything. What a pity that you have to go back to America.
Майк	Да ... Но ведь у вас есть погово́рка: "Без разлу́к не быва́ет встреч". Ско́ро мы бу́дем вме́сте рабо́тать в Нью-Йо́рке. Yes ... But you have a saying, don't you: "Without partings, there are no meetings". Soon we'll be working together in New York.
Ната́ша	Да, пра́вильно. Зна́ете, я бу́ду о́чень мно́го рабо́тать, чтобы всё зако́нчить до своего́ отъе́зда. Yes, that's right. You know, I'm going to do a lot of work in order to finish everything before my departure.
Майк	Я был здесь то́лько три с полови́ной неде́ли, а вы бу́дете у нас полго́да. Мы смо́жем осмотре́ть весь Нью-Йо́рк. И не то́лько! Мои́ роди́тели уже́ проси́ли меня́ пригласи́ть вас к ним в Лос-А́нжелес. I was only here for three and a half weeks, but you'll be with us for half a year. We'll be able to explore all New York. And not only that. My parents have already asked me to invite you to visit them in Los Angeles.
Ната́ша	Отку́да они́ мо́гут знать обо мне́? How could they know about me?
Майк	Я мно́го говори́л им о вас по телефо́ну. Им не те́рпится познако́миться с ва́ми ли́чно. I spoke to them a lot about you on the phone. They can't wait to get to know you in person.

(Го́лос из громкоговори́теля) Пассажи́ры, сле́дующие ре́йсом 341 в Нью-Йо́рк! Вас про́сят пройти́ на регистра́цию в зал вы́лета, сто́йка но́мер три!
(Voice from the loud-speaker) Passengers bound for New York on flight 341! Please proceed to check-in in the departure hall, desk number three!

Ната́ша	Объявля́ют ваш ре́йс, Майк! Вам на́до идти́! They're announcing your flight, Mike! You have to go!
Майк	Да. Пора́ ... Ната́ша, у меня́ к вам одна́ про́сьба. Я был бы сча́стлив, е́сли бы мы могли́ перейти́ на "ты". Но, коне́чно, я не зна́ю ва́ших тради́ций и не хочу́ ника́к вас оби́деть! Yes. It's time ... Natasha, I'd like to ask you a favor . I would be glad if we could change over to "ты" (informal you). But of course, I don't know your traditions and I don't want to offend you in any way!

Ната́ша	Спаси́бо, Майк! Вы ника́к не мо́жете меня́ оби́деть! Напро́тив! Я сама́ ду́мала об э́том и вы, то́ есть, коне́чно, ты! – про́сто прочита́л мои́ мы́сли. А тепе́рь пора́ проща́ться. До свида́ния, Майк! Я бу́ду о́чень ждать встре́чи с тобо́й!
	Thank you, Mike. You can't offend me in any way. On the contrary. I was thinking about it myself, and you – that is, of course, ты! – simply read my thoughts. And now it's time to say farewell. Goodbye Mike! I really look forward to seeing you again.
Майк	До свида́ния, Ната́ша! Мне бу́дет о́чень не хвата́ть тебя́.
	Goodbye Natasha! I'll miss you a lot.

Grammar

1. POSSESSIVES

мой *m.*/моя́ *f.*/моё *n.* **my/mine** and наш *m.*/на́ша *f.*/на́ше *n.* **our/ours** are declined as follows:

	Singular			Plural
	Masculine	Feminine	Neuter	All genders
Nom.	мой/наш	моя́/на́ша	моё/на́ше	мои́/на́ши
Acc.	мой/наш моего́/на́шего	мою́/на́шу	моё/на́ше	мои́х/на́ших мои́/на́ши
Gen.	моего́/на́шего	мое́й/на́шей	моего́/на́шего	мои́х/на́ших
Dat.	моему́/ на́шему	мое́й/ на́шей	моему́/ на́шему	мои́м/ на́шим
Instr.	мои́м/на́шим	мое́й/мое́ю/ на́шей	мои́м/на́шим	мои́ми/ на́шими
Prep.	моём/на́шем	мое́й/на́шей	моём/на́шем	мои́х/на́ших

The possessives **твой** **your/yours** (informal) and **ваш** **your/yours** (formal or plural) follow the same pattern.

Его́ means **his** (**of him**) or **its** (**of it**), её means "**her**" (**of her**), and их means **their** (**of them/ theirs**). Unlike regular pronouns or adjectives, they do not change according to the gender of what is **possessed**, nor do they decline:

Я разгова́риваю с мои́м студе́нтом.
I am talking with my student (male).

Я разгова́риваю с его́ студе́нтом/студе́нткой.
I am talking with his student (male/female).

Я разгова́риваю с её студе́нтом.
I am talking with her student (male).

Я разгова́риваю с их студе́нтом.
I am talking with their student (male).

Я разгова́риваю с их студе́нтами.
I am talking with their students.

Он разгова́ривает с мои́ми студе́нтами.
He is talking with my students.

Она́ рабо́тает недалеко́ от моего́ до́ма.
She works not far from my house.

Она́ рабо́тает недалеко́ от его́ до́ма.
She works not far from his house.

Она́ рабо́тает недалеко́ от её да́чи.
She works not far from her (some other female's) country house.

Она́ рабо́тает недалеко́ от их до́ма.
She works not far from their house.

свой *m.*/своя́ *f.*/своё *n.* means **one's own** and is used to denote possession of something by the subject of the verb. Look at the following examples:

Она́ разгова́ривает со свое́й попу́тчицей.
She is chatting with her traveling companion.

Майк сра́зу уви́дел табли́чку со свои́м и́менем.
Mike right away saw the sign with his name.

У неё своя́ отде́льная кварти́ра в Москве́.
She has her own separate (non-communal) apartment in Moscow.

In the last example, the impersonal **У неё** means **she has**, and **she** can be regarded as the subject of the sentence, even though **she** is not in the nominative **онá**.

Similarly:

Мне нýжно взять своþ кни́гу.	I have to take my book.
Тебé нýжно взять своþ кни́гу.	You have to take your book.
Емý нýжно написáть свой доклáд.	He has to write his report.
Им нýжно взять свой кни́ги.	They have to take their books.

Now, look at some examples of the use of **мой** *m.*/**мoя́** *f.*/**моё** *n.* from the course:

Балéт - моё люби́мое искýсство.
Ballet is my favorite art form.

Мы должны́ обсуди́ть вопрóс с мои́м начáльником.
We must discuss the question with my boss.

Смотрéть телеви́зор, по-мóему(мнéнию), потéря врéмени.
To watch television is, in my opinion (**мнéние**), a waste of time.

In these sentences, the subject of the sentence is not the **possessor**: the object of the sentence does not belong exclusively to the subject. However, sometimes **мой** *m.*/**мoя́** *f.*/**моё** *n.*, and **свой** *m.*/ **своя́** *f.*/**своё** *n.* are interchangeable:

Я приéду с мои́м начáльником./Я приéду со свои́м начáльником.
I will come with my boss.

Онá в кабинéте своегó начáльника./Онá в кабинéте её начáльника.
She is in the office of her boss.

This interchangeability seems to be possible because one cannot really **possess** a boss, but he or she is, after all, one's own boss!

However, **Онá в кабинéте её начáльника** can mean both **She is in the office of her (own) boss** and **She is in the office of her (some other female's) boss**. The sentence **Онá в кабинéте своегó начáльника** is unambiguous, as are the sentences **Он в кабинéте её начáльника** and **Онá в кабинéте егó начáльника**.

2. ВЕСЬ

весь *m.*/вся *f.*/всё *n.*/все (plural) **all, whole** is declined as follows:

	Singular			Plural
	Masculine	Feminine	Neuter	All genders
Nom.	весь	вся	всё	все
ǎcc.	весь/всего́	всю	всё	все/всех
Gen.	всего́	всей	всего́	всех
Dat.	всему́	всей	всему́	всем
Instr.	всем	всей	всем	всеми
Prep.	всём	всей	всём	всех

Here are some examples of **весь** *m.*/**вся** *f.*/**всё** *n.* and **все** (plural). Note that **всё** can mean **everything** as well as **all**:

Ша́пка – две ты́сячи, перча́тки – одна ты́сяча и четы́ре ты́сячи за сапоги́. Всего́ семь ты́сяч. (in all)
The hat, two thousand, the gloves, one thousand, and four thousand for the boots. In all, seven thousand.

Там так мно́го экспона́тов! И все – шеде́вры! (all of them)
There are so many exhibit items there! And they're all masterpieces!

Вся информа́ция есть в но́мере. (all)
All the information is in the (hotel) room.

Мы смо́жем осмотре́ть весь Нью-Йо́рк. (all, the whole of)
We can explore (lit. look around) all New York.

Я бу́ду стара́ться всё зако́нчить до своего́ отъе́зда. (everything)
I will try to finish everything before my departure.

Всё can also combine with other words for emphasis:

Сего́дня она́ всё ещё в Санкт-Петербу́рге. (still, even yet)
Today, she is still in St. Petersburg.

И всё равно́ бы́ло ма́ло. (all the same)
And, all the same, it was (very) little.

Всё лу́чше и лу́чше. (gradually)
Better and better.

Vocabulary

располо́женный m./располо́женная f./
располо́женное n. situated

над above

доста́точно sufficiently, enough

ла́дить друг с дру́гом to get along well with one another

получи́ть рабо́ту to get a job

ми́лый m./ми́лая f./ми́лое n. nice, sweet

обая́тельный m./обая́тельная f./ обая́тельное n. charming

же́нщина woman

о́бщество society, company

быть в ва́шем о́бществе to be in your company

говори́ть о чём уго́дно to talk about anything

жаль pity, what a shame

ведь after all, you see

разлу́ка parting

осма́тривать (impf) to examine, to visit, to inspect

осмотре́ть (perf) to examine, to visit, to inspect

не то́лько not only

роди́тели parents

обо мне́ about me

терпе́ние patience

Мне/Нам/Им не те́рпится. I/We/They (etc.) can't wait.

ли́чно in person

пассажи́р passenger

сле́довать (impf) to follow, to be bound for

после́довать (perf) to follow, to be bound for

сле́дующий m./сле́дующая f./
сле́дующее n. following, next, bound for

про́сьба a request

У меня́ к вам про́сьба. I'd like to ask you a favor.

гора́здо much, far

просто́й m./проста́я f./просто́е n. simple, easy

про́ще simpler, easier

счастли́вый m./счастли́вая f./
счастли́вое n. happy, fortunate

сча́стлив m./сча́стлива f./сча́стливо n. happy, fortunate (short form)

сча́стье happiness

переходи́ть (impf) to cross, to go over; to change over to

перейти́ (perf) to cross, to go over; to change over to

тради́ция tradition

ника́к in no way

оби́да insult, injury

обижа́ть (impf) to offend

оби́деть (perf) to offend

напро́тив quite the opposite, on the contrary

мысль f. thought

проща́ться (impf) to say goodbye

прости́ться (perf) to say goodbye

не хвата́ть to lack, to miss

го́лос voice

гро́мко loudly

громкоговори́тель m. loudspeaker

да́ча country house

Exercises

Exercise A

Translate the following sentences into English.

1. Мы прие́хали сюда́ о́чень ра́но, и у нас есть мно́го вре́мени, что́бы поговори́ть.

   ....

2. Я сиде́л в рестора́не и пил ко́фе.

   ....

3. Мы мо́жем говори́ть о мно́гих веща́х.

   ....

4. Майк с Ната́шей о́чень хорошо́ ла́дят друг с дру́гом.

   ....

5. Мне о́чень прия́тно рабо́тать с тобо́й.

   ....

6. Я почти́ ничего́ не зна́ю о жи́зни в Аме́рике.

   ....

7. Майк получи́л рабо́ту в о́фисе в Москве́.

   ....

8. Ната́ша о́чень ми́лая и обая́тельная же́нщина.

   ....

9. Нам бы́ло о́чень прия́тно в их о́бществе.

   ....

10. Когда́ им на́до возвраща́ться в Аме́рику?

   ....

11. **Мы мно́го говори́ли Ната́ше об Аме́рике по телефо́ну.**

....

Exercise B

Put the words in parentheses into the correct form.

1. **Ско́ро они́ (быть)** .... **вме́сте рабо́тать в (Росси́я)**

    ....

2. **Я хочу́ всё зако́нчить до (свой отъе́зд)** ....

3. **Майк был здесь в (Вашингто́н)** .... **то́лько три с (полови́на)**

    .... **(неде́ля)** ....

4. **Мои́ роди́тели уже́ проси́ли (я)** .... **пригласи́ть (он)**

    .... **к (они́)** .... **в Ло́ндон.**

5. **Отку́да они́ зна́ли обо (я)** .... **?**

6. **У (я) к (вы)** .... **одна́ про́сьба.**

7. **Я бу́ду о́чень ждать (встре́ча)** .... **с (ты)** ....**!**

8. **У (мы)** .... **мно́го (вре́мя)** .... **, чтобы поговори́ть.**

9. **Мы мо́жем говори́ть о (мно́гие ве́щи)** ....

10. **Они́ о́чень хорошо́ ла́дят друг с (друг)** ....

11. **Мне о́чень прия́тно рабо́тать с (вы)** ....

12. **Они́ получи́ли (рабо́та)** .... **в (рестора́н) в (Минск)**

    ....

13. **(Я)** .... **бы́ло о́чень прия́тно в их (о́бщество)** ....

14. **Мы мно́го говори́ли (Ната́ша)** .... **об (Аме́рика)**

    .... **по (телефо́н)** ....

Exercise C

Translate the following sentences into Russian.

1. **We are sitting in the restaurant and drinking wine.**

   ....

2. **I arrived there very early.**

   ....

3. **I have a lot of time.**

   ....

4. **I love to drink coffee.**

   ....

5. **They get along with each other very well.**

   ....

6. **It's pleasant for me to work with them.**

   ....

7. **I know almost nothing about him.**

   ....

8. **He knows almost nothing about her.**

   ....

9. **It is very pleasant for me to be in your company.**

   ....

10. **In a month we will work together in Moscow.**

    ....

11. **She was here for six and a half weeks only.**

    ....

12. I can't wait to get to know you in person.

....

Exercise D

True or false?

1. Майк и Ната́ша одина́ково ду́мают о мно́гих веща́х.   T/F

2. Они́ не о́чень хорошо́ ла́дят друг с дру́гом.   T/F

3. Ма́йку о́чень неприя́тно рабо́тать с Ната́шей.   T/F

4. Ната́ша родила́сь в Новосиби́рске, но учи́лась в Моско́вском

   госуда́рственном университе́те.   T/F

5. Майк ду́мает, что Ната́ша о́чень ми́лая и обая́тельная же́нщина.   T/F

6. С Ма́йком Ната́ша мо́жет говори́ть о чём-уго́дно.   T/F

7. Майк с Ната́шей осмо́трят весь Нью-Йо́рк.   T/F

8. Роди́тели Ма́йка живу́т в Вашингто́не.   T/F

20. Review: Lessons 17-19

Well done, you have reached the end of the course! This review section is a revision of the last few chapters. Take the time to listen to the audio dialogues again and see how far you have come. The language should flow more naturally now, with easy comprehension and a solid foundation in grammar and vocabulary.

DIALOGUE 17: МАЙК ПРИГЛАШÁЕТ НАТÁШУ В РЕСТОРÁН

Майк прóбыл в Москвé ужé óколо двух недéль. Чéрез пять-шесть дней он возвратúтся в Соединённые Штáты. Сегóдня вéчером он приглосúл Натáшу пообéдать с ним ...

Натáша	Большóе спасúбо за приглашéние, Майк!
Майк	Я ужé двáжды был здесь. Онú вкýсно готóвят. Обéд из пятú блюд с вóдкой, винóм, шампáнским и коньякóм. Что вы хотúте на закýски?
Натáша	Давáйте посмóтрим меню́.
Майк	Есть рýба, икрá, колбасá, салáты ...
Натáша	Я бы хотéла всегó – понемнóжку.
Майк	А пéрвое? У них здесь óчень вкýсная солянка по-москóвски.
Натáша	Я люблю́ солянку.
Майк	Хорошó, две солянки. А что на горячее? Рýба или мясо?
Натáша	А что вы посовéтуете?
Майк	У них сегóдня осетрúна – э́то óчень вкýсно!
Натáша	Осетрúна мне подхóдит. А что вы решúли, Майк?
Майк	Я, пожáлуй, возьмý мясо. Здесь óчень хорошó готóвят котлéты по-кúевски ... Хотя нет. Сегóдня я попрóбую беф-

	стро́ганов. Говоря́т, он счита́ется лу́чшим в Москве́.
Ната́ша	Это впечатля́ет.
Майк	А на десе́рт …
Ната́ша	Нет, нет, не сейча́с! Посмо́трим, чего́ нам захо́чется к концу́ обе́да. Вот тогда́ и реши́м.
Майк	Что бу́дем пить? Шампа́нское? Коне́чно! А та́кже бока́л бе́лого вина́ к ры́бе и бока́л кра́сного к мя́су.
Ната́ша	Замеча́тельно!
Майк	Официа́нт! Мы гото́вы сде́лать зака́з.

DIALOGUE 18: ВЕ́ЧЕР В ТА́ТРЕ

Ната́ша пригласи́ла Ма́йка в Моско́вский Худо́жественный Теа́тр. Там они́ посмотре́ли дра́му Анто́на Че́хова "Вишнёвый Сад" в но́вой постано́вке. Спекта́кль был великоле́пный.

Ната́ша	Вам понра́вилась пье́са?
Майк	Ещё бы! Это бы́ло замеча́тельно! Актёры о́чень хорошо́ игра́ли. А как в Москве́ с биле́тами? Тру́дно доста́ть?
Ната́ша	По-ра́зному. У нас пье́сы Че́хова о́чень лю́бят и ча́сто прихо́дится стоя́ть в о́череди. Обы́чно все биле́ты быва́ют распро́даны за не́сколько дней до спекта́кля и остаю́тся то́лько стоя́чие места́.
Майк	А вы ча́сто хо́дите в теа́тр?
Ната́ша	Да, но мне бо́льше нра́вится бале́т. Бале́т – моё люби́мое иску́сство. О́чень люблю́ та́кже кино́. Но смотре́ть телеви́зор, по-мо́ему, поте́ря вре́мени.
Майк	По пра́вде сказа́ть, бале́т не о́чень люблю́. По-мо́ему, кино́ интере́снее, чем теа́тр. Что сейча́с идёт в кинотеа́трах? Не могли́ бы вы посове́товать, како́й хоро́ший ру́сский фильм я могу́ посмотре́ть?
Ната́ша	Мой люби́мый, ру́сский фильм – э́то "Война́ и Мир" Бондарчука́. Вы смотре́ли?
Майк	Да. Зна́ете, мно́го лет наза́д я посмотре́л америка́нскую инсцениро́вку рома́на Толсто́го "Война́ и Мир", но ду́маю что ру́сский фильм лу́чше.
Ната́ша	Я по́лностью согла́сна с ва́ми. Мы одина́ково ду́маем о мно́гих веща́х, Майк. А сейча́с, ча́ю хоти́те?
Майк	Ну что вы? Я угощу́ вас бока́лом шампа́нского! Пошли́!

DIALOGUE 19: МАЙК ВОЗВРАЩА́ЕТСЯ В АМЕ́РИКУ.

Майк с Ната́шей сидя́т в рестора́не, располо́женном над за́лом вы́лета в Шереме́тьево-2. Они́ прие́хали туда́ о́чень ра́но, и у них доста́точно вре́мени, чтобы вы́пить ко́фе и поговори́ть …

Майк	Мы одина́ково ду́маем о мно́гих веща́х, Ната́ша. Мы о́чень хорошо́ ла́дим друг с дру́гом, и мне прия́тно рабо́тать с ва́ми. Но я почти́ ничего́ не зна́ю о вас.
Ната́ша	Да почти́ и не́чего знать, Майк. Я родила́сь в Новосиби́рске, учи́лась здесь, в Москве́, в Моско́вском госуда́рственном университе́те. Пото́м получи́ла рабо́ту в ба́нке.
Майк	Вы о́чень ми́лая и обая́тельная же́нщина, Ната́ша. Мне о́чень прия́тно быть в ва́шем о́бществе.
Ната́ша	И мне то́же легко́ с ва́ми. С ва́ми я могу́ говори́ть о чём-уго́дно. Жаль, что вам на́до возвраща́ться в Аме́рику.
Майк	Да … Но ведь у вас есть погово́рка: "Без разлу́к не быва́ет встреч". Ско́ро мы бу́дем вме́сте рабо́тать в Нью-Йо́рке.
Ната́ша	Да, пра́вильно. Зна́ете, я бу́ду о́чень мно́го рабо́тать, чтобы всё зако́нчить до своего́ отъе́зда.
Майк	Я был здесь то́лько три с полови́ной неде́ли, а вы бу́дете у нас полго́да. Мы смо́жем осмотре́ть весь Нью-Йо́рк. И не то́лько! Мои́ роди́тели уже́ проси́ли меня́ пригласи́ть вас к ним в Лос-А́нжелес.

(Го́лос из громкоговори́теля) Пассажи́ры, сле́дующие ре́йсом 341 в Нью-Йо́рк! Вас про́сят пройти́ на регистра́цию в зал вы́лета, сто́йка но́мер три!

Ната́ша	Отку́да они́ мо́гут знать о́бо мне?
Майк	Я мно́го говори́л им о вас по телефо́ну. Им не те́рпится познако́миться с ва́ми ли́чно.

Э́то наибо́лее интере́сный фильм.
Э́то наибо́лее краси́вая страна́.
Э́то наибо́лее ску́чное ме́сто.

Ната́ша	Объявля́ют ваш ре́йс, Майк! Вам на́до идти́!
Майк	Да. Пора́ … Ната́ша, у меня́ к вам одна́ про́сьба. Я был бы счастли́в, е́сли бы мы могли́ перейти́ на "ты". Но, коне́чно, я не зна́ю ва́ших тради́ций и не хочу́ ника́к вас оби́деть!
Ната́ша	Спаси́бо, Майк! Вы ника́к не мо́жете меня́ оби́деть! Напро́тив! Я сама́ ду́мала об э́том и вы, то-есть, коне́чно, ты! – про́сто прочита́л мои́ мы́сли. А тепе́рь пора́ проща́ться. До свида́ния, Майк! Я бу́ду о́чень ждать встре́чи с тобо́й!
Майк	До свида́ния, Ната́ша! Мне бу́дет о́чень не хвата́ть тебя́.

Exercises

Exercise A

Listen again to the dialogue from Lesson 17 and repeat.

Exercise B

Translate the dialogue from Lesson 17 into English and check your translation against ours on pages 205–207.

Exercise C

Listen again to the dialogue from Lesson 18 and repeat.

Exercise D

Translate the dialogue from Lesson 18 into English and check your translation against ours on pages 216–217.

Exercise E

Listen again to the dialogue from Lesson 19 and repeat.

Exercise F

Translate the dialogue from Lesson 19 into English, and check your version against ours on pages 225–227.

Answer Key

It does not matter if your translations into English are not the same, word for word, as in the book. The important thing is that the *meaning is the same*.

Lesson 1

A.

1. Tennis   2. Dollar   3. Basketball   4. Doctor   5. New York   6. California   7. Baseball   8. University
9. Address   10. Cola   11. Office   12. Football   13. President Obama   14. President Bush
15. Telephone   16. Bar   17. Restaurant   18. Vladimir Putin   19. Mafia   20. Taxi

B.

1. А а   2. Я я   3. Э э   4. Е е   5. Ы ы   6. И и   7. О о   8. Ё ё   9. У у   10. Ю ю

C.

1. з   2. м   3. с   4. р   5. т   6. р   7. к   8. ь   9. ф   10. я   11. р   12. с   13. о … д
14. ф   15. й   16. т

D.

1. четы́ре   2. де́сять   3. де́вять   4. во́семь   5. нуль   6. четы́ре   7. де́сять
8. семь   9. пять   10. шесть

LESSON 2

A.

1. vodka   2. fact   3. plan   4. professor   5. class (= class/classroom)   6. Lenin   7. Gorbachev
8. canal   9. student   10. Bolshoi Ballet   11. port   12. film   13. baggage/luggage   14. bazaar

B.

1. Это кни́га   2. Это бага́ж   3. Это стол   4. Это ру́чка   5. Это стул

C.

1. Да, э́то Пол.

2. Нет, э́то не кни́га. Это стол.

3. Да, э́то ру́чка.

4. Нет, э́то не А́нна Ива́новна. Это Пол.

5. Да, э́то стол.

6. Нет, э́то не стол. Это стул.

7. Нет, э́то не Пол. Это А́нна Ива́новна.

D.

1. Аме́рика   2. президе́нт   3. университе́т   4. ко́ка-ко́ла   5. бейсбо́л
6. во́дка   7. до́ктор   8. студе́нт/студе́нтка   9. Калифо́рния

LESSON 3

A.

1. sport, sport   2. film, feel'm   3. taxi, tahk-see   4. telephone, tee-lee-fon   5. center, tsentr   6. car, ahf-tah-mah-beel'   7. football, food-bol   8. tsar, tsahr'   9. excursion, eks-koor-see-yah
10. theater, tee-ahtr   11. iceberg, ies-byerk   12. author, ahf-tahr

B.

1. Нет, я не из Ло́ндона.

2. Нет, он не из Новосиби́рска.

3. Нет, она́ не из Москвы́.

4. Нет, они́ не из Аме́рики.

5. Нет, я не из А́нглии.

6. Нет, он не из Берли́на.

7. Нет, она́ не из Сан-Франци́ско.

8. Нет, они́ не из Нью-Йо́рка.

C.

1. Да, я профе́ссор.

2. Да, он бухга́лтер.

3. Да, она́ студе́нтка.

4. Да, они́ врачи́.

5. Да, я преподава́тель.

6. Да, он пило́т.

7. Да, она́ преподава́тель.

8. Да, они́ пило́ты.

D.

1. А   2. Б   3. Б   4. А   5. В   6. В   7. А   8. В

E.

1. I am very glad to meet you.

2. Natalya Petrovna works in a bank.

3. Paul lives in Moscow, but he was born in San Francisco.

4. Anna Ivanovna is not an accountant. She teaches at the university.

5. He is not from Moscow, but he works in Moscow.

6. I work in America.

7. Anna is not an American, nor a Russian. She is a Belarusian.

8. Is she Russian or an American?

9. Is this book in Russian or in English?

F.

1. T   2. F   3. T   4. F   5. F   6. T   7. T   8. T   9. F   10. T

Did you understand question 10 "You are learning Russian"? If so, you really are making progress!

LESSON 4

A.

1. в командиро́вку	6. свою́рабо́ту	11. на Кавка́з самолётом
2. в Москве́	7. на рабо́те . . . в университе́те	12. с Ива́ном по телефо́н
3. в ба́нке	8. от Москвы́ до Ми́нска	13. из Ми́нска . . . в Москве́
4. самолёт	9. по у́члице	14. о матема́тике
5. у Ива́на	10. у меня́ . . . по́езд	15. Москву́ч . . . Нью-Йо́рк

B.

1. иду́   2. е́дет   3. лети́м   4. лета́ете   5. рабо́тает   6. люблю́   7. лю́бит   8. идёт
9. хо́дим   10. живу́чт

C.

1. I am an American (female).
2. I live in an apartment in New York.
3. My father and my mother do not live in New York.
4. They live and work in California.
5. My father is an accountant, and my mother is a doctor.
6. I work in an office.
7. I like my work very much.
8. Usually I go to the airport by bus, but today I am going there by taxi.
9. My work is hard [heavy], but very interesting.
10. Now I am going home from work.

D.

1. Мо́й оте́ц и моя́ мать живу́чт в Москве́.
2. Как ва́ша мать?
3. Я не люблю́ Санкт-Петербу́чрг.
4. Большо́й чемода́н тяжёлый.
5. Чемода́нчик лёгкий. (Ма́ленький чемода́н - лёгкий.)
6. Я быва́ю в Москве́ три-четы́ре дня ка́ждый ме́сяц.*
7. Ната́лья у Ива́на.
8. Мы лети́м в Москву́ч че́рез три часа́.

* Note that "a month" in English here means "every month".

E.

1. F   2. T   3. T   4. F   5. F   6. T   7. F   8. F   9. F   10. T

LESSON 5

A.

1. Майк живёт и рабо́тает в Нью-Йо́рке.

2. Ната́ша рабо́тает в ба́нке в Москве́.

3. Её оте́ц и её мать живу́чт в Ми́нске.

4. У меня́ есть своя́ отде́льная кварти́ра.

5. Сейча́с Ната́ша в гости́нице.

6. Ей тру́чдно позвони́ть своему́ч колле́ге Воло́де.

7. Воло́дя и Майк бы́ли о́чень за́няты.

8. Когда́ мы мо́жем встре́титься?

B.

1. домо́й   2. в кабине́те   3. до́ма   4. на столе́   5. Мне . . . в Москве́   6. её   7. меня́

8. у нас   9. Его́ . . . в Москве́

C.

1. бу́чду   2. рабо́тали   3. говори́т   4. бы́ли   5. иду́ч   6. е́здит   7. живёт   8. бу́чдет

9. был   10. звони́л

D.

1. I do not like working in Moscow.

2. It is now eight o'clock.

3. Is it convenient for you to meet at three?

4. They will wait for us at five thirty in the bank.

5. Mike sent us a lot of wine.

6. My father likes his job (work) very much.

7. I have four tickets for the theater.

8. Where is Andrei? He's not at home.

9. Volodya will go with you, if you wish.

E.

1. T   2. T   3. F   4. F   5. T   6. T   7. F   8. T

LESSON 6

A.

1. Аме́рика   2. Нью-Йо́рк   3. президе́нт   4. о́фис   5. студе́нт   6. студе́нтка

7. во́дка   8. пило́т   9. студе́нты   10. аэропо́рт

B.

А. 8	Й. 22	У. 14	Э. 83
Б. 3	К. 36	Ф. 12	Ю. 19
В. 7	Л. 40	Х. 15	Я. 29
Г. 4	М. 55	Ц. 44	
Д. 2	Н. 69	Ч. 71	
Е. 1	О. 70	Ш. 18	
Ё. 5	П. 100	Щ. 68	
Ж. 6	Р. 94	Ъ. 37	
З. 9	С. 80	Ы. 42	
И. 10	Т. 73	Ь. 11	

C.

1. Москву́ч . . . командиро́вку   Москвы́.

2. рабо́те . . . ба́нке . . . Ми́нске   7. Новосиби́рска

3. свою́ рабо́ту . . . университе́те   8. домо́й . . . рабо́ты

4. Ма́йком   9. вам

5. Ива́на   10. мне

6. кварти́ре . . . це́нтре . . .   11. Ива́на

12. удово́льствием

13. ва́ми

14. командиро́вке . . . Ната́ши

15. В конце́ концо́в.

D.

1. лю́бит . . . люблю́   4. бы́ли . . . рабо́тают   7. бу́чду . . . был/была́

2. живёт . . . живу́ч   5. звони́л . . . бы́ло   8. бу́чдем

3. рабо́тали . . . рабо́таем   6. бу́чдете . . . бы́ли

LESSON 7

A.

1. impf   2. perf   3. impf   4. perf   5. impf   6. perf   7. impf   8. impf   9. perf   10. perf

B.

А. 5 Пять   3. 45 со́рок пять   П. 85 во́семьдесят пять

Б. 10 де́сять   И. 50 пятьдеся́т   Р. 90 девяно́сто

В. 15 пятна́дцать   Й. 55 пятьдеся́т пять   С. 95 девяно́сто пять

Г. 20 два́дцать   К. 60 шестьдеся́т   Т. 100 Сто

Д. 25 два́дцать пять   Л. 65 шестьдеся́т пять   У. 101 сто оди́н

Е. 30 три́дцать   М. 70 се́мьдесят   Ф. 111 сто оди́ннадцать

Ё. 35 три́дцать пять   Н. 75 се́мьдесят пять   Х. 200 две́сти

Ж. 40 Со́рок   О. 80 во́семьдесят   Ц. 222 две́сти два́дцать два

C.

1. Do you want tea, coffee, mineral water or vodka?

2. What date is it today?

3. Today is the 29th of April.

4. Excuse me, please. Is there a toilet here?

5. When will you be free?

6. We will be free on Tuesday, at 6 o'clock in the evening.

7. On the way to Volodya's, Natasha bought a newspaper.

8. Volodya gave Natasha copies of some American promotional brochures.

9. Before (earlier), I drank tea in the morning(s), but now I drink mineral water.

10. Volodya gave Natasha the/some brochures, and she thought that they were just what she needed.

D.

1. Вчера́ я говори́л?/говори́лаfc Ма́йком в о́фисе.
2. Ната́ша хо́дит в банк пешко́м ка́ждый день.
3. Ра́ньше я пил?/пила́fчай по утра́м, а тепе́рь я пью ко́фе.
4. Ру́ччка и ключ на столе́.
5. В про́шлом году́ч мы е́здили в Нью-Йорк ка́ждую неде́лю.
6. Я откры́л?/откры́лаfдверь.
7. Мы поговори́ли с Ма́йком.
8. Ско́ро я бу́чду е́здить в Москву́ч ка́ждый ме́сяц.

E.

1. F   2. F   3. T   4. F   5. F   6. F   7. F   8. T   9. F

LESSON 8

A.

1. Я пишу́ч
2. Они́ чита́ют
3. Мы поём
4. Они́ пьют
5. Вы ждёте
6. Он преподаёт
7. Я зна́ю
8. Они́ гуля́ют
9. Она́ понима́ет
10. Вы идёте
11. Мы е́дем
12. Вы де́лаете
13. Я пою́
14. Они́ отвеча́ют
15. Я слу́чшаю

B.

1. Я хожу́ч
2. Они́ говоря́т
3. Она́ кричи́т
4. Мы хо́дим
5. Вы говори́те
6. Они́ крича́т
7. Я смотрю́
8. Мы сиди́м
9. Он лети́т
10. Она́ молчи́т
11. Они́ звоня́т
12. Мы покупа́ем
13. Она́ стои́т
14. Я ви́жу
15. Я вожу́ч

C.

1. зна́ем (зна́ли)
2. стоя́ли
3. говори́т
4. показа́л
5. сто́или ... стоя́т ... бу́чдут сто́ить
6. смо́трит
7. зна́ет
8. покупа́ет ... счита́ет ... бу́чдет сто́ить
9. заплати́ла
10. реши́ла

D.

Boris works not far from his home in Moscow. He has a car, but he walks to work. Every morning, on the way to the office, he buys a newspaper. But yesterday there were no newspapers. What did he do? He bought a book. He very much likes to read newspapers, books and magazines. He likes the movies, but does not like to watch television at all: he doesn't even have a television. Now it is winter. It's cold outside [on the street]. But Boris is not cold when he walks to work. He has a warm coat, a hat, woolen gloves and a pair of good boots.

E.

1. Ка́ждое у́чтро по пути́ в о́фис я покупа́ю газе́ту.

2. Сейча́с она́ говори́т с Ива́ном.

3. Мо́жно посмотреть ша́пку, пожа́луйста.

4. Я возьму́ч её, хоть и до́рого.

5. Пожа́луйста, покажи́те мне э́ти перча́тки.

6. Мо́жно посмотре́ть э́то пальто́, пожа́луйста.

7. Сего́дня у нас есть немно́го свобо́дного вре́мени.

8. Где ка́сса?

9. Ка́сса вот там, нале́во.

F.

1. T 2. T 3. F 4. T 5. F 6. F 7. T 8. T

LESSON 9

A.

1. fax

2. calculator

3. boutique

4. snowboard

5. computer

6. telephone

7. xerox (in Russian = any photocopier)

8. music center

9. printer

10. cartridge

11. player

12. scanner

13. diving

14. automobile

B.

1. До́брый ве́чер. Дава́йте знако́миться.

2. Меня́ зову́чт . . . . А вас?

3. Я америка́нец?/америка́нкаf(англича́нин/ англича́нка,...).

4. Я роди́лся?/родила́сьfв (Филаде́льфии, Ло́ндоне...)

5. Я рабо́таю в...

6. Мне нра́вится...

7. Мне не нра́вится...

8. Я учу́ч ру́сский язы́к.

C.

1. I would like to open the window.

2. We would like to set up a company in Minsk.

3. He would like to be there every day.

4. She would like to buy a newspaper.

5. She would like to drink (some) mineral water.

6. They would like to go shopping.

7. They would like to live in America.

8. I would like to speak Russian well.

9. I would like to go home.

10. Would you like to work in Moscow?

D.

1. Он е́дет домо́й.

2. Она́ покупа́ет биле́т.

3. Они́ гуля́ют по на́бережной Невы́.

4. Они́ проща́ются в гости́нице.

5. И́горь в двухме́стном купе́ в по́езде.

6. Ната́ша и И́горь разгова́ривают об Эрмита́же.

7. И́горь живёт в Ирку́чтске.

8. Мы обе́даем в рестора́не.

9. Что вы де́лаете?

E.

1. F   2. F   3. T   4. T   5. F   6. T   7. F   8. F   9. F   10. F   11. T   12. F

LESSON 10

A.

1. Today is Sunday, yesterday was Saturday, and tomorrow will be Monday.
2. The work is finished. Go home.
3. Yesterday evening, Ivan flew into Moscow by plane.
4. I didn't manage to buy any gloves.
5. What's the name of this train?
6. At 10 o'clock in the morning, I drank coffee in a/the restaurant with Natasha.
7. May I close the door? It's terribly cold here.
8. Vladimir went to the Hermitage almost every day for a whole week.
9. The wine was good — it would have been nice to have more (still more was wanted).
10. I don't have my own car, but I have my own (non-communal) apartment.
11. Mike lives very far from Moscow - in America.
12. I would live in Philadelphia with pleasure.
13. How will they go home? (by transport)
14. What are you going to do tomorrow evening?
15. Yesterday we bought a new car.

B.

1. Иди́/Иди́те сюда́
2. Сади́сь/Сади́тесь
3. Извини́/Извини́те ; Прости́/Прости́те
4. Покажи́/Покажи́те мне
5. Поду́чмай/Поду́чмайте
6. Реша́й/Реша́йте
7. Одева́йся/Одева́йтесь
8. Не кури́/Не кури́те
9. Не подпи́сывай/Не подпи́сывайте
10. Чита́й/Чита́йте
11. Рабо́тай/Рабо́тайте
12. Не покупа́й/Не покупа́йте
13. Не кричи́/Не кричи́те
14. Не носи́/Не носи́те
15. Не плати́/Не плати́те

C.

1. хочу́ч   2. хотя́т   3. хо́чет   4. хоти́м   5. хотя́т   6. хо́чешь   7. хо́чет   8. хотя́т

D.

1. два … второ́й
2. три … тре́тий
3. четы́ре … четвёртый
4. четы́рнадцать … четы́рнадцатый
5. пять … пя́тый
6. пятна́дцать … пятна́дцатый
7. шесть … шесто́й
8. семь … седьмо́й
9. во́семь … восьмо́й
10. де́вять … девя́тый

E.

1. T   2. F   3. T   4. F   5. F   6. T   7. F   8. F   9. T   10. T

LESSON 11

1. рабо́тает … гости́ницы
2. кни́гу
3. пил … утра́м, пьёт
4. чай, ко́фе, во́дку … минера́льную во́ду
5. вре́мени … о́череди
6. ва́ми
7. бу́чдут … вас … гости́нице
8. э́ту газе́ту … собо́й
9. удово́льствием … це́лую неде́лю … Эрмита́же

LESSON 12

A.

1. vendetta
2. ventilation
3. gas
4. hamburger
5. gangster
6. handicap
7. garage
8. megalomania
9. racism

B.

1. In Russia it is cold in winter and hot in summer.
2. I work by day and sleep at night.
3. Yesterday they were in New York, and tomorrow they'll be in Moscow.
4. I've never been to America, but I want to go there sometime.
5. It's good here, but it's better there.
6. The bank is on the right, and the hotel is on the left.
7. Now I'm going home. At home I'm going to watch television.
8. Where are you going?
9. Where are you from?

C.

1. Днём … но́чью
2. за́ле … наро́ду
3. табли́чки … свои́м и́менем
4. ней
5. ним
6. хоте́л
7. стака́на джи́на … то́ником
8. Тверско́й у́члице
9. Кра́сной пло́щади

D.

1. Извини́те, что э́то тако́е?
2. Здесь мно́го наро́ду.
3. Я совсе́м не уста́л?/уста́лаf.
4. Ты о́чень уста́ла, Ната́ша?/Вы о́чень уста́ли, Ната́ша?
5. Э́то на́ша но́вая студе́нтка?
6. Я о́чень хочу́ч встре́титься с ва́ми.
7. Она́ рабо́тает в на́шем отделе́нием в Вашингто́не.
8. Она́ пришла́ к нам приме́рно пять ме́сяцев наза́д.
9. Он прилете́л в Нью-Йорк из Москвы́ ночны́м ре́йсом.

E.

1. F   2. F   3. T   4. F   5. T   6. T   7. F   8. T   9. F

LESSON 13

A.

1. My house is not far from the Zvezda (Star) Hotel.
2. Can you tell me where the registration desk is, please?
3. I booked a room by e-mail.
4. You confirmed the booking. [that the order was accepted]
5. Here is my passport. When can I have it back? [receive it]
6. Is there a radio, television and telephone in the room?
7. When do they broadcast the news in English?
8. I want to buy both English and American newspapers.
9. I want to have breakfast in my room.

B.

1. письма́
2. но́мере
3. кото́рому
4. но́мере … ру́чсском … англи́йском
5. получа́ют … газе́ты
6. рестора́на
7. ва́шем
8. Зна́ете … передаю́т

C.

1. Гости́ница "Звезда́" недалеко́ от моего́ до́ма.
2. У меня́ есть больша́я но́вая маши́на.
3. В но́мере есть телеви́зор?
4. Зака́з при́нят?
5. Мо́жно ли смотре́ть переда́чи по-англи́йски?
6. Мы здесь бу́чдем три-четы́ре дня.
7. Я там быва́ю два дня ка́ждый ме́сяц.
8. В гости́нице есть химчи́стка?

D.

32,400 rubles

E.

1. F   2. T   3. T   4. F   5. T   6. T   7. T   8. F   9. T   10. T

LESSON 14

A.

1. In Russia it's cold in winter, but for the last five to seven years the winters were not (have not been) very cold.
2. In winter in Russia, the temperature is often above freezing (zero).
3. There is often a strong wind and sleet.
4. When the sky is cloudless and blue, and the sun is shining, and the snow is sparkling, it is wonderful in Russia.
5. At the beginning of March, the weather is very variable in New York.
6. Mike came to Moscow at the very beginning of spring.
7. We decided to set off on a trip around Moscow.
8. What's that building?
9. The Cathedral of St. Basil is an absolutely unique building.
10. Pushkin, Tolstoy and Dostoyevsky were great writers.
11. Let's go back to the car.
12. Novodevichy is a convent on the banks of the Moscow River.

B.

1. Извини́те, вы не ска́жете, как прое́хать к Третьяко́вской галлере́е?

2. Извини́те, вы не ска́жете, как пройти́ к ближа́йшей ста́нции метро́?

3. Извини́те, вы не ска́жете, как пройти́ к ближа́йшему универма́гу?

4. Прости́те, вы не ска́жете, как пройти́ к ближа́йшей це́ркви?

5. Прости́те, вы не ска́жете, как прое́хать к ближа́йшей больни́це?

6. Прости́те, вы не ска́жете, как пройти́ к ближа́йшей апте́ке?

7. Скажи́те, пожа́луйста, как пройти́ к Мавзоле́ю Ле́нина?

8. Скажи́те, пожа́луйста, как прое́хать к Тверско́й учи́лице?

9. Скажи́те, пожа́луйста, как прое́хать к университе́ту?

10. Прости́те, вы не ска́жете, как прое́хать к гости́нице "Украи́на"?

C.

1. Как вы уже́ зна́ете, в Росси́и хо́лодно зимо́й.

2. Температу́ра ча́сто вы́ше нуля́.

3. Ча́сто быва́ет си́льный ве́тер.

4. Идёт снег.

5. Температу́ра - ми́нус де́сять гра́дусов.

6. Не́бо голубо́е, и со́лнце сия́ет.

7. Здесь чуде́сно!

8. В нача́ле ма́рта пого́да о́чень неусто́йчива.

9. Температу́ра бы́стро меня́ется.

10. Но́чью - ми́нус два́дцать, а днём - плюс де́сять.

11. Майк прие́хал в Москву́ч в са́мом нача́ле весны́.

12. День так прекра́сен, что про́сто невозмо́жно сиде́ть в гости́нице.

13. Собо́р был постро́ен при Ива́не Гро́зном.

14. Это прекра́сная страна́.

15. Толсто́й был вели́кий писа́тель.

D.

1. F   2. F   3. T   4. F   5. T   6. T   7. F

LESSON 15

A.

1. I intend to live in Moscow.

2. I decided to study Russian seriously.

3. A/The professor agreed to give me private lessons.

4. Natasha has just arrived at his house and is ringing the doorbell.

5. Come in, please.

6. Where did Mike learn Russian? In America?

7. Yes, but now he must improve his Russian [know Russian better].

8. She must broaden her vocabulary.

9. When she watches television, she understands quite a lot.

10. He has good Russian pronunciation.

11. She speaks Russian badly.

12. I have a problem.

13. When people speak quickly, I don't understand.

14. Natasha prepared dinner.

15. The book will be useful to you.

B.

1. Майк мог бы проводи́ть в Москве́ от шести́ ме́сяцев до го́да.

2. Я реши́л всерьёз заня́ться ру́чсским языко́м.

3. А́нна согласи́лся дава́ть Ма́йку ча́стные уро́ки.

4. Где вы изуча́ли англи́йский?

5. Я не бу́чду жить в Москве́ до́лго.

6. Нам ну́чжно лу́ччше знать ру́чсский.

7. Когда́ я смотрю́ телеви́зор, я понима́ю довольно мно́го.

8. Я ду́чмаю, что я могу́ч помо́чь вам.

C.

1. По́лночь.

2. По́лдень.

3. Пятна́дцать часо́в пять мину́чт OR: пять мину́чт четвёртого.

4. Четы́ре часа́ де́сять мину́чт.

5. Семна́дцать часо́в пятна́дцать мину́чт OR: пятна́дцать мину́чт шесто́го.

6. Шесть часо́в два́дцать мину́чт.

7. Девятна́дцать часо́в три́дцать мину́чт OR: полови́на восьмо́го.

8. Семь часо́в со́рок мину́чт.

9. Два́дцать часо́в со́рок пять мину́чт OR: без че́тверти де́вять.

10. Де́вять часо́в пятьдеся́т семь мину́чт OR: без трёх (мину́чт) де́сять.

D.

1. F 2. T 3. T 4. T 5. T 6. T 7. F 8. T 9. T 10. T 11. T 12. T 13. T 14. T 15. F

LESSON 16

1. нахо́дится … кабине́те … нача́льника

2. телефо́ну.

3. ве́чером … гуля́ли … у́члицам … це́нтре Москвы́

4. Ната́шей … господи́ну Ро́джерсу

5. часо́в ве́чера … во́дку … рестора́не … Ива́ном.

6. ска́жете … Америка́нскому посо́льству?

7. ска́жете … Кра́сной пло́щади?

8. ска́жете … ближа́йшему ба́нку?

9. ска́жете … ближа́йший туале́т?

10. сле́дующем поворо́те … це́рковью.

LESSON 17

A.

1. We have already been in Minsk for about five weeks.

2. In three days I am returning to Russia.

3. Yesterday I invited him to have dinner with me.

4. They have very tasty meat today.

5. What do you recommend today?

6. I'll have a bottle of red wine.

7. We're returning to Russia in a week.

8. This evening we invited Ivan to have dinner with us.

9. Thanks a lot for the invitation.

10. We've never been there.

11. May I/we have a look at the menu?

12. I like fish and meat very much.

13. Sturgeon is a fish. It's very tasty.

14. Our Chicken Kiev is considered to be the best in Moscow.

15. I want a bottle of red wine with the meat, and a bottle of white with the fish.

B.

1. Че́рез шесть дней они́ возвратя́тся в Соединённые Шта́ты.

2. Я пригласи́л свои́х друзе́й пообе́дать со мной сего́дня ве́чером.

3. Большо́е спаси́бо за приглаше́ние.

4. Обе́д из пяти́ блюд, с во́дкой, вино́м, шампа́нским и коньяко́м.

5. Мы бы́ли здесь вчера́.

6. Я никогда́ там не́ был?/былаf.

7. Мо́жно посмотре́ть меню́?

8. У вас есть ры́ба?

9. У вас есть мя́со?

10. Я люблю́ кра́сное вино́.

11. Что вы посове́туете?

12. За на́шу дру́чжбу!

C.

1. Москве́ . . . двух неде́ль

2. ве́чером . . . пригласи́л Ната́шу с на́ми

3. четырёх . . . во́дкой, вино́м, шампа́нским и коньяко́м

4. не́ была

5. ры́бы, икры́, колбасы́, сала́тов

6. них . . . лу́ччшим . . . Москве́

7. чего́ . . . концу́ч обе́да

8. бу́чдем . . . буты́лку кра́сного вина́

D.

1. F   2. T   3. F   4. T   5. T   6. T   7. F   8. F

LESSON 18

A.

1. I am going to invite Natasha to the Bolshoi Theater, to the ballet, every week.

2. Yesterday evening, the performance in the theater was magnificent.

3. Many years ago, I lived in Africa.

4. I very much want to see the film War and Peace.

5. This movie is more interesting than the other.

6. This book is more interesting than the other.

7. My life is getting worse and worse.

8. My father's life got better and better when he lived in America.

9. What do you prefer, the movies or television?

B.

1. пригласи́ли . . . пье́су

2. лет . . . смотре́л(а)

3. ви́дели . . . им . . . понра́вился

4. нас . . . Че́хова . . . лю́бят

5. ве́чером . . . угоща́ли . . . меня́. . . шампа́нского

6. мне . . . вам

7. пра́вде . . . ры́бу

8. ду́чмаем . . . мно́гих . . . вре́мени

C.

1. Ива́н пригласи́л меня́ в теа́тр на бале́т.

2. О́пера была́ великоле́пная.

3. Э́то замеча́тельно!

4. Мно́го лет наза́д я жил(а) в Росси́й.

5. Я то́же ви́дел?/ви́делаfэтот фильм.

6. Я о́чень люблю́ смотре́ть телеви́зор.

7. Теа́тр бо́лее интере́сный чем и о́пера и бале́т.

8. Не могли́ бы вы посове́товать хоро́шую, ру́чсскую пье́су?

D.

1. F   2. T   3. T   4. F   5. T   6. F   7. F   8. T

LESSON 19

A.

1. We came here very early, and we have a lot of time to talk.
2. I sat in the restaurant and drank coffee.
3. We can talk about a lot of things.
4. Mike and Natasha get along very well together.
5. It's very nice for me to work with you.
6. I know almost nothing about life in America.
7. Mike got a job in an/the office in Moscow.
8. Natasha is a very nice and charming woman.
9. It was very pleasant for us to be in their company.
10. When do they have to go back to America?
11. We talked a lot about America to Natasha on the phone.

B.

1. бу́чдут ... Росси́и
2. своего́ отъе́зда
3. Вашингто́не ... полови́ной неде́ли
4. меня́ ... его́ ... ним
5. мне
6. меня́ ... вам
7. встре́чи ... тобо́й
8. меня́ ... вре́мени
9. мно́гих веща́х
10. дру́чгом
11. ва́ми
12. рабо́ту ... рестора́не ... Ми́нске
13. Мне ... о́бществе
14. Ната́ше ... Аме́рике ... телефо́ну

C.

1. Мы сиди́м в рестора́не, и пьём вино́.
2. Я прие́хал?/прие́халаf(пришёл?/пришла́f) туда́ о́чень ра́но.
3. У меня́ мно́го вре́мени.
4. Я люблю́/Мне нра́вится пить ко́фе.
5. Они́ о́чень хорошо́ ла́дят друг с дру́чгом.
6. Мне прия́тно рабо́тать с ни́ми.
7. Я почти́ ничего́ не зна́ю о нём.
8. Он почти́ ничего́ не зна́ет о ней.
9. Мне о́чень прия́тно быть в ва́шем о́бществе.
10. Че́рез ме́сяц мы бу́чдем рабо́тать вме́сте в Москве́.
11. Она́ была́ здесь то́лько шесть с полови́ной неде́ль.
12. Мне не те́рпится познако́миться с ва́ми ли́чно.

D.

1. T 2. F 3. F 4. T 5. T 6. T 7. T 8. F

Glossary

а

а: *and, but*
автобус: *bus*
автобусная: остановка: *bus stop*
áдрес: *address*
америкáнец *m.*/**америкáнка**f **American**
англи́йский *m.*/**англи́йская** *f.*/**англи́йское** *n.*: *English*
англичáнин: *Englishman*
англичáнка: *Englishwoman*
анкéта: *questionnaire*
архитéктор architect
аэровокзáл: *air terminal*
аэропóрт: *airport*

б

багáж baggage
балéт: *ballet*
банк: *bank*
бáнка: *jar, can, tin*
баскетбóл: *basketball*
безóблачный: *cloudless*
бейсбóл: *baseball*
белорýс *m.*/**белорýска** *f.* **a Belarusian**
Бéлые Нóчи: *White Nights*
бéлый *m.*/**бéлая** *f.*/**бéлое** *n.*: *white*
бéрег: *bank (of a river, lake)*
беспокóить *(impf):* *to disturb, to trouble*
беспокóиться *(impf):* *to be disturbed, to be troubled, to be*

uneasy
беф-стрóганов: *beef stroganoff*
билéт: *ticket*
билéт на самолёт: *a plane ticket [ticket onto plane]*
благополýчно: *safely*
бли́зко close
блю́до: *dish, course in a meal*
бóлее more
бóлее-мéнее: *more or less*
брать *(impf):* *to take*
букéт: *bouquet*
буты́лка: *bottle*
буфéт: *buffet*
бухгáлтер: *accountant*
бывáть: *to be in/to visit/to go*
бы́стро: *quickly*
быть: *to be*

в

в ... вéке: *in the ... century*
в делáх: *on business, working*
в командирóвку: *on a business trip*
в концé концóв: *in the end [in the end of ends]*
в рукáх: *in (one's): hands*
в сáмом начáле: *at the very beginning*
в спéшке: *in a hurry, in a rush*
в течéние: *during*
в течéние цéлого мéсяца: *for a whole month*

Verbs marked *perf* = perfective, *impf* = imperfective; nouns are only marked *m.*, *f.* or *n.* if the gender is not apparent from the form (see Lesson 3). Adjectives are given in the masculine, feminine and neuter forms.

в углу́: *in the corner*
вдруг: *suddenly*
ведь: *after all, you see*
век: *century*
вели́кий *m.*/вели́кая *f.*/вели́кое *n.*: *great*
великоле́пно: *wonderfully, it's wonderful/splendid/ magnificent*
великоле́пный *m.*/великоле́пная *f.*/великоле́пное *n.*: *wonderful, splendid, magnificent*
Ве́рно: *It is true/correct*
верну́ться *(perf)*: *to return, go back*
вести́ *(impf)*: *to lead, to take*
ве́тер: *wind*
ве́чер: *evening*
ве́чером: *in the evening*
вещь *f.*: *thing*
взять *(perf)*: *to take*
ви́деть *(impf)*: *to see*
ви́за: *visa*
визи́т: *visit*
визи́т состои́тся: *the visit will take place*
вино́: *wine*
вку́сно гото́вить: *to prepare something tasty*
вку́сно: *tasty*
вме́сте: *together*
внести́ *(perf)*: *to carry into, to bring into*
внести́ в счёт: *to put on expenses, on account*
вноси́тс *(impf)*: *to carry into, to bring into*
вода́: *water*
во́дка: *vodka*
возврати́ться *(perf)*: *to return, come back*
возвраща́ться *(impf)*: *to return*
возмо́жно: *it is possible*
война́: *war*
вопро́с: *question*
вот: *there is/are, here is/are*
впечатля́ть *(impf)*: *to impress*
вре́мя *n.*: *time, period of time*
всегда́: *always*
всего́: *in all, of all*
всего́: до́брого *all the best*
всего́ понемно́жку: *a little of everything*
всерьёз: *seriously*
всё: *all*
всё возмо́жно: *anything is possible, all is possible*
Всё норма́льно: *Everything is OK*
всё равно́: *all the same, in any case*
всё-таки: *all the same, nevertheless*
вспоте́ть *(perf)*: *to perspire, to get sweaty*
встре́тить *(perf)*: *to meet*

встре́титься *(perf)*: *to meet (one another)*
встре́ча: *meeting, get together*
встреча́ть *(impf)*: *to meet*
встреча́ться *(impf)*: *to meet (one another)*
вто́рник: *Tuesday*
вчера́: *yesterday*
вы: *you (formal or plural)*
выдава́ть *(impf)*: *to hand out, to give, to issue*
вы́дать *(perf)*: *to hand out, to give, to issue*
вы́нести *(perf)*: *to carry out, to remove*
вы́пить *(perf)*: *to drink up*
высоко́: *high*
вы́ше ноля́: *above zero (freezing)*
вы́ше: *higher*
вы́яснить *(perf)*: *to clear up, to explain*
выясня́ть *(impf)*: *to clear up, to explain*

г

гла́сность *f.*: *openness*
глубо́кий *m.*/глубо́кая *f.*/глубо́кое *n.*: *deep*
газе́та: *newspaper*
где́-то: *somewhere*
Где?: *Where?*
геро́й: *hero*
говори́ть о чём-уго́дно: *to talk about anything*
говоря́: *speaking*
го́лос: *voice*
голубо́й *m.*/голуба́я *f.*/голубо́е *n.*: *blue*
гора́здо: *much, far*
го́рдость *f.*: *pride*
го́рничная: *maid, cleaner*
го́род: *town*
горя́чее (блю́до): *hot (dish, course)*
горя́чий *m.*/горя́чая *f.*/горя́чее *n.*: *hot*
господи́н: *Mister*
госпожа́: *Madam, Mrs., Ms*
гости́ница: *hotel*
гость?: *guest*
гото́в *m.*/гото́ва *f.*/гото́во *n.*: *ready (short form of the adjective)*
гото́вить *(impf)*: *to prepare, get ready, make*
гото́вый *m.*/гото́вая *f.*/гото́вое *n.*: *ready*
гра́дус: *degree (temperature)*
грани́ца: *frontier/border*
гро́мко: *loudly*
громкоговори́тель *m.*: *loudspeaker*
гря́зный *m.*/гря́зная *f.*/гря́зное *n.*: *dirty, filthy*
гуля́ть: *to walk, stroll*

д

да: *yes*
Да нет!: *Oh, no! (stronger than нет)*
давайте: *give, let us, let's*
давать: *уроки to give lessons*
даже: *even*
далеко: *far, a long way, far away*
далёкий *m./*далёкая *f./*далёкое *n.: distant, remote*
даль *f.: distance, expanse*
дата: *date*
дача: *country house*
двадцать: *twenty*
дважды: *twice*
два *m. f. n.,* две *f.: two*
двухместный *m./*двухместная *f./*двухместное *n.:*
two-place, two-seater
делать покупки: *to go shopping [to be doing purchases]*
дело: *affair, work, business*
деньт: *day*
десерт: *dessert*
дешевле: *cheaper*
дешёвый *m./*дешёвая *f./*дешёвое *n.: cheap*
джин: *gin*
длинный *m./*длинная *f./*длинное *n.: long*
днём: *by day*
до: *until, to*
До свидания: *Goodbye*
до сих пор: *until now, up to now*
До скорой встречи: *See you soon*
добавить *(perf): to add*
добро: *good*
Добро пожаловать!: *Welcome!*
добрый *m./*добрая *f./*доброе *n.: good, kind*
Добрый вечер: *Good evening*
довольно: *enough, sufficiently, rather*
договариваться *(impf): to agree*
договориться *(perf): to agree*
дождьт: *rain*
дозвониться: *to ring the phone until it is answered, to get through to someone*
дойти *(perf): to go up to, to reach*
доктор: *doctor*
долго: *a long time*
долететь *(perf): to fly to, to fly here*
должен *m./*должна *f./*должно *n.: have to, must, ought to*
доллар: *dollar*
дом: *house*
дома: *at home*
дорого: *it's expensive*

дорогой *m./*дорогая *f./*дорогое *n.: expensive*
досадно: *frustrating*
достаточно: *sufficiently, enough*
доходить *(impf): to go up to*
дочьf: *daughter*
другой *m./*другая *f./*другое *n.: other*
дружба: *friendship*
думать *(impf): to think*
душ: *shower*
дыхание: *breathing, breath*
дядя: *uncle*

е

его: *him*
её: *her*
если: *if*
ехать *(impf): to go (by transport), to drive*
ещё: *also, again*
Ещё бы!: *I should say so!*

ж

Жаль!: *It's a pity!/What a shame!*
жаркий *m./*жаркая *f./*жаркое *n.: hot*
жарко: *it is hot*
ждать *(impf): to wait, to await*
же: *no specific meaning it serves to emphasize another word*
жена: *wife*
женщина: *woman*
жизньf: *life*
жить *(impf): to live, to be alive; to spend time somewhere*
журнал: *magazine*

з

За дружбу!: *To friendship!*
за компанию: *for the company*
за продуктами: *for food, groceries*
за углом: *around the corner*
забывать *(impf): to forget*
забыть *(perf): to forget*
заведение: *establishment, institution*
заезжать *(impf): to call in*
зависеть *(impf): to depend (on)*
зависеть от: *того, как . . . : to depend on how . . .*
завтра: *tomorrow*
завтракать *(impf): to have breakfast*
заехать *(perf): to call in*
заехать за: *to call on, to collect*
заказ: *an order*
заказан *m./*заказана *f./*заказано *n.: booked, ordered (short form of adjective)*
заказать *(perf): to book, to order*

заказывать (*impf*): *to book, to order*

закончен *m.*/закончена *f.*/закончено *n.*: *finished (short form of adjective)*

законченный *m.*/законченная *f.*/законченное *n.*: *finished*

закуска: *snack*

зал: *hall*

зал прибытия: *arrivals hall*

Замечательно!: *Great!/Wonderful!*

замечательный *m.*/замечательная *f.*/замечательное *n.*: *remarkable*

замёрзнуть (*perf*): *to freeze*

занимать (*impf*): *to take up, to occupy*

заниматься (*impf*): *to be engaged in, to study*

занят *m.*/занята *f.*/занято *n.*: *busy, engaged (short form of adjective)*

занять (*perf*): *to take up, to occupy*

занять много времени: *to take a lot of time*

заняться (*perf*): *to be engaged in, to study*

заняться языком: *to study a language*

запас: *store, stock*

заполнить (*perf*): *to fill, to fill up, to complete (a form)*

заполнять (*impf*): *to fill, to fill up, to complete (a form)*

заранее: *in advance, earlier*

затем: *after that*

зато: *but, however*

захотеть (*perf*): *to desire, to want*

захотеться (*perf*): *to desire, to want*

звать: *to call (a name)*

звонить (*impf*): *to phone, to call*

звонить в дверь: *to ring at the door, to ring the doorbell*

здание: *building*

здесь: *here*

здороваться (*impf*): *to greet*

Здорово!: *It's great/nice!*

Здравствуйте: *Hello*

земля: *earth, land*

зеркало: *mirror*

зима: *winter*

зимой: *in winter*

зло: *evil*

знакомая: *female acquaintance*

знакомить (*impf*): *to introduce*

знакомиться (*impf*): *to meet, to be introduced, to get to know*

знакомство introduction, acquaintance

знакомый: *male acquaintance*

знать (*impf*): *to know*

значить: *to mean*

зовите: *call (imperative)*

золотой *m.*/золотая *f.*/золотое *n.*: *golden*

зря: *for nothing, to no purpose*

и

играть: *to play*

Идёт дождь: *It is raining*

Идёт снег: *It is snowing*

Идите сюда: *Come here*

идти пешком: *to go on foot, to walk*

идти: *to go*

Идут переговоры: *Negotiations are going on/taking place*

из: *from, out of*

из аэропорта: *from/out of the airport*

Извините: *Excuse me/I'm sorry*

извинить: *to forgive, to excuse*

изменение: *a change*

изображение: *image, picture*

икра: *caviar*

или: *or*

именно: *precisely, specially*

иметь (*impf*): *to have, to own*

имея при себе: *having with you*

имя *n.*: *first name*

иногда: *sometimes*

иностранец *m.*/иностранка *f.*: *foreigner*

интеллигенция: *intelligentsia*

Интересно: *It is interesting*

интересный *m.*/интересная *f.*/интересное *n.*: *interesting*

информация: *information*

искренний *m.*/искренняя *f.*/искреннее *n.*: *sincere*

искриться (*impf*): *to sparkle*

история: *history*

к

к: *to, towards, up to*

к: *сожалению unfortunately, regrettably*

к: *счастью fortunately*

кабинет: *office*

каждый *m.*/каждая *f.*/каждое *n.*: *every, each*

как: *as, how, like, how is/are*

Как ваши дела?: *How are things? How goes it?*

как всегда: *as always, as usual*

Как насчёт…?: *What about…?*

как раз то, что …: *just what …*

какой *m.*/какая *f.*/какое *n.*: *what sort of, what a, which*

какой-нибудь *m.*/какая-нибудь *f.*/какое-нибудь *n.*: *some or other, any*

канал: *channel*

касса: *cash register*

кварти́ра: *apartment/flat*
кино́: *movie/movie theater*
ключ: *key*
кни́га: *book*
Когда́?: *When?*
колбаса́: *sausage*
колле́га: *colleague (male or female)*
коммуника́бельный *m.*/**коммуника́бельная** *f.*/
коммуника́бельное *n.*: *approachable*
ко́мната: *room*
компью́тер: *computer*
коне́ц: *end*
коне́чно of course
ко́нсульство: *consulate*
контро́льт: *control*
конфере́нция: *conference*
конья́к: *cognac*
ко́пия: *copy, duplicate*
коро́ткий *m.*/**коро́ткая** *f.*/**коро́ткое** *n.*: *short,.brief, concise*
коро́че говоря́: *in short, briefly speaking*
котле́ты по-ки́евски: *Chicken Kiev (breaded chicken with butter)*
кото́рый *m.*/**кото́рая** *f.*/**кото́рое** *n.*: *which*
ко́фе: *coffee*
кра́йт: *border, edge*
краси́вый *m.*/**краси́вая** *f.*/**краси́вое** *n.*: *beautiful*
кремль: *castle, fort, kremlin*
крича́ть *(impf)*: *to shout*
Кто вы по национа́льности?: *What is your nationality?*
Кто?: *Who?*
купе́: *compartment*
ку́пол: *cupola, dome*
кури́ть *(impf)*: *to smoke*
курс: *course*
ку́хня: *kitchen*

л

ла́дить друг с дру́гом: *to get along well with one another*
ла́дно: *right, all right, fine*
легко́: *easy*
лес: *a forest, woods*
ле́то: *summer*
ле́том: *in summer*
лёгкие заку́ски: *light snacks*
лёгкий *m.*/**лёгкая** *f.*/**лёгкое** *n.*: *light*
лицо́: *face*
ли́чно: *in person*
лу́чше: *better*
любо́й *m.*/**люба́я** *f.*/**любо́е** *n.*: *any*
лю́ди: *people*

м

магази́н: *shop, store*
ма́ло: *little, few*
мать: *mother*
маши́на: *car*
ме́дленно: *slowly*
меню́: *menu*
Меня зову́т. . .: *My name is. . .*
меня́ть *(impf)*: *to change*
меня́ться *(impf)*: *to change*
меня́ющийся *m.*/**меня́ющаяся** *f.*/**меня́ющееся** *n.*: *changing*
ме́рять *(impf)*: *to try on, to measure*
ме́сто place, seat
ме́сяц: *month*
мех fur
мехово́й *m.*/**мехова́я** *f.*/**мехово́е** *n.*: *fur, of fur*
ми́лый *m.*/**ми́лая** *f.*/**ми́лое** *n.*: *nice*
минера́льный *m.*/**минера́льная** *f.*/**минера́льное** *n.*: *mineral*
ми́нус: *minus*
мину́та: *a minute*
Мне/Ему́/Им *(etc.)* **подхо́дит:** *It suits me/him/them (etc.)*:
Мне всё равно́: *It's all the same to me*
Мне на́до: *I must/It is necessary for me*
Мне хо́чется: *I want*
Мне/Нам/Им не те́рпится: *I/We/They (etc.): can't wait*
мно́го: *a lot, many*
мо́жет: быть: *perhaps, maybe*
Мо́жно: *It is possible*
мо́крый *m.*/**мо́края** *f.*/**мо́крое** *n.*: *wet*
молодо́й *m.*/**молода́я** *f.*/**молодо́е** *n.*: *young*
монасты́рь *m.*: *monastery, convent*
мо́ре: *sea*
моро́з: *frost*
мочь *(impf)*: *to be able to*
мой *m.*/**моя́** *f.*/**моё** *n.*: *my*
муж: *husband*
мча́ться *(impf)*: *to hurry away, to zip*
мы: *we*
мысль *f.*: *thought*
мя́со: *meat*

н

на: *on (can be the equivalent of "in")*
на горя́чее: *for the hot course (main course)*
на авто́бусе: *by bus, on a bus*
на берегу́: *on the bank*
на заку́ски: *for starters*
на рабо́те: *at one's work, at the office*

на ру́сском языке́: *in Russian*
на сле́дующий день: *on the next day*
на экску́рсию: *on a trip*
на́бережная: *embankment, waterfront, wharf*
наве́рное: *surely, certainly*
над: *above*
На́до: *It is necessary*
называ́ть *(impf)*: *to call, to address (someone)*
нале́во: *to the left*
напро́тив: *quite the opposite, on the contrary*
наро́д: *people, the people*
наско́лько: *as . . . as, as far as, as much as*
находи́ть *(impf)*: *to find*
находи́ться *(impf)*: *to be, to be situated*
намерева́ться: *to intend*
национа́льность *f.*: *nationality*
нача́ло: *beginning, start*
нача́льник: *chief, boss*
наш: *our*
не *used to form negative sentences as in* Я: **не ру́сский** *(I'm not Russian),* **Не́ было мест** *(There were no seats/places)*
не ме́нее: *not less*
не то́лько: *not only*
не хвата́ть: *to lack, to miss*
не́бо: *sky*
небольшо́й *m.*/**небольша́я** *f.*/**небольшо́е** *n.*: *not big, small, little*
Невозмо́жно: *It's impossible*
неда́вно: *not long ago, recently*
недалеко́: *not far*
неде́ля: *week*
незнако́мый *m.*/**незнако́мая** *f.*/**незнако́мое** *n.*: *unknown*
нельзя́: *not allowed*
немно́го: *not much, a little*
необходи́мый *m.*/**необходи́мая** *f.*/**необходи́мое** *n.*: *unavoidable, necessary*
не́сколько: *a few, several*
не́сколько раз: *several times*
нести́ *(impf)*: *to carry*
нет: *no*
Нет вре́мени: *There is no time*
неусто́йчив *m.*/**неусто́йчива** *f.*/**неусто́йчиво** *n.*: *variable (short form of adjective)*
неусто́йчивый *m.*/**неусто́йчивая** *f.*/**неусто́йчивое** *n.*: *variable*
ни́зкий *m.*/**ни́зкая** *f.*/**ни́зкое** *n.*: *low*
ника́к: *in no way*
никако́й *m.*/**никака́я** *f.*/**никако́е** *n.*: *none, not any*
никогда́: *never*

никто́: *nobody*
никуда́: *nowhere [to nowhere]*
Ничего́ не понима́ю: *I understand nothing/I don't understand anything*
но: *but, however*
но́вости: *the news*
но́вый *m.*/**но́вая** *f.*/**но́вое** *n.*: *new*
нога́: *leg, foot*
но́мер: *number*
но́мер в гости́нице: *hotel room*
норма́льно: *O.K., normal, all right*
носи́ть *(impf)*: *to wear, to carry*
ночно́й *m.*/**небольша́я** *f.*/**небольшо́е** *n.*: *night*
но́чью: *at night, by night*
Ну́жно: *It is necessary*
Ну что́ вы!: *Oh, come on!*

о

обая́тельный *m.*/**обая́тельная** *f.*/**обая́тельное** *n.*: *charming*
обе́д из пяти́ блюд: *a five course meal*
обе́дать *(impf)*: *to dine, to have a meal/ lunch (dinner)*
оби́да: *insult, injury*
оби́деть *(perf)*: *to offend*
обижа́ть *(impf)*: *to offend*
о́блако: *cloud*
о́блачный *m.*/**о́блачная** *f.*/**о́блачное** *n.*: *cloudy*
обрати́ться *(perf)*: *to address (someone)*
обра́тно: *back (direction, movement)*
обра́тный *m.*/**обра́тная** *f.*/**обра́тное** *n.*: *return*
обраща́ться *(impf)*: *to address (someone) frequently*
обсуди́ть *(perf)*: *to discuss*
обсужда́ть *(impf)*: *to discuss*
о́бувь *f.*: *footwear*
о́бщество: *society, company*
обы́чно: *usually*
одина́ково: *the same*
одева́ться *(impf)*: *to dress oneself*
оде́жда: *clothing*
оди́н: *one*
оди́н: раз *one time, once*
ожере́лье: *necklace*
ожида́ть *(impf)*: *to wait, to expect*
окно́: *window*
о́коло: *about*
онт: *he, it*
она́f: *she, it*
они́: *they*
оно́ *n.*: *it*
описа́ть *(perf)*: *to describe*

описывать *(impf)*: to describe
оплата: *payment, settlement*
освежиться *(perf)*: to freshen oneself up
осетрина: *sturgeon*
ослепить *(perf)*: to blind, to put out someone's eyes
осматривать *(impf)*: to examine, to visit, to inspect
осмотреть *(perf)*: to examine, to visit, to inspect
остальной *m.*/остальная *f.*/остальное *n.*: *remaining*
остановиться *(perf)*: to stop, to stay
остановлен *m.*/остановлена *f.*/остановлено *n.*: *stopped (short form of adjective)*
от: *from*
ответ: *answer*
отвечать: *to answer, to reply*
отдать *(perf)*: to hand in, to give back, to return
отделение: *section, division, branch*
отдельный *m.*/отдельная *f.*/отдельное *n.*: *separate, individual*
отец: *father*
открывать *(impf)*: to open
открыть *(perf)*: to open
Откуда?: *Where from?*
Отлично: *It's excellent/great*
отправиться *(perf)*: to set off
офис: *office*
официальный *m.*/официальная *f.*/официальное *n.*: *official*
оформление: *preparation, processing*
очень: *very*
очередь *f.*: *line, queue*

п

пара: *pair*
пальто: *coat*
паспорт: *passport*
пассажир: *passenger*
пачка: *packet*
пачка сигарет: *packet of cigarettes*
перевести *(perf)*: to translate, to transfer
переводить *(impf)*: to translate, to transfer
переговоры: *negotiations, talks*
передавать *(impf)*: to broadcast
передавать новости: *to broadcast the news*
передача: *program*
переделать *(perf)*: to change
перейти *(perf)*: to cross, to go over
переставать *(impf)*: to cease, to stop
перестать *(perf)*: to cease, to stop
переходить *(impf)*: to cross, to go over
перчатка: *glove*

песня: *song*
петь *(impf)*: to sing
пешком: *on foot*
пилот: *pilot*
писатель *m.*: *writer*
письмо: *letter*
пить *(impf)*: to drink
пицца: *pizza*
плата: *payment, cost*
платить *(impf)*: to pay
плохой *m.*/плохая *f.*/плохое *n.*: *bad*
площадь *f.*: *square*
по: *on, by*
по московскому времени: *by/according to Moscow time*
по набережной: *on/along the bank*
по пути: *on the way*
по радио: *by radio, on the radio*
по телевизору: *on television*
по телефону: *on the phone, by phone*
по-английски: *in English*
по-моему: *in my opinion*
по-русски: *in Russian*
по-старому: *as before, as usual*
побывать: *to be in, to spend some time in, to visit*
повести *(perf)*: to lead, to take
повести обедать: *to take out for a meal, for lunch/dinner*
поговорить: *to speak, to have a talk*
поговорка: *a saying*
пограничный *m.*/пограничная *f.*/пограничное *n.*: *frontier/border*
пограничный: *контроль*: *border control*
под ногами: *under the feet*
подешевле: *a bit cheaper*
поднимать *(impf)*: to lift, to raise
поднять *(perf)*: to lift, to raise
подойти *(perf)*: to suit, to match, to approach
подолгу: *a long time*
подтвердить *(perf)*: to confirm
подтверждать *(impf)*: to confirm
подходить *(impf)*: to approach, to go up to; to suit, to match
поездом: *by train*
пожалуй: *perhaps, very likely, I dare say*
пожалуйста: *please*
позавтракать *(perf)*: to have breakfast
позвонить *(perf)*: to phone, to call
познакомить *(perf)*: to introduce
познакомиться *(perf)*: to meet, to be introduced, to get to know someone
пойти *(perf)*: to go

пойти́ по магази́нам: *to go around the shops*
пока́: *until*
пока́ нет: *not yet*
показа́ть *(perf)*: *to show*
покупа́ть *(impf)*: *to buy*
поку́пка: *a purchase*
по́ле: *field*
поле́зен *m.*/**поле́зна** *f.*/**поле́зно** *n.*: *useful, beneficial (short form of adjective)*
поле́зный *m.*/**поле́зная** *f.*/**поле́зное** *n.*: *useful, beneficial*
полови́на: *half*
получа́ть *(impf)*: *to receive*
получе́ние: *acquisition, obtaining*
получи́ть *(perf)*: *to receive*
поме́рить *(perf)*: *to measure, to try on*
по́мнить *(impf)*: *to remember*
помога́ть *(impf)*: *to help*
помо́чь *(perf)*: *to help*
понима́ть *(impf)*: *to understand, to comprehend*
поня́тно: *(it is) understood/clear*
поня́ть *(perf)*: *to understand, to comprehend*
пообе́дать *(perf)*: *to dine, to have dined, to have a meal/lunch/(dinner)*
попада́ться *(perf)*: *to be caught*
попроща́ться *(perf)*: *to say goodbye*
попу́тчик *m.*: *traveling companion*
попу́тчица *f.*: *traveling companion*
Пора́: *It is time*
порекомендова́ть *(perf)*: *to recommend*
после́дний *m.*/**после́дняя** *f.*/**после́днее** *n.*: *last*
после́довать *(perf)*: *to follow, to proceed*
посмотре́ть *(perf)*: *to have a look at, to see*
посове́товать *(perf)*: *to advise, to recommend*
постира́ть *(perf)*: *to wash (clothes)*
постро́ен *m.*/**постро́ена** *f.*/**постро́ено** *n.*: *built (short form of adjective)*
постро́ить *(perf)*: *to build*
посчита́ть *(perf)*: *to calculate, to add up*
посыла́ть *(impf)*: *to send*
пото́м: *then*
потому́ что: *because*
Почему́?: *Why?*
почи́стить *(perf)*: *to clean*
почти́: *almost*
пра́вда: *truth; it is true*
пра́вильно: *correct, right*
предлага́ть *(impf)*: *to suggest*
предприя́тие: *venture, undertaking*
пре́жде всего́: *first of all*
пре́жде чем нача́ть: *before starting*

прекра́сен *m.*/**прекра́сна** *f.*/**прекра́сно** *n.*: *beautiful, pretty (short form of adjective)*
прекра́сный *m.*/**прекра́сная** *f.*/**прекра́сное** *n.*: *beautiful, pretty*
преподава́тель: *teacher*
при себе́: *with you, on you*
прибыва́ть *(impf)*: *to arrive*
при́бывший *m.*/**при́бывшая** *f.*/**при́бывшее** *n.*: *arrived, having arrived*
прибы́тие: *arrival*
приглаше́ние: *invitation*
пригото́вить *(perf)*: *to prepare, get ready, make*
приезжа́ть *(impf)*: *to arrive*
прие́хать *(perf)*: *to come (by transport)*
приземли́ться *(perf)*: *to land*
прилета́ть *(impf)*: *to fly to, to arrive by air*
приме́рно: *approximately, about*
принима́ть *(impf)*: *to accept*
приня́ть *(perf)*: *to accept*
приня́ть душ *(perf)*: *to take a shower*
присла́ть: *to send*
приходи́ть *(impf)*: *to come, arrive*
прийти́ *(perf)*: *to come, arrive*
Прия́тно: *It's pleasant*
пробле́ма: *problem*
пробы́ть *(perf)*: *to stay, to spend time, to stop (for a time)*
провести́ *(perf)*: *to accompany, to take (on foot), to see off; to spend time*
проводи́ть *(impf)*: *to accompany, to take (on foot), to see off; to spend time*
програ́мма: *program*
продаве́ц: *sales assistant*
проду́кт: *product, grocery*
проезжа́ть *(impf)*: *to go through (by transport)*
прое́хать *(perf)*: *to go through (by transport)*
произноше́ние: *pronunciation*
проспе́кт: *brochure, prospectus; prospect, long, wide road*
прости́ть *(perf)*: *to pardon, forgive*
прости́ться *(perf)*: *to say goodbye*
про́сто: *simply*
просто́й *m.*/**проста́я** *f.*/**просто́е** *n.*: *simple, straightforward, easy going*
про́сьба: *request*
проти́скиваться *(impf)*: *to force one's way, to squeeze through*
профе́ссор *(male or female)*: *a professor*
проходи́ть *(impf)*: *to travel through, to pass (time)*
проща́ть *(impf)*: *to pardon, forgive*
проща́ться *(impf)*: *to say goodbye*
про́ще: *simpler, easier*

пря́мо: *straight*
путьm: *way*
пыта́ться: *to try*

р

рабо́та: *work*
рабо́тать *(impf)*: *to work*
рад *m.*/ра́да *f.* pleased
разгова́ривать *(impf)*: *to talk, to chat*
разлу́ка: *parting*
ра́но early
распакова́ть *(perf)*: *to unpack*
располо́женный *m.*/располо́женная *f.*/
располо́женное *n.*: *situated*
регистра́ция: *registration*
рейс: *flight*
река́: *river*
рекомендова́ть *(impf)*: *to recommend*
рестора́н: *restaurant*
реша́ть *(impf)*: *to decide*
реши́ть *(perf)*: *to decide*
роди́тели: *parents*
рожде́ние: *birth*
рольf: *role*
росси́йский *m.*/росси́йская *f.*/росси́йское *n.*: *Russian (pertaining to the Russian state)*
ру́сский *m.*/ру́сская *f.*/ру́сское *n.*: *Russian (for a person/place/thing)*
ру́чка: *pen*
ры́ба: *fish*

с

с: *with*
с и́скренним уваже́нием: *with sincere respect*
с тех пор: *from that time, since then*
с трудо́м: *with difficulty*
с удово́льствием: *with pleasure*
сади́ться *(impf)*: *to sit down*
сала́т: *salad*
са́мое нача́ло: *the very beginning*
самолёт: *airplane*
самолётом: *by plane*
са́мый *m.*/са́мая *f.*/са́мое *n.*: *the very, the most*
сапо́г: *boot*
сара́йm: *shed*
свобо́дный *m.*/свобо́дная *f.*/свобо́дное *n.*: *free*
свой *m.*/своя́ *f.*/своё *n.*: *one's own*
сде́лан *m.*/сде́лана *f.*/сде́лано *n.*: *done, finished (short form of adjective)*
сде́ланный *m.*/сде́ланная *f.*/сде́ланное *n.*: *done, finished*
сде́лать: *to do*
себя́: *oneself*
сего́дня: *today*
сейча́с: *right now, immediately*
село́: *village*
семья́: *family*
сестра́: *sister*
сигаре́та: *cigarette*
си́льный *m.*/си́льная *f.*/си́льное *n.*: *strong*
ситуа́ция: *situation*
сия́ть *(impf)*: *to shine*
ска́жем: *let's say, we'll say*
сказа́ть *(perf)*: *to say*
сквозь: *through*
Ско́лько?: *How much?, How long?*
Ско́лько сейча́с?: *What time is it now?*
Ско́лько сто́ит?: *How much does it cost?*
скоре́е: *faster; rather*
скро́мность *f.*: *modesty*
сле́довать *(impf)*: *to follow, to be bound for*
сле́дующий *m.*/сле́дующая *f.*/сле́дующее *n.*: *following, bound for*
словарьm: *dictionary*
сло́во: *word*
сло́жный *m.*/сло́жная *f.*/сло́жное *n.*: *difficult, complicated*
слу́шать: *to listen*
слы́шать *(impf)*: *to hear*
сля́коть *f.*: *slush*
смесь: *mixture*
смея́ться *(impf)*: *to laugh*
смотре́ть переда́чу: *to watch a program*
смотре́ть телеви́зор: *to watch television*
смочь *(perf)*: *to be able to*
смысл: *sense, meaning*
снача́ла: *at first*
снег: *snow*
снима́ть *(impf)*: *to take off, to remove*
снять *(perf)*: *to take off, to remove*
собо́р: *cathedral*
собра́ние: *meeting*
соверше́нно: *completely*
сове́товать *(impf)*: *to advise*
совме́стное предприя́тие: *joint venture*
совме́стный *m.*/совме́стная *f.*/совме́стное *n.*: *joint*
совсе́м: *completely*
совсе́м не: *not at all*
согла́сен *m.*/согла́сна *f.*/согла́сно *n.*: *agreed, according to, in conformity with*

согласи́ться (perf): to agree
соглаша́ться (impf): to agree
сожале́ние: regret
созда́ние: establishing, setting up
созда́ть: to found, to set up
со́лнце: sun
соля́нка по-моско́вски: Moscow style solyanka soup
сосе́д m./**сосе́дка** f.: neighbor
состоя́ться (perf): to take place
спаси́бо: thank you
спать (impf): to sleep
спекта́кль m.: performance
спеши́ть: to hurry
спе́шка: a rush
спра́шивать (impf): to ask
спроси́ть (perf): to ask
сра́зу: at once, right away, immediately
стака́н: a glass
станови́ться (impf): to get, to grow, to become
ста́рый m./**ста́рая** f./**ста́рое** n.: old
стать (perf): to get, to grow, to become
стена́: wall
стира́ть (impf): to wash (clothes)
сто́имость f.: cost, value
сто́ить (impf): to cost, to be worth
стол: table
стол регистра́ции: check in desk
стоя́ть (impf): to stand
стоя́ть в о́череди: to stand in line
страна́: country
строи́тельство: building, construction
стро́ить (impf): to build
студе́нт m./**студе́нтка** f.: student
стул: chair
суди́ть (impf): to judge, to criticize
существова́ть (impf): to exist
сча́стлив m./**сча́стлива** f./**сча́стливо** n.: happy, fortunate (short form of adjective)
счастли́вый m./**счастли́вая** f./**счастли́вое** n.: happy, fortunate
сча́стье: happiness, good fortune
счита́ть (impf): to consider
счита́ться (impf): to be considered, to consider

т

табли́чка: a card, notice (as held up in airports with the name of a person)
так so
та́кже also
тако́й m./**така́я** f./**тако́е** n.: so, such, such a one

тала́нт: talent
там: there
тамо́женный: досмо́тр customs check
тамо́жня: customs
теа́тр: theater
телеви́дение: television
телеви́зор: television (set)
телефо́н: telephone
те́ло: body
температу́ра: temperature
те́ннис: tennis
тепло́: warmth
терпе́ние: patience
теря́ть (impf): to lose
тече́ние: flow, course (of time); trend; current (river, etc.)
тёплый m./**тёплая** f./**тёплое** n.: warm
тира́н: tyrant
то же са́мое the very same
това́рищ m.: comrade, friend
тогда́: then
то́же: also, too
толпа́: crowd
то́лько: only
то́ник: tonic
тост: toast
то́чно: exactly
тради́ция: tradition
тра́нспорт: transport
три: three
труд: labor, toil, work, exertion
тру́дно: difficult, hard
тру́дность f.: difficulty, hardship
туда́: there (to there)
ты: you (informal)
тяжёлый m./**тяжёлая** f./**тяжёлое** n.: heavy
тут: here

у

у: at; beside; by; near; on
У меня́ всё хорошо́: Everything's fine
У меня́ есть . . .: I have . . .
У меня́ к вам про́сьба: I'd like to ask you a favor
у неё: she has/at her place [at her]
у себя́ в кабине́те: in one's office
уваже́ние: respect
уве́рен m./**уве́рена** f./**уве́рено** n.: convinced (short form of adjective)
уви́деть (perf): to see, to have seen
у́гол: corner
угости́ть (perf): to treat, to pay for somebody

угоща́ть (impf): to treat, to pay for somebody
удо́бно: convenient
удово́льствие pleasure
ужа́сен m./ужа́сна f./ужа́сно n.: awful, terrible (short form of adjective)
ужа́сный m./ужа́сная f./ужа́сное n.: awful, terrible
уже́: already
украи́нец m./украи́нка f.: a Ukrainian
улета́ть: to fly out [to depart]
у́лица: street
умыва́ться (impf): to wash oneself
университе́т: university
уника́льный: unique
упражне́ние: exercise
уро́к: lesson
устра́иваться (impf): to arrange, put in order, settle in
устро́иться (perf): to get organized
у́тро: morning

ф

фа́брика: factory
факс: fax
фами́лия: surname
фильм: film
фи́рма: firm, company
францу́зский m./францу́зская f./францу́зское n.: French

х

химчи́стка: dry cleaning
Хо́лодно: It is cold
хоро́ший m./хоро́шая f./хоро́шее n.: good
Хорошо́: It is good/fine
хорошо́ пообе́дать (perf): to have eaten well
хоте́ть (impf): to want
хоть: even though
хотя́: although, despite
худо́жник m./худо́жница f.: artist
ху́же: worse

ц

цвето́к: flower
це́лый m./це́лая f./це́лое n.: entire, whole, complete
це́льсий: centigrade/Celsius
цена́: price
центр: center
це́рковь f.: church

ч

ча́й: tea
час: hour
ча́стный m./ча́стная f./ча́стное n.: private
ча́сто: often
чемода́н: suitcase
чемода́нчик: little suitcase (a diminutive form of чемода́н)
че́рез: in, after
че́рез неде́лю: in a week
че́рез четы́ре часа́: in four hours
чернови́к: a draft
чёрный m./чёрная f./чёрное n.: black
число́: number, date
чи́стить (impf): to clean
чита́ть (impf): to read
что: that
Что ещё?: What else?
Что вы посове́туете?: What do you recommend?
Что но́вого у вас?: What's new(lit with you)?
что-то: something
чу́вство: feeling
чуде́сный m./чуде́сная f./чуде́сное n.: wonderful, marvelous
Чуть не забы́л!: I almost forgot!
чуть-чуть: just a little, a tiny bit

ш

шампа́нское: champagne
ша́пка: hat
шеде́вр: masterpiece (from the French "chef-d'oeuvre")
шко́ла: school
шоссе́: highway
шум: noise
шу́мно: noisy

э

экску́рсия: trip, excursion
экспона́т: exhibit item
электро́нное письмо́: e-mail
электро́нный а́дрес: e-mail address
э́то: this, that, it; this is, that is, it is

я

язы́к: language, tongue
яйцо́: egg